About the Author

Wendy DeVere-Austin was born in Bath, England. She was schooled at La Sainte Union Convent. She then went to Exeter University. After four years modelling for Chanel, Escada, Valentino and Dior, she entered the film industry, working on films such as *Run Wild, Run Free*, *Nicholas and Alexandra*, *Conduct Unbecoming*, *The Internecine Project*, *The Life Story of D.H. Lawrence* and many more. She and her husband now live in Virginia.

No Way to Treat a Child

Wendy DeVere-Austin

No Way to Treat a Child

Olympia Publishers
London

www.olympiapublishers.com
OLYMPIA PAPERBACK EDITION

A CIP catalogue record for this title is available from the British Library.

ISBN: 978-1-78830-192-3

First Published in 2018

Olympia Publishers
60 Cannon Street
London
EC4N 6NP

Printed in Great Britain

Dedication

This is for my darling husband, Raymond, who brought me into the sunshine of my life, and has given me so much love and happiness. A believer that all things are possible, he is my true soulmate.

To my wonderful friend, Judith Halsall, who helped me through some of the darkest days of my teens. She is forever in my heart.

I thank, Austin, my stepson, so much for his computer knowledge and great patience in helping me at various stages of this book.

FOREWORD

With this generously candid account, Wendy allows us heartfelt access to the astonishing details of her life. It takes great courage to reveal not just the events of one's life, but the hidden secrets of our inner lives; our hopes and aims, as well as our regrets. Wendy's story is ultimately one of resilience and success, despite adversity. We can have hope that happiness is possible, even with the most difficult of beginnings. As one of the many victims of childhood trauma, neglect and abuse, Wendy's story is also a horribly painful and sad tale. Her mother died when Wendy was a baby, and she was left vulnerable. Fortunately for Wendy, she was blessed with intelligence, a sense of humour and an appreciation of nature; so as soon as she was able to make her own way in life, her situation began to improve. However, Wendy's account helps us to understand the pervasive impacts abuse can have on the developing mind and personality of survivors that can endure well beyond childhood and the time of the abuse itself.

As a clinical psychologist, I value knowledge of someone's early learning and individual context to appreciate who they are as a person, and I am grateful to Wendy for sharing this with us through her writing. Before reading this book I'd only known Wendy as a warm and happy adult. Her concern with tidiness, and her gently self-mocking jokes, take on a whole new depth of meaning when understood in the context of her history with the woman who betrayed the role of an adoptive parent with breath-taking cruelty. Some might find it hard to believe that someone could go through all that Wendy did and still eventually come out of it as a reasonably well-balanced and happy adult. However, many people do achieve this recovery with time and (dare I say) often without the help of a therapist, as Wendy did.

Wendy's resilience in the face of such suffering can be partly explained by her positive personal qualities, and having experiences of love and safety before being placed in the hands of the woman. This gave Wendy something nourishing to cling to when all else was bleak, but her snippets of memories became abstract fantasies with time. Wendy emphasises the importance of this fantasy life in keeping her sane, but it also had its downside. By finding solace in fantasy, Wendy acknowledges that she was often distracted from reality, even into early adulthood. While the woman was around there were few opportunities to develop a sense of capability and independence in the real world. Sadly, Wendy's cautious steps toward autonomy were too frequently discovered, and fiercely punished or destroyed. Consequently, her developing self was inhibited by a frightening and dangerous world that could only be escaped in make-believe.

Within this context, the importance of others' care, belief and support to develop becomes apparent. Wendy's story celebrates the many loving individuals and relationships that enabled her to grow and develop confidence in adulthood. Because Wendy was lucky enough to meet a man who was a film producer, and charismatic enough to attract his interest, in this book we also learn about Wendy's escape into an adult world of fantasy in the film industry. Wendy found that a combination of reality and fantasy, socialising and solitude, gradually helped her to develop and mature in time to meet the love of her life, Raymond. There is beauty in Wendy's account of healing childhood fears with Raymond, as he values her emotional experience and supports her to overlay ingrained terrors with a new sense of safety in the world. While experiences of authentic intimacy are a vital part of the journey, ultimately it is Wendy's own sense of her true nature, and following her desires to fulfil her essential needs, that enables her to find much deserved happiness.

Dr Sharron Smith, Clinical Psychologist (DClinPsy; CPsychol)

ABOUT THE AUTHOR

Don't look to these pages for the answer to the question *"Why?"* Even when Wendy became an adult this torment continued! What we do know is, it's happening to millions all over the world as you read these pages. Unspeakable cruelty to children, wives and husbands.

No way to treat a child contains the painful memories written on these pages by the woman who was once that child, Wendy Marie Knight-Wilton, memories that still generate waking nightmares and many sleepless nights. Wendy's mother died of tuberculosis at the age of twenty-four, leaving Wendy motherless at the age of fourteen months old. She never knew her estranged father. At the time, her grandmother became her guardian, but sadly not her protector. Her uncles had families of their own, and so were very reluctant to take on their young niece. Her aunt, already in declining health, was excused the burden. Eventually, her widowed grandmother, who had suffered chronic asthma all her life, decided she could no longer shoulder the burden of bringing up a child alone. So arrangements would need to be made and Chris and Ken Brisley were brought into this innocent life, eventually adopting her into a hell on earth for the next eighteen years.

From that first day forward the Brisleys made her life a living nightmare. Chris Brisley was the main abuser, but her husband stood by, basically condoning Wendy's daily, everlasting terror. Wendy was unwanted, abused verbally and physically over the years, and always alone. No one knew, or, if they did, no one came forward to help. For self-preservation, she shut herself away in a world of make-believe, conjuring up the images of her dead parents, who would carry her through her childhood and well into her late teens. Each night they would dry her tears and bring comfort to her lonely and isolated world, with her desperate need to be wanted and longing to be loved.

This is the story of one child's agonizing day-to-day torment. Her suffering, though now long past, still often creeps unwanted into her thoughts, casting long dark shadows of her past that will never be forgotten.

She wonders about other children in the world today, enduring what she went through, and, sadly, probably far worse. God keep them safe, and *please* let someone be there to save them.

IN THE BEGINNING

I was caught roughly under the arms and swung up on to a large kitchen table. My small bony legs hung over the side, as I held my hands together with tiny fingers interlaced, ready for the fight that was once again about to begin.

I closed my eyes tightly, clamping my mouth shut as the bottle was pressed hard against my already bruised lips, forcing them open, but not making it past the clenched teeth. The white liquid poured down my chin and pooled onto my lap, soaking the floral cotton dress. Then, gradually, it made rivulets across the table, eventually plopping noisily into a pool on the floor. I hated milk almost as much as I hated the person who now stood before me trying, as she had done for the last two weeks, to make me drink it.

Tears welled in my eyes as I fearfully looked up into the cold, chiseled face of the woman who, not long ago, had become my guardian, and now governed my life.

"I'll make you drink it if it's the last thing I do." Her voice was hard and grating as she smacked me across my face, making me lose my balance and land in a heap on the floor beside the table. "Get up and go to bed. If you won't drink the milk, you're obviously not hungry. There will be no dinner for you tonight. There will be no more food for you until I say so."

My tummy growled with hunger as I scuttled up the stairs and into my room. I undressed and slipped into bed, but not before firmly closing the door. A place to run to, to shut the world away and feel safe. My sanctuary as long as the door remained *closed*. To this day it's very difficult for me to sleep in a bedroom with the door open.

This was the very first recollection of my young life with *her*, and I was not quite five years old, but it remains in glorious technicolor, as vivid today as it was all those years ago.

***

There were strange and wonderful memories that surfaced when the bedroom light went out. A garden. Smiling faces looking down at me. Outstretched fingers, touching my cheeks, puckered lips kissing my eyes, my nose, and my mouth. A young boy with curly auburn hair running in circles around me, teasing and pulling at my hair. Happy days, long and bright. Birdsong, country smells, and the carpeted lawn I would frequently pat, velvet-soft to tiny palms. Laughter and a babble of voices all discussing things I didn't understand, too young to comprehend. Sufficient to know though, even at a very young age, that I was loved and safe.

Those memories, too precious to let go, stayed with me long into each night, stamping a seal of insomnia that would follow me throughout my adult life. Where did they go, those halcyon days? Why were they not still mine to sample and enjoy? What dreadful deed had I perpetrated, taking me from that life into this frightening, unloved setting? Again, too young to understand, but with unfettered knowledge that somewhere, sometime, I *must* have committed something so terrible for this to happen to me. Still, unwilling to pack away the cloak of security, a deft imagination emerged, mingling fact with fiction to create a world in which I could exist throughout the long arduous task of growing from a skinny child into a leggy teenager. Lonely, introverted, and very much unwanted, I grappled with my private world, often letting it lap over into reality when the realism of my existence was too much to endure.

To the two adults who now inhabited my life I was a quiet girl, not prone to childish bursts of exuberance or laughter. Trained as one would train an animal. A command once given never had to be repeated. A task performed to perfection or redone until the adult satisfaction was fulfilled. Those cold, empty eyes spat rage and frustration, trying to control, but *never* owning the small child who most days stood before her, stone-faced and passive, while she vented her feelings upon me and her unfulfilled life.

***

I was born at my grandmother's home on the 5th of January, in the City of Bath, England. I had been christened Wendy Vere Knight-Wilton, but, for some reason, my grandmother always called me Marie. I learned much later that she disliked the name Wendy. My great grandfather was a baron. My grandfather died of tuberculosis before I was born. Eileen, my mother, had already contracted the deadly disease from him. But at the time, her condition was not known. In fact, it was not diagnosed until it was too late. My mother's younger sister Vere also died of tuberculosis, at the age of twenty-one. When I was only fourteen months old, my mother sadly succumbed, and died at the tender young age of twenty-four. Much later in my life I was told by my grandmother that, soon after my mother died, my father was killed in a motorcycle accident. Fact or fiction would only partially come to light many years later. So there it was: at the ripe old age of fourteen months, I was an orphan, with my grandmother still in mourning for her husband and two young daughters. She was now faced with the daunting task of bringing up a baby alone. My grandmother suffered all her life with chronic asthma, which, as she grew older, got worse, leaving her with no option but to look for alternative care for her young grandchild.

A FAMILY SUMMIT

Unknown to me, there were now frantic discussions at the home of my grandmother. Her two sons, Cyril and Bob, along with Maude, the remaining daughter, each with their respective spouses, came to talk about Eileen's child, and what was to be done about her. Not one of the three had come forward to look after me during their sister's illness, and, as tuberculosis was so contagious, it had been imperative that the young baby be removed from the home as soon as possible. To my grandmother's everlasting sadness and embarrassment, I was eventually taken to the local orphanage, where I was cared for until my mother's death. It was while I was there that it was discovered that I had a shadow on my chest, and I was immediately removed to a children's hospital for treatment. Luckily, it was caught early on, and my recovery was quick, though for years I was monitored to make sure that nothing recurred.

So now all the family sat scared witless that one of them would be saddled with a baby they didn't want. Maude was already not in the best of health, so she was excused the burden. Uncle Cyril, the eldest son, had only recently married, and felt it unfair to his new wife to take on someone else's child, albeit his so-called favorite sister's child. Uncle Bob, the youngest son, had a daughter of his own, who was roughly the same age as me. He felt he could not give his niece the affection and attention he so lavishly bestowed upon his own beloved infant. It was a sad betrayal of family unity, and the first betrayal in a litany of events that would virtually separate me from my family forever. In the end, my grandmother decided to care for me herself.

I'm told I was an easy baby to look after. I was a happy, but now fast becoming an inquisitive, toddler. Running from room to room, eager to open drawers for hidden delights. Tiny arms outstretched to reach for treasured ornaments, and family heirlooms. A woman was hired to come in each day to help, and for a while, life was interesting, fun; and in later years, my grandmother confessed that these were some of the happiest days of her life. But that old saying, 'Nothing lasts forever' reared its ugly head. In the winter of my third year, my grandmother became seriously ill. She was rushed to hospital with a chronic asthma attack, and stayed there for six weeks while I once more was shipped off to the local orphanage. Her life expectancy was pronounced as not great, and she was still very frail when she came home. So again, a frantic search began as to where the *child* should go. Again, none of the family rushed to help, so my grandmother soldiered on, knowing that at some time she would have to make a decision as to what should be done about me.

* * *

Confusion, uncertainty and insecurity began in those few short years of my young life, and would follow me well into my middle years. Nothing was ever said, but I learned very quickly to pick up on tensions and atmospheres surrounding me during my stay with my grandmother, even at a very young age, I sensed that nothing was forever.

Even though my grandmother was only in her sixties, she developed arthritis in her hands, it soon became almost impossible for her to do a lot of the things she most liked to do, such as knitting and gardening. Eventually she found someone who would look after the garden and come most weekends. I remember following him around and watching him pulling weeds, pruning roses; and later I would stand close, as he cut those blooms heavy with perfume for the house, letting me bury my nose in each one before giving him my approval. In those balmy days it seemed that it never rained, when he was there I could always be found trailing after the old gardener, watching him work and digging my small fingers into the soft brown earth, loving the feel, the smell, and most of all, loving the green lawn where I would lie looking up at the clear blue sky. I had no idea that, yet again, my world was about to change forever, most certainly not for the better.

LIFE-CHANGING EVENTS

A lot of this story is told retrospectively, for, as a young child, there was much I didn't know, or didn't learn until I was older. By then, I was allowed to visit my grandmother alone, and at those times many questions were asked, and, I hope, were answered honestly. Though as I now look back on my life, it's quite incredible how many incidents I *do* remember: every detailed account, every look, and every heart-stopping dread of what would happen next.

The day of my final departure from my grandmother's home was a Saturday. It was grey, wet and cold. It *must* have been, for such a terrible day could not be any other. I was just four years old.

One Saturday morning, I was brought into my grandmother's sitting room to meet a woman who was to control the next seventeen years of my life. She was a tall, heavy-set woman, with a striking face, dark hair, and black, *black* eyes boring into me; and I knew, even then, that I was frightened of her. I moved closer to my grandmother, and slipped my hand into hers.

In a kind, soft voice, my grandmother leaned toward me and said. "Go to her Marie. This is a very kind lady who is going to take care of you. Eventually she will become your guardian."

My first thought was that she must be someone who had come to look after me. It was only then that I saw a man sitting at the far end of the room, clutching a walking stick. He looked distant, as if he wasn't part of this meeting. I thought then that he was the ugliest man I'd ever seen. Even at a very young age, I could hardly bear to look at him. Sadly, for the rest of my traumatic time spent with this man, I never felt any different, though in later years we came to an understanding.

"This is Chris and Ken Brisley," my grandmother said brightly. "Chris went to the same school as your dear mother, and they stayed friends until Chris and Ken married and moved to London.

"They cannot have children of their own and so..." She then dropped the bombshell that changed my life forever. "After much thought, and a great desire on their part, I have agreed you will live with them. You should have a mother and father to look after you, not live with an old woman who is afraid that each winter will be her last. I want to see you settled before I die." Incidentally, she lived well into her eighties.

I stared up at her in horror. I was still so young but, again, this memory is so clear that I can remember every detail. The utter fear that welled up inside me threatened to explode and split me in two. I opened my mouth and screamed at the top of my voice, then fled from the room. Still screaming, I ran out of the house and into the arms of the gardener. He carried me to a wooden bench and cradled me on his lap, while I sobbed my story out to him. He couldn't bring himself to tell me it would be alright, because I guess he knew it wouldn't. I was told many years later that he informed my grandmother that she had done a terrible thing, and that she would live to regret it one day. Little did he know how true those words were. Try as I might, I can't remember his name, but today, if I close my eyes, I can see him as if he was standing next to me: his weathered face, with clear blue eyes that twinkled as he told me stories about fairies coming out at the stroke of midnight to play in the garden. And the two of us picking strawberries and eating some of them before lunch. He must have been well into his seventies, bent from too many hours digging, weeding, and planting. I will remember him until the day I die, that kind old man who cried with me on the very last carefree day of my childhood.

***

The wheels were duly set in motion, and within a couple of weeks, I left the warmth and security of my grandmother's home. I don't remember her ever talking to me about these two people who were about to take over my life. My cases were packed, and one morning, Mr and Mrs Brisley came to collect me. I stood sobbing as I said goodbye, not knowing whether I would ever see my grandmother again.

***

It was the first time I had been on a train. I sat opposite the man and woman as they silently stared across at me and, I'm sure, wondered what the hell they were going to do with me. I learned that Ken Brisley had lost a leg in the Second World War, though at the time the word war meant nothing to me; but I was reminded on many occasions, this day being the first, of the great sacrifice which he and thousands of others had made for our country. As I looked out of the train window, and watched my countryside disappear, to be replaced by rows of grey buildings, I vaguely remember wondering whether this too was to be *my* sacrifice.

So here I was now, in London – Hampton Hill to be precise – with two people I didn't know, who, though they spoke to each other, never really bothered to speak to *me*. I was alone. No garden to run and play in. No wonderful old man to teach me how to plant flowers and watch them grow. Just a flat above a post office, managed by the man and woman. I have a photographic memory of all the places I stayed in while living with them, and if I think about it now I can still feel the utter panic I felt then, of never being able to get away from these two strangers who now controlled me. Within the first few days, I was given a rigid daily routine, which I had to follow without question.

One morning, after I had been living with them for a couple of months, *the woman* said that they both needed to speak to me. This usually meant that I was in some sort of trouble. As I followed them into the sitting room, I searched my mind, trying to think what I could have done to upset either one. I was told to sit. It was then *the woman* informed me that it was time I started calling them *Mother and Father*. To this day, I can remember being quite stunned by this. The thought of having to call them *anything* was bad enough, but to have to pretend they were my parents was unthinkable. I sat and stared at them. They weren't my parents; I didn't belong to them. I belonged far away with my grandmother, and I knew that one day soon she would come and get me. It was the first time *she* called me an unfeeling block of wood, for outwardly I showed no reaction at all. I was learning, even from a very early age, that whatever happened in my life I would never let anyone know how I was feeling. It was a shield which protected me from the outside world. From then on I would go out of my way not to use those coveted titles; these two people were not worthy of them. It wasn't because I wanted to hurt them; it was because I couldn't bring myself to ever think of me being a part of them. On looking back, it's strange to think that, even before I was five, *I knew I was different.*

Again, years later, I learned from my Uncle Cyril that the post office and buildings in the surrounding area where we were living at the time were to be pulled down, to make way for a housing estate. The Brisleys were soon to be out of a home, and a job.

***

It was Christmas, and we were still living in London. I knew all about Father Christmas. I remembered the last year when my grandmother told me about him coming down the chimney on the twenty-fourth of December when everyone was asleep. It worried me a lot, because from the pictures I'd seen of him, I could tell he was fat, and I wasn't sure he would make it down my grandmother's chimney without getting stuck. But he did come, and the next day all my presents were there under the tree. What a magical time of the year! Even to this day, I still love Christmas, and all the trappings that go with the festive season.

However, this year was different. My grandmother was no longer in my life. The warm happy home was gone, and here I was, wondering whether Father Christmas would still remember me, and bring me presents. I also remember being very concerned I had not told him I had moved. These were a lot of problems for a child who was not quite five years old.

"Until Christmas day you must not go into the front sitting room."

I looked up at *the woman*, not understanding. It had never been a forbidden area before. "Why?" I asked. I still hadn't learned never to ask questions.

"Because I said so," she replied, swatting the back of my head.

Curiosity seared into my senses. What was so important, or so dreadful, that I was not allowed to enter that well-trodden room? Was it because Father Christmas wouldn't get as far as London? Suddenly I couldn't remember what the fireplace was like, and I had a terrible feeling that it had an electric fire fitted into the surround. I had to make sure so that night I crept down the hall from my bedroom and into the prohibited room. There by the window was a small Christmas tree, all decorated ready for the twenty-fifth. I could hardly believe my eyes. Father Christmas would be coming. I rushed over to the fireplace and pulled the electric fire away, peering up the chimney. It looked very small. Still I felt he would manage it. Suddenly the light went on, and *the woman* was standing in the doorway. I ran and cowered behind an armchair.

"You have disobeyed my instructions. You're a bad and hideous child, so there will be no presents for you this year." She stared across at me with those dark black eyes. "You've managed to spoil everything for us all." It was a sentence she would use a lot, and it always made me feel so hopeless and wicked. But I still couldn't believe what I was hearing.

I stuck my head out from behind the chair. "But Father Christmas loves me and I know *he* will give me presents," I answered, in a timid voice.

"There's no such person as Father Christmas, he's just an imaginary figure, and the sooner you learn that the better. You refused to follow a command, and will now be punished for it." She ordered me to stand in front of her then smacked me hard across my face. "You will do as I say, when I say it, or you will get far worse than that." I remember thinking how terrible it was to have so-called parents, and wondered whether all parents hit their children as these people did. I was sure they did, and felt sorry for every child I saw along my journey of growing up.

She was correct. There were no presents for me that year. The tree was dismantled the next day. My grandmother's gift was given to me on my birthday, along with my birthday present. I received no other presents. It was a salutary lesson to learn, and I never disobeyed her again.

A couple of weeks later, and to mark the occasion of my fifth birthday, my grandmother apparently requested that I had a professional photograph taken. On the fifth of January, I was taken to a studio in the City. I remember it being quite dark and bare, except for a small stool in the middle of the room and a flowered screen behind it. The photographer was a large man, though at my age I expect every grown man looked big. He told me to sit on the stool while he straightened my dress and tidied my hair. He pointed to a strange object in front of me, and told me to watch for the birdie; if I was a good girl, and remained very still, the birdie would fly out and sit on my hand. I was so excited I didn't take my eyes off of the camera waiting for the little fluffy creature to fly out.

Of course, it didn't, and I sat there in complete and abject misery, knowing that I obviously *was* a very bad girl, and maybe *she* was right. I ached for the little creature to fly out, to come to me and sit on my hand, for even at a very young age I always adored them, especially English robins. I thought about the visit on and off for years. I always hoped that, one day, I would meet the photographer and it would have given me immense pleasure to give him a piece of my mind. What a stupid and very careless thing to say to any child! I still have the photograph and the memories that go with it.

These were dark cold days for me, for I simply had no one to talk to. I was completely regimented by this time, and would get up each morning, make my bed, then go to the kitchen, where my breakfast was laid out on the table, which I would eat then wash and put away the dishes. I had been taught from the very first day how to wash dishes. After that, there was simply nothing for me to do. I would sit on a chair until lunch, when the Brisleys would come up to the flat from the post office. Nothing was said to me; it was as if I didn't exist. After lunch, they would leave me to wash up again and wait in my bedroom until they returned. They had put some children's books by the side of my bed, but I couldn't read, so I contented myself with looking at the pictures over and over again. I must have become almost monosyllabic because after a few weeks I would only speak if spoken to, which was usually a command to either do or not do something. What a very strange child I was turning into, and, oh, I was so lonely, and so very afraid!

GRANDPA LEWIS

After just a few short months, our time in London came to an end. We were all packed up, and heading back to Bath. I was deliriously happy. For some reason, I thought I would be given back to my grandmother, and this horrendous period of my life would be over. After arriving at the City station, the suitcases were piled into the back of a taxi. We ended up in a tiny street at the home of Mr and Mrs Lewis Chalker. I later found out that they were *the woman's* parents. They turned out to be the sweetest couple on earth: old-fashioned, humble and quiet people, who had never controlled, and still didn't know how to control, their only daughter. Even as a small child I could see the pain in their eyes as she ranted on about her ruined life with the husband, who was now half a man, and whom she detested.

She would point to me, and I remember clearly her saying, "She was a huge mistake; I was never meant to be a mother, and should not have agreed with Cecily Knight to have her. All this talk of her mother's money coming to us for her upbringing has still not materialized. It's probably been divided between the family, and we won't see a penny." Throughout the years she would often say this as if I was a delivered package, who most certainly hadn't lived up to their expectations. I didn't understand what she meant. I only knew I was a great disappointment to everyone, including my grandmother.

Grandpa Lewis, as I called him, was a tiny man with a balding head, but the hair he had left was carefully waved each morning into a sausage curl at each side of his head. He was soft and gentle, always trying to shield me from his daughter's anger for whatever misdemeanour I'd perpetrated at any given time.

I remember that, one evening, I was sent to bed without supper, and Grandpa Lewis crept up the stairs with a huge chicken sandwich and a hot chocolate drink. Pressing his fingers to his lips, he told me it would be our secret. I know this mild-mannered man was *very* intimidated by his loud overpowering daughter. In the next few months, while his daughter and son-in-law looked for a house to rent, Grandpa Lewis could always be relied upon, at any missed meal, to bring me supper and tuck me up in bed. His wife, Florence Chalker, was a stout woman, with long white hair which she would twist up into a bun each morning. I used to sit mesmerized by the way she would twirl her hair around her fingers, securing it to the nape of her neck with large black pins. She was kind but a fairly distant woman. I'm sure she never did understand why her daughter had taken on the burden of looking after someone else's child, when her own life was in such disarray. I don't think she ever knew why and I most certainly didn't.

It is now incredible to know that, whilst living in the tiny over-crowded terrace house in Bath, I was virtually within walking distance from my grandmother's home. Yet during the almost eighteen months of my stay there, I never saw her once.

***

Grandpa Lewis was a gardener. I had found another soul mate. At the rear of his house, he had a narrow, but long garden, which he filled with flowers. It was the first time I'd seen or heard of Lilies of the Valley. They are a small white bell flower, with an incredible perfume. He'd planted a huge patch of them outside the kitchen window. When they were in bloom, the smell was almost overpowering. I would kneel down and bury my head in them. At the other side of the path, he had a strawberry bed. During the summer, the bed produced some of the sweetest fruit I have ever tasted, and – ah yes! – that strawberry patch. On one hot summer afternoon, I was in the garden and the sight of those bright red strawberries was too much for me. I looked up and down the path to see if anyone was looking and then set to work eating those succulent berries. Suddenly the back door opened, and *she* was standing there. I was asked whether I had eaten any of the strawberries, and, shaking my head, I emphatically answered no. Never in my young life had I seen such a look of fury and hate. I had been caught out in a lie. She was upon me like a wild animal before I had time to move, and beat the living daylights out of me. My head, my body, my arms and legs. Nothing was safe from her rage. Grandpa Lewis rushed out of the house pulling her off and hurrying me inside. I was in a terrible mess. One black eye, a bleeding nose, and a lot of bruising to my body, which came out in a rainbow of painful colors during the next few days. I hobbled to my room, and lay fully clothed, shivering with fear under the bed covers. I was in so much pain that I couldn't even undress. It was the only time I ever heard Grandpa Lewis raise his voice, as I lay crying uncontrollably in my bed. I couldn't hear all the shouting that went on between them but every now and then *she* would scream out things like, "She's a liar. She no good, a bad lot." I was simply terrified. I heard Grandpa Lewis tell her that I was a mere child, and that all children told lies; and he also said that he could see I was simply petrified of her. I didn't understand what he was saying but somehow his words summed up what I was feeling at that very moment. Later on, during the evening, when she had calmed down, I heard Grandpa Lewis tell her that, one day, if she wasn't careful, she would kill me. I was in awe about this, and wondered what it meant. He told her he wanted to go to my grandmother and ask her to take me back. I sat up, straining my ears; sheer electrifying excitement welled up inside of me. I was going home! But by then, they had both calmed down, and I couldn't hear any more of the conversation. Sadly, Grandpa Lewis never did go to my grandmother. *She* never hit me again in his presence. But when he was away, I was always fair game for her moods. I still loved Grandpa Lewis's garden, but from then on kept well away from the strawberry patch.

***

It was at this time that I started helping him weed various beds, and would spend hours watering the lavender bushes, rose bushes, and other flowers and shrubs, too numerous to mention. When he

27

returned from work in the evenings, I would join him in the garden. We would potter, as he called it, up and down the path, spraying the roses or pruning any shrub or plant that needed pruning. He could see how much I enjoyed being with him. So one Saturday morning, he asked his daughter if he could take me with him to the allotment, which she readily agreed to. I was completely mystified by this word 'allotment', but the thought of spending time with this sweet man and away from *her* made me almost sick with excitement. I soon found out that the allotment was a piece of land owned by the city, which was divided up and rented out so that people could grow vegetables to feed their families. The practice was started during the war by Winston Churchill when fresh food was scarce, and carried on through the fifties and sixties, though I believe some are still in England to this day.

Grandma Chalker packed us a lunch, and off we went. It took about half an hour to walk through the back lanes to this place called the allotment. We were like two children let out of school, and determined to enjoy every precious minute. When we arrived, I stood gazing in wonderment at the sight before me. There must have been around thirty men, some with their children, either digging, planting, talking, or drinking tea. They were a noisy and happy bunch. Some were showing off their vegetables with pride, while others were packing fruit, vegetables, and various assortments of flowers into the back of a van. It was a hive of activity.

Grandpa Lewis was watching me and suddenly burst out laughing. "It's obvious you've never seen an allotment before," he said, ruffling my hair as he passed me, leading the way to his patch of land. I think my eyes must have grown as big as saucers as I looked at all the various things he had growing there. At my young age, I didn't know or recognize what most of the foliage was, but I can tell you his patch was crammed full of the most interesting and exciting greenery. At one end, he had a double row of what I learned were bamboo canes stuck in the earth and tied together at certain places. They were for runner beans. He walked me up and down paths he made from paving slabs, showing me what he was growing.

There were potatoes, cabbages, sprouts, kale, turnips, carrots, and cauliflowers. I was struck dumb. My first thought was that he must be so rich to have all of this wonderful food. Even way back then, I was a hearty eater. I was as thin as a bean pole, but I could certainly pack it away. I know without a doubt that in the short time I spent living with the Chalkers, I acquired the taste for all vegetables.

From then on, rain or shine, Grandpa Lewis would take me with him to *our* allotment each Saturday morning, and we would spend those glorious days digging, weeding, and bringing home baskets laden with goodies to last us throughout the following week.

***

Not long after I returned to Bath, I was told by Ken and Chris Brisley that they had become my legal guardians. They showed me a piece of paper, which I couldn't read, to prove it. I was confused and deeply troubled by this new turning in my life. I didn't understand why my grandmother had given me to these people in the first place. I was still too young to grasp the meaning of life and death; I knew I didn't want to live with the Brisleys. Sadly, though, after some time had passed I began to accept they must now be part of my life. Even then I always hated this knowledge. I would look at them and almost cringe. I could never bear to be too close to them. I would watch other children with their parents, and although they were laughing and playing together, I was absolutely sure they were not happy; how could they be? All parents, and so-called parents like mine must treat their children in the same way; if not, why were these two people so different? I was coming up to six years old.

Because of our move from London, I was late starting school, but soon I was enrolled into a kindergarten school, which was virtually a ten minute walk away from the Chalkers' home. After a few weeks, I was allowed to walk to the school by myself each morning and home each afternoon. In those days, life wasn't fettered with all the dreadful problems we have today. A child could walk to school without the fear of being kidnapped, or offered drugs. From my first day at school, I was in love with it. Not necessarily for the learning, but the chance to spend time away from home and with other children, who all seemed so happy and carefree. I distinctly remember that for the first few weeks I would stand in the corner of the playground watching them, wondering why they laughed so much, for I simply knew they must secretly be as unhappy as me. I was still much too young for envy, as I observed them interacting with their chosen friends. But there was a great yearning inside of me for a friend of my own, though I had no idea how to achieve this.

It was probably a couple of months into my first term when I became friends with a plump little girl with huge brown eyes and a very freckled face. Or rather, she became friends with me.

As usual, I was sitting on one of the playground benches, watching a group of children playing together. I was never asked to join in. I think I was known as *the weird one*. If either child or adult tried to speak to me, I would blush beetroot red and stammer over each word. You see I had never been taught how to interact with other people.

Susan Bishop became my friend through hard work. At first, I think I was quite rude to her. I found her attention much too complicated, and although I desperately wanted someone of my own, I hadn't the first idea how to go about getting to know that someone. Susan, bless her heart, never gave up. I firmly think I became a challenge to her.

On this particular morning break she came over and sat next to me. I immediately wanted to leave, yet found myself rooted to the spot.

"Hello, Marie." She smiled across at me. "We've all talked about you, and decided you're not very friendly."

I stared back at her. How could I tell her that I didn't know *how* to be friendly? Instead, I shook my head and suddenly, to my horror, I felt tears well up and run down my face. She stood, and at first I thought she was leaving me. But she turned to face me and put out her chubby arms, pulling me up and holding me tight. I then sobbed until there were no more tears left. From that day on, Susan Bishop was my constant companion at school. On a school morning, she would wait for me at the corner of my road, and we would walk the rest of the way together. We were the same age with birthdays just a month apart. Incredible to think how independent we were at such a tender age. Many mornings I wouldn't talk to her. I couldn't talk, probably because the night before had been so traumatic. So we would walk together in silence. What on earth made this particular child so wise beyond her years I will never know, but somehow on those mornings she seemed to understand and we would walk hand in hand, in silence, until we reached the school gates. It's strange: I can remember those very early days with such clarity, and even at such a young age I became so deeply locked up into a world of my own. It often became difficult, no, almost impossible, for me to re-enter the harsh reality of my existence. I realize now that I have a photographic memory of my life as a child. I know some children block out their horrors of childhood, and there are still some days when I wish that I could do the same.

I would sit and daydream at school, with only Susan to completely understand this solitary girl. Luckily, I was a bright student. Learning to read came easily and quickly. Apart from Susan, books were to become my constant companions. I knew all about Enid Blyton's famous five. I read *Little Women* and *Good Wives* twice before I was eight. I simply loved Aesop's Fables, and JM Barrie's Peter Pan and Wendy. Reading took me out of my solitary and lonely world into journeys of excitement and adventure. Looking back now, I realize that I very rarely lived in reality. I was always off on some dramatic adventure, where I was loved, admired and always the center of attention.

***

I was seven when once again my life changed. Ken got a position in the Admiralty, which had offices in Bath at the time. With help from his job, they managed to get a mortgage for a lovely house situated at Odd Down, one of the seven Downs of Bath. It was a far cry from the Chalkers' terrace house, and had a fair-sized rear garden overlooking the local cricket field. I certainly never understood cricket, and still don't, but it was so exciting to watch the players on a Saturday afternoon, all dressed in their whites, hitting a ball and running around like mad people trying to catch it. It wasn't long before Chris and Ken Brisley became involved in the community's activities. Ken loved to watch the cricket, and I loved helping to assemble the deck chairs around the field. I think the best part of those afternoons was also being allowed to help the cricketers' wives make the sandwiches for afternoon tea, though I'm quite sure I was more of a nuisance than a help. It was such pleasure sitting in a deck chair munching thin egg and watercress sandwiches and drinking ice cold lemonade.

There was, though, a terrible downside to the new home because it meant my Saturdays with Grandpa Lewis were at an end. Sadly, I didn't see him very much after the move, and I often wondered if he missed me as much as I did him.

Soon after we moved into the new house, *the woman* took me to see my grandmother. It must have been over a year since I had last seen her. My only thought was that I hoped she would remember me. Before the meeting, I was constantly prepped as to how I would behave, and told what to say if asked how I was, and if I was happy. I sat nodding my head like a puppet, suddenly feeling very tense and agitated, worried I would say something that would be considered absolutely wrong. I decided I would say nothing at all. That way I would not get into trouble when I left my grandmother's house.

This meeting, yet again, is indelibly stamped into my memory bank. The sheer emotional turmoil of walking into the house that had once been my home was all too much for me. I simply broke down the minute I saw my grandmother. Running over to her, I buried my head in her skirt, and sobbed until I could hardly breathe. There was much agitation, with my grandmother getting very upset and Chris Brisley assuring her it was because I had been ill with a stomach upset for the last two days, which of course was completely untrue. It was the very first time I experienced what became known to me as *the look.* Whilst tea was being organized, *the woman,* which I now secretly called her, stared at me with those large black empty eyes. She said nothing, but continued to bore through me, closing those eyes until they were mere slits in her head. I knew I was in deep trouble. From then on *the look* never failed to absolutely terrify me, and was used by her until the day I left her and would always leave me almost immobilized with fear and dread, knowing it was a prelude of worse things to come.

The minute she closed the front door of our home she hit me. "That's for making such a scene. God knows what your grandmother must have thought of you." She continued hitting me, not caring where the blows landed, as I ran like a frightened rabbit up the stairs. I knew I must never cry again when visiting my grandmother.

MY CHRISTMAS ANGEL

We had been living in the new house for about a month when I was sent to another school nearer home. Unlike my first school, I didn't seem to fit into this one. It was a much bigger school, with children ranging from five to ten years old. I can't remember making any new friends while I was there, which thankfully turned out to be for only a short time. I remember being absolutely desolate that I would be leaving Susan Bishop. Apart from Grandpa Lewis, Susan was the only friend I had in the world. I never saw or heard from her again, and only saw Grandpa Lewis when we were invited to visit, which sadly wasn't very often.

It was getting near the end of term, with Christmas a couple of weeks away. One of the teachers at my new school, with the help of some of the older girls, put up a Christmas tree in the main hall. It was lovely. The whole school gathered to help decorate it with handmade decorations that had been made over the years and we all watched while it was lit. The first thing that caught my eye was the angel at the top of the tree. She was dressed in white satin and had a luminous halo with wings as sheer as a butterfly. She was so pretty and I desperately wanted her. Each morning before the holidays we would assemble in the hall for morning prayers and I would look up at the angel. I simply had to have her. On the Friday evening just before the end of term, when the hall was empty, I climbed onto a chair, reached up, unplugged and pulled the angel from the tree. As I held her in my hands I thought she was even more beautiful and now she was mine. I tucked her away in my school satchel and set off for home.

She looked wonderful on our Christmas tree, and I told *the woman* she had been a present from school. There was no excuse for what I'd done. I only say that maybe if I'd had more toys of my own, I wouldn't be looking at other objects, or maybe I took it because I wanted it? Anyway, Christmas came and went. For me it was always a fairly solitary event. Another ordinary day with a tree in the front room. No joy of opening presents, though I did get some, mainly books, which I loved.

A few days into my return to school for the new term, I was given a letter to take home. Chris Brisley was asked to come to the school to see the headmistress. I had a lead feeling in the pit of my stomach and I knew it wasn't good, though I had no idea what the pending visit would be about. Sadly, one of the teachers had seen me taking the angel off the tree. She didn't say anything at the time, because she was hoping that I would bring it back. After the head mistress and *the woman* had finished their meeting, I was brought into the room and asked about the angel. I remember shaking with fear not daring to look at either of them. I cried and said I was sorry and I would bring it back. The head mistress was so kind, and knew I was repentant. She was told by *the woman* that I would get a good talking to when I got home. *She* didn't talk to me on the way home and her silence was ominous. As we entered the house, I was commanded to go to my room and lay across the bed and wait for her. She then beat me with a belt, buckle side to my body, which seemed to go on forever, but I kept telling myself that this time I deserved to be punished. When she'd finished I was so bruised with welts that stood out on my back like thick ridges. I rose stiffly from the bed. I could hardly walk let alone sit down. She had now learned to hit me in places where it didn't show. Needless to say I was sent to bed without food, but bed was my refuge and I was used to not eating for long periods so I hardly thought about it. Much later on that night *she* came back into the bedroom and told me to get dressed. It was still mid winter, dark and very cold outside. We left the house and walked in silence to a wooded area called Kilkenny Woods which was about twenty minutes away from where we lived. I had no idea why. I knew it was very late, very dark with an icy cold wind that almost took my breath away. I was not dressed for such weather, wearing just a thin blouse and skirt, and soon could hardly feel my extremities. My body was also so bruised with some of the welts now bleeding, making my clothes stick to my skin, so that it became almost impossible to walk. When we got to the edge of the woods I suddenly felt very afraid. We walked on in silence until we were well into the woods. She then turned to me telling me I needed to be taught a lesson and she was going to leave me there to think about the terrible thing I'd done, and then... *she walked away*. It was so black that I couldn't even see my hand in front of my face. I don't think I'd ever been so terrified in all my young life. I remember standing there, listening to the night sounds of animals and the cacophony of the trees and underbrush as the wind howled through the branches. I stood shivering with the cold, crying pitifully. Eventually I curled myself into a small ball trying to keep warm, shutting my eyes tightly so I wouldn't see any of the hideous creatures I was so sure roamed those woods at night. My imagination ran into overdrive and I stayed there trembling with dread, willing myself to stay as still as possible. I don't know how long I remained there, but I know it was well into the early hours of the morning. I told God I was so sorry and would never ever take anything again. But, I knew whatever happened to me after this night I would always fear and hate *the woman* far more than I ever thought possible. From that evening on, I could not bear dark places. Looking into unlit areas always scared me. It sounds silly but even to this day there are certain rooms in my home that have to be lit; if not, they are dark holes filling me with uncertainty and an almost choking unreasonable fear. I have tried to be logical about these feelings, but they are buried so deep within me and I know I will never be free of them. Eventually, on that terrible night, she returned and we walked back to the house in silence. The next day while eavesdropping, which I did often, I overheard Ken arguing with her about leaving me alone and unprotected. Her answer was, that she had only been a few feet away and had been watching me the whole time; and anyway, if something untoward had happened, she would have said that I had slipped out of the house and ran away. It seemed to satisfy him, and made me feel more alone and frightened than ever.

Ken wasn't as cruel as his wife, but he did have a flash point and if it was reached, then he would lash out at anyone and anything. I think he was too wrapped up with his own problems. Losing a leg, plus three years in a prisoner of war camp had taken their toll on him. He just wanted a quiet life; also being married to her must have been hell for him and now a child whom he most certainly didn't want.

Soon after this incident, there was another summit meeting at my grandmother's home. It was decided that I should be sent to a private school. Later my grandmother told me she had become greatly concerned about me being so introverted, and thought it best I spend more time with children of my own age.

***

A couple of weeks later, I was taken on the bus by Chris Brisley to the Parade, a circular paved area where all the buses ended their journey into the centre of the city from various parts of Bath. We then walked over the Pulteney bridge which crossed the Avon river toward a large building at the end of a long road. It was the only time I ever entered the building through the front door. My family were all Catholics, and, apparently at my grandmother's insistence, I was to be sent to a convent.

CONVENT

We were shown into a large, high-ceilinged room with mahogany walls, deep soft armchairs, and a large desk at the far end. We were offered tea and biscuits by a motherly looking woman. As usual, I wasn't told why I was there, so I sat with mounting apprehension wondering what I'd done wrong this time, to be brought here. Sadly, I spent most of my childhood and young adult life always thinking I'd done something bad whenever circumstances were beyond my control, or no knowledge of what was happening to me. Eventually, a nun entered the room. It was the first time I had ever met one in person, but I immediately knew who she was. I must have read about them in a book somewhere. I remember thinking that she was very beautiful, and the black robe she wore made her look not of this world, for she seemed to float across the room. She and Chris Brisley talked for a few minutes, I was then informed that I would be taking a small exam. Completely mystified, I followed her into another room where I sat at a desk and was given pen and paper along with a written questionnaire. For a few minutes, I remember sitting there completely dumbfounded not knowing what to make of it. However after a few minutes I read the exam paper and answered all the questions.

I was then taken back to the first room, which I later found out was the Reverend Mother's private study.

Remember that, even then, I still didn't know why I was there, so it came as a complete surprise when the Reverend Mother asked me if I would like to be a weekly boarder at their school. She could see by my reaction that I had no clue. She took both my hands in hers and told me in a very soft voice, I would be very happy there, and I was obviously a highly intelligent child. Oh God, I completely fell in love with her from that moment on. My spirits soared. I really had no idea what the future had in store for me, and didn't care for I now knew I would be away from *the woman* and her husband for long periods of time. I was completely euphoric. From then on my school days were to become the happiest of my young life.

***

The next few weeks were a whirl of activity. I was attired in my maroon-coloured winter uniform. The list included everything, right down to vest and knickers. The uniform had to be *exact*. Later on, I remember arriving at school one Monday morning only to be sent home because I was wearing white socks instead of beige. The rules were very strict, and there were no excuses. On looking back, I totally agree with school uniforms. It makes everyone feel the same. No one looks richer or poorer than the next child. And for me, it gave me a sense of belonging.

On the Saturday morning, two days before I was due to start at my new school, we were sitting down to a breakfast of boiled eggs and toast. I was having great difficulty cracking open the top of my egg. *The woman* told me to take a knife and slice the top off. I tried but the egg was too hot for me to hold. She was furious. She caught both of my hands and held my fingers around the egg until I screamed out in pain. She then cuffed me on the side of my head, knocking me off the chair, something she did at fairly regular intervals. It was the first time I saw Ken get really angry with her. I don't think it was because he felt sorry for me, but he could see my fingers were already beginning to blister and he was worried they wouldn't heal before I started my new school. He was correct. My fingers were in a terrible state on my first Monday morning. When we arrived at the convent, *she* went into overdrive, telling the nun, who met us, that I had picked up a hot pan from the stove. The nun believed her. Why wouldn't she? I, along with my suitcase, was now a weekly boarder at La Sainte Union Convent school. My life had changed yet again.

***

I found the next few hours traumatic. I was handed over to yet another nun and taken up to the dormitory and shown a bed at the end of a long line of beds that was to be mine. I was told that when I was not sleeping in it, it had to be made at all times and kept neat. There was a bedside cabinet next to it. I was then shown a small wardrobe for my clothes. The nun, who I later learned was the dormitory nun, then glided out of the room, telling me to come downstairs when I had finished unpacking. I cried as I hung my coat, blazer, and the extra blouses up in the wardrobe, and put the folded underwear and socks away on the shelf at the top. I'm not sure if it was from fear of the unknown or from the dreadful pain in my fingers as I fumbled to keep everything neat. Yes, I was a neat freak even at a very young age.

I stood at the door of the dormitory for at least five minutes, steeling myself to go down those stairs, hoping and praying that I wouldn't get lost. Luckily the nun was waiting for me at the end of the corridor. She smiled as I walked toward her, telling me all the nuns at the convent were called Madam, and she was Madam Mary and suddenly I felt secure. I followed her out of the building, across a grass square and into another building, where I could hear children's voices, so I knew this must be where the classes were. My stomach churned and I felt sick. And remember, at that age I was still so shy that I was almost mute. Words didn't come easily; also, I had started my convent life in the middle of a term. So, as the saying goes, I would be the new kid on the block. I was simply dreading it. I looked pleadingly up at her. She must have sensed my fear, for she took my hand in hers and gave it a squeeze. Needless to say I cried out with pain. She turned both my hands palm up and looked in horror at the still huge watery blisters adorning most of my fingers. Again tears rolled down my cheeks. This was a terrible way to start a new life.

Madam Mary, who had dedicated herself to God, was to become a very important person in my young life. She whisked me back to the main building and into a small office where the Matron of the school sat sipping tea. Matron took one look at my fingers and started asking questions. I couldn't remember what *the woman* had said so I stood looking at the two women, completely speechless.

Then suddenly I said. "I think I picked up something hot from the stove."

"*Just* with your fingers?" Matron asked. "And not using your thumbs at all?"

I nodded miserably. Shaking her head, she then made a quick arm movement over my head to get to a medicine cabinet. I immediately flinched and ducked. I remember both women staring at me and I knew *they* knew. Again, in those years people didn't voice their concerns to the appropriate authorities. It wasn't the time where you couldn't smack a child or chastise them for being naughty, mind you I think they would have spoken out at criminal mistreatment, but I was someone who clearly was slipping through the cracks. Matron bandaged both hands while they talked in whispers about whether I was well enough to start classes yet. I quickly assured them I was. I couldn't bear to be closeted somewhere waiting for my fingers to heal, not knowing when I had to face the new class. I would much rather get the inevitable over with. So once again, I followed Madam Mary across the grass square toward the room that was to be my class.

I was taken in and introduced to a teacher called Miss Ryder. She was a tiny little person, wearing incredibly high heeled shoes and I guess, to an adult, would have been considered quite attractive, but for her extremely large nose, which seemed to dominate her whole body. She quickly acknowledged me, telling me to find a desk, then continued on with the lesson, which was English History. I gazed around the room at the sea of faces all staring back at me with open curiosity. I started to shake with embarrassment. Not one single desk was free, so I stood there feeling extremely silly, now aware that along with me my bandaged hands were causing a lot of attention. After what seemed an eternity, Miss Ryder suddenly realized that I was still cowering beside her. I opened my mouth to speak but no sound came out. Thankfully a young girl with masses of frizzy red hair came to my rescue, explaining to the teacher that all the desks were taken. Soon there was a hive of activity with children and teacher moving desks around, while a maintenance man brought in a new one. It was placed right at the front of the class. I felt conspicuous and silly, knowing that the whispers emanating from the girls could only be about me.

It seemed that no sooner had I sat down than a bell sounded, heralding the end of the lesson and the beginning of the morning break. All the girls made an *en masse* dash for the door, leaving me still sitting at my desk. A few minutes later the girl with the red frizzy hair came rushing back, grabbed my arm and navigated me toward the playground.

Ah, the playground! It was beyond my imagination. Indeed there *was* a playground at one end, but the rest of it was in lawns with shrubs and hedges dividing the playing area from the tennis and netball courts. Running along the other side was a larger hedge backed by a high wall with a gate. There was another building on the other side of this hedge, which I later learned was the nuns residence. Their private garden looked out on to a field used for hockey and other sporting activities. The whole place was absolutely beautiful. I stared around in wonderment; even at my young age, surroundings completely governed my moods. I knew I was going to love this school.

The frizzy haired girl, who was called Elizabeth, and, yes, was nicknamed *Frizzy Lizzie* by all her friends, had obviously taken charge of me. In some ways she reminded me of Susan Bishop, though I was in no way inclined to rush into any friendship with her. I truly resented her at the time, feeling that she was trying to manipulate me. I remember being extremely cold and distant with her. Her show of friendship bounced off of me like a tennis ball to a racquet, yet, like Susan, she didn't give up, and in her girlish way told me that we were going to be friends, and she would look after me. It's strange when I think about it, but all through my life, people have come into it and often had to fight hard to get to know me; and yes, at first, I always shied away from these attachments. Some were good and others were not. There were a number of females who were overly possessive, some of them even trying to control me. A lot were very jealous of what they thought my life was. To them, because I was so distant, I was from some sort of privileged background and worthy of a certain amount of jealousy. God, how wrong they were! Also, during all my years at school, no one knew how terrible my life was at home. I always lied about it, making out how loved I was and how terrifically wonderful everything was at home. For a very long time, I always thought that somehow it was my fault, and that maybe I deserved to be treated badly. Also I was always told by *her* how ugly I was, so naturally I *felt* ugly and uncoordinated, and, to this day, find it difficult and almost embarrassing when anyone pays me a compliment. My biggest handicap throughout my childhood and young teens, though, was being so shy, and usually completely tongue-tied. I *hated* meeting new people, and would immediately put up a barrier. It was as if I was telling the world that no one was going to get to know me or hurt me. I would never let it happen. So you see, poor Frizzy Lizzie truly had her work cut out for her, yet she soldiered on, God knows why.

For the first month, I stayed as a full time boarder at the convent. I think it was for me to get used to my surroundings. It was amazing how quickly I settled into this new life. I loved the order of it all. Up at seven a.m.: shower, dress, and make our beds. Down to the chapel for morning prayers, then to the refectory for breakfast and school at nine a.m. sharp. Though I still wasn't aware of my family being Catholic, it was at this time I became interested in the catholic religion. Not difficult really, when I was completely surrounded by all things catholic. Again, it gave me a sense of belonging and stability, something I greatly needed in my young life. I simply soaked it all up, and loved the religious lessons. Again, at the time, if a child went to a convent whether or not she was a catholic, it was mandatory she was included in all the religious lessons. I also *loved* the mass on Sunday morning, even though at the time it was all in Latin. I found the whole ceremony quite amazing: all the glitz that went along with it; the robes worn by the priests; the sound of the choir as their voices reverberated around the church; the altar boys walking up and down the aisles holding the incense in a burner on a long chain and wafting it over the congregation. The smell would stay in my nostrils throughout the Sunday, and I felt so very holy.

My first weekend home was a complete disaster. I hated leaving the warmth and love I found at my school, and dreaded the return to *her*. On that Friday evening, I kept telling myself that it was only for two days, but at the age of seven, two days is a lifetime away. I walked along the road and over the Putney bridge toward the Parade where the bus would take me home. I paid the fare and sat stiff with overwhelming dread, wondering what sort of welcome I would receive.

I arrived home around five p.m., and stood trembling before the front door. I was to stand at various front doors for many years to come, wondering what mood *she* would be in. My stomach was tied in knots, and I felt sick. It was the first time, since I'd been sent to live with her, that I'd been away from her for so long. I didn't have a key, so I knocked timidly on the door; there was no answer. There was no one at home. I waited until around seven p.m. for her to come home. When she finally arrived, she looked at me as if I was an insect that should be exterminated.

"So you've decided to grace us with your presence," were her first words, shoving me through the front door and into the kitchen. As I looked at the mess before me, I couldn't believe my eyes. It was obvious the room hadn't been touched in days. I was told Ken was away on business and would not be home until the following week. She had taken a job as a nurse at a private nursing home, looking after elderly patients. I was somewhat surprised by this information. I knew she was a lot of things, but the nurse information was new; still, at the time, I didn't think to query it, even in my mind. She was always what she said she was. I was then told that she was tired and needed a rest. The kitchen had to be cleaned before I would get any supper. I think it was around this time I started to learn how to become a good housekeeper. From then on, whenever I was at home, it was always my job to wash up, clean, and keep the house tidy. I was seven years old going on forever. She didn't wake up to get supper, so I ate bread and jam and put myself to bed.

Soon after my night in Kilkenny Woods, the woman knew I was now petrified of the dark, so from then on her new punishment for anything I did that wasn't to her liking was to lock me in the hall cupboard under the stairs for hours as a punishment. One afternoon, after washing the lunch dishes I dropped a plate which smashed, scattering fragments over the kitchen floor. She was there in a flash smacking my head and body while dragging me off to the now dreaded cupboard. I heard the key turn and crouched down in the corner, shutting my eyes tight and once again willed myself not to open them until the door was unlocked. I thought she must have forgotten me for I stayed huddled in that corner until the morning came and I heard the lock turning. Stiff and cold I crawled out to face a new day. I soon realized she had not forgotten me for there were many nights to come when I knew I wouldn't be let out of that cupboard until the morning.

Whenever I slept at home, I always knew what mood she was in by the call from her bedroom to mine in the morning. If she was in a bad mood she would yell out, saying that I was a lazy good for nothing little cow, and I was to get up and make her breakfast. This I did at top speed, trying not to incur any more of her wrath. If she was in a good mood, she would call to me in a soft voice, asking me nicely if I would make her breakfast. It made my flesh crawl.

Throughout my years at the convent, my weekends at home were like an unexploded bomb of emotions. Never quite knowing how to please *the woman*, always hoping that she was in a good mood, and always scurrying around like an ill-treated dog, cringing away from her, watching her body language to see where I stood for the next few hours. Although Ken lived in the same house, it was as if he didn't exist. I usually managed to keep out of his way, and I guess he did the same with me. It's very strange but looking back on those years I never actually knew these two people. Even though, years later, I met Ken again, I still never truly knew him.

Around this time, as regular as clockwork, every Sunday

morning I would wake up with a dreadful headache, so much so that I could hardly bare to move. It was only much later that I realized that it was because on the Saturday, there was shopping to be done, which meant me getting out of the house, because it was me who did all the shopping. On the Sunday, I was closeted with *her and Ken* for the whole day, and there was simply no way of getting away from them. I always seemed to be the fuse for their arguments, which were too numerous to count. I remember one Sunday morning, the argument started off as usual, with both saying how much they hated one another. I'm not sure how it escalated into a full blown war, but at the time I thought they were going to kill each other. Let's put it this way, I *hoped* they would kill each other. How terrible for such a young child to desire another person's death. But I didn't think of it like that. I thought that, if they were gone, then I would have to go back and live with my grandmother. Yes, I was still obsessed with returning home to my Grandmother. On that day, I remember seeing Chris Brisley standing in the kitchen, with her head stuck between two cupboard door handles, and Ken trying to throttle the life out of her. The fight went on for sometime, until at last Ken realized he was out of control. He let her go, and she fell to the ground gasping for air. I was very disappointed.

VELVET SKIRT

There was one bright spot on those dark weekends, and it was the present my grandmother gave me for my eighth birthday. It was a lovely velvet skirt with a yellow and gold sweater. The skirt was a multi-colour mixture of autumnal shades. They were the most beautiful colours I had ever seen, and I think that, right then and there, it started my love of rustic shades: marigold oranges, deep reds and sunburnt browns. The velvet material made the skirt fall around my legs in soft folds, and had a slight swishing sound as I walked. I felt like a princess each time I wore it. I was only allowed to wear it on Saturdays, and again, only if I was at home and not at school. It certainly made my home weekends much more tolerable. It's strange how small things can bring such joy to a very introverted child, but when those Saturdays came around I would take the skirt from my wardrobe and the sweater from the drawer and lay them out on the bed, before I had my morning bath. It was a weekend ritual that never ceased to bring me an incredible feeling of joy and self-worth. I knew I looked very special in my Saturday outfit, and went to great lengths to keep it looking as lovely as the day I had received it. I wore my outfit for about a year, and it looked as new then as it did when I opened the present.

It was inevitable that some disaster would befall my precious outfit. One Saturday morning, I quickly bathed and returned to my bedroom to dress, but the skirt and sweater I'd so neatly laid out ready for me to wear were nowhere to be seen. I rushed downstairs, only to find Chris Brisley washing them in the sink in extremely hot water. Her black eyes almost danced with pleasure when she saw the look of horror on my face. "The skirt was dirty and needed washing," she said smiling as she lifted the now out-of-shape mass from the water. Even I knew it had to be dry cleaned and not washed. I also knew instantly that it was completely ruined. The sweater had also suffered the same fate, and was now discoloured and half its original size. Both could never be worn again. "It's probably for the best. You looked quite ridiculous in them anyway. Not a colour you could carry off, with your pasty complexion and your skinny body," came her happy reasoning as she wrung them out and threw them into the trash bin. I was completely heartbroken, yet I knew I mustn't cry, mustn't let her see what my Saturday outfit had meant to me, for I knew that's what she wanted. I would cry later, when I was safely in my bedroom. I had learned control years before and would stand looking at her with no emotion showing on my face. She could hit me again and again, and shout until she went purple in the face and I would stand there wordless waiting for her to cease her verbal and physical abuse. Only when I reached my bedroom with the door firmly closed would I give way to my emotions, usually slamming myself onto the bed and smashing my fist into my pillow until I was too exhausted to even move and only then I would cry. From then on, I did my best always to have an excuse to stay at school for as many weekends as possible. That way I wouldn't have to see her, or mourn my special present from the only person in the world I loved. In the wee small hours of the night I often wondered whether my grandmother loved me as much as I loved her.

***

There wasn't a weekend that went by without some sort of conflict between the two Brisleys, or me. I think she hated me as much as she hated her husband. I could do nothing right. If I stayed in my room, I was bone idle and shirking my duties. If I cleaned the house, it wasn't done to her satisfaction. I was still very young and to do the washing up, which I had to do each evening; I stood on a chair. Ken was a stickler for cleanliness, in fact I would say he was bordering on the fanatic. One evening I had just finished washing up the dinner things when he came into the kitchen to inspect my work. He scrutinized the saucepans, and saw they had not been cleaned correctly. He got so mad that he hit me, pushing me off the chair, which tipped over, and I hit my head on the edge of the kitchen table and knocked myself out. That was the first time. There would be many other times. My friends will laugh when they read this and say now they know what's wrong with me: too many bumps on the head.

I think the worst head bashing I got was when I was ordered, never asked, to clean the garden shed, and I couldn't get the lawn mower out to sweep under it. Inspection time came around, and the mower was moved to reveal a healthy mound of grass clippings. To this day I'm amazed she didn't kill me. Those black eyes burned into me as she told me that I was a lazy filthy creature, and she then banged the side of my head with a garden shovel. I hit the floor of the shed with a resounding thud, and was left there as punishment for being so slovenly. I'm not sure how long it was but it was dark when I regained consciousness. I lay there for a long time, gingerly feeling the side of my face which was so swollen with a cut running down one side of it. Ken eventually came to look for me, and even as a child I could see that he was scared witless by the state I was in. I was taken to the outpatient ward of St Martin's hospital, and was classed as an accident-prone child, because they were so used to seeing me there for various injuries. Not once in all those years, when I went to hospital, did anyone ask any questions. This time they were told I had slipped in the garden shed and fallen on to the lawn mower.

***

It was now the summer holidays, and the return to school seemed an eternity away. Still, both Ken and *the woman* were working, so apart from the daily duties which had to be done before they got home, I was left to my own devices. One afternoon, I was swinging on the back gate when I saw a young boy walking toward me. As usual I wanted to run and hide, but something kept me swinging on the gate. He was a most beautiful boy, with tight curly auburn hair. He stopped and smiled at me.

"My name is Peter and I know your name is Wendy."

I stared solemnly across at him. "My name is Marie not Wendy."

He laughed. "No, Wendy really is your name. It's just that everyone calls you Marie. Aunt Maude told me." I was silent as I continued to swing on the gate. He then said, "I'm your brother." I stared open-mouthed at him, and I was suddenly very frightened. I almost fell off the gate and ran into the house. He called after me. "I am your brother, Peter. Peter Pan and Wendy, get it?" I remember running upstairs to my room and burying my head into my pillows. Who was this strange boy? And why was he teasing me?

A couple of days went by and then I saw him again. I was in town with *the woman*. We were shopping for my school summer uniform, and there he was, walking by the shop with a woman, presumably his mother. I was so scared, and thought I must be seeing things and couldn't wait to get home. For the next two days I didn't venture out of the house, in case he reappeared.

I genuinely didn't factor in Ken and Chris's life, so I found it amazing when they actually realized something was wrong, but it seems they did. I was due to visit my grandmother on the following day, so I think they were worried that I might say something untoward to her. The evening before the visit, Ken asked me to come to his study. I knew, yet again, that I had done something bad for this to happen. I slunk into the room, only to find that *she* was also there. God, this was trouble, with a capital T! They then asked me what was wrong with me? Was I feeling sick? I had no intention of telling another living soul about my encounter with the boy, but suddenly the words came spilling out.

It started an avalanche. Strange looks passed between them, and I was quickly sent off to bed. As I undressed I saw them leave the house by the kitchen door, and hurry along the back lane. I was consumed with curiosity, and I must say a little excited, though I didn't know why. It was almost dark before they returned home.

The next day I was told the visit to my grandmother was postponed. I was almost beside myself with grief; yes, genuine grief. Yet again, it had been months since I had last seen her. For the next few days I noticed a lot of coming and going along the back lane. Sometimes I used to stand on the gate to watch Chris and Ken Brisley, but they disappeared around the bend of the lane, and I lost sight of them. I knew there was something brewing and I knew it was about me.

***

The following Saturday morning, armed with a list, I was sent to do the weekly shopping. As always, I would be laden down with bags of groceries for the week. They were so heavy that I could hardly carry them. Sometimes I even had to drag them along the road to the bus stop. It was around that time that I developed yet another complex, a feeling that everyone was looking and laughing at me. It got so bad that there were times when I could hardly put one foot in front of the other. In my mind, I would morph into a hideous creature. I wanted to get home and hide myself away from the world.

I was still a skinny kid with thin legs and big feet. I knew people were laughing at me. Especially as I lugged those heavy bags on and off the bus, then up the road to the house. When I look back on those days, I guess people *were* staring at me, but it must have been with compassion that such a small child would be sent out on such an unkind errand.

I arrived home, hot, tired and exhausted, only to be summoned into my bedroom by the screaming woman. The *look* was in place. Those black eyes were once again mere slits as I entered my room. She pointed to a mark on my dressing table.

"When did you do this?"

I stared at it. It was a white circle on the top right hand side of the highly polished dressing table. I shook my head, telling her that I'd not seen it before, and I hadn't done it. Then she started to hit me. When she was mad, and I do mean *mad*, there was no stopping her. Although, now, she was usually very careful where she hit, there were times when she didn't care, and this time she lost control. Head, body, legs, I was fair game. She called me a liar, an ugly little runt, one of her favorite words for me. It was then a miracle happened. In her rage, she told me she was so glad I was no part of her, and also glad that my parents were dead; they would never see what an ugly little liar they had produced. I stood there, staring up at this horrid woman. My heart was racing and my head spinning. I kept repeating her words over and over again in my mind. I knew it all along; I was nothing to do with her or Ken. In that moment, it was as if I stood beside myself and watched the beating taking place, and it didn't hurt. I had been told so many times that I was their property that I had come to believe being adopted actually meant I had now become *their* child. I was completely euphoric with the now absolute certainty I was *not* theirs. I really *did* belong to someone else. I remember my grandmother telling me that I needed a mother and father. For a long time, I thought that children who didn't have parents were given new parents, and they took over where the others left off. It's very easy to brainwash a very young child. If you're told something enough times, no matter how difficult it is, eventually you believe. Half an hour later, Ken arrived home and was summoned to the bedroom to find out what I'd done this time. Yet again I listened to their screaming at each other but I was too wrapped up in my own beautiful realization that I really and truly didn't belong to them. Still, I'm quite sure that, on that morning, she would have done considerably more damage to me if Ken hadn't come home when he did. She was shaking with rage as she showed him the mark on the dressing table, telling him what a destructive little liar I was. He then calmly told her that he had put a hot cup on it a couple of days before, while replacing a drawer hinge. There was no apology from either of them as they rushed from the room, leaving me sitting on my bed yet again nursing my battered body and trying to absorb this wonderful new-found information. Later I learned that she had told Ken of her outburst about my parents, and it was at last decided to tell me about my mother and father.

WHO AM I

The family gathering was held at my grandmother's home a couple of weeks later. The boy and the woman who I thought was his mother were also there. My grandmother looked tired and drawn. As usual, I was told to keep my mouth shut and also to tell her I had fallen off a swing, for my face was badly bruised down one side. I firmly think that they were all too preoccupied to truly notice what state I was in. Anyway that's what I tell myself.

I didn't look at Peter, although I wanted to. To me, he was so incredibly beautiful, and here was I, all arms and legs, wearing a simply hideous dress, and ugly, oh so ugly. How could he even want to pretend to be my brother?

The woman who sat beside him turned out to be Maude Fletcher. She was not Peter's mother, she was his aunt. She was also my aunt. She was my mother's sister. I sat on the edge of the settee opposite my grandmother, waiting for her to say something. She had been watching me intently while Maude and *the woman* talked quietly together.

It had now become imperative that I should be told who I was. This would never have happened if Peter had not been staying with his aunt while on his school holidays. He was two years older than me, and yes, he was my brother, or half-brother! Though I still have some faded photographs showing me as a baby with Peter, I have no memory of him, except for the little boy who used to tease me when I sat on my grandmother's lawn when I was not quite two years old. When Chris and Ken Brisley came into my life, they apparently talked about Peter, but it was decided it would be best not to ever mention him to me, as at the time it was thought we would never meet. Apparently Peter had gone to live with his father. If his father was my father, why hadn't I gone to live with him as well? And I thought my father was dead, and if he was, why did Peter say he was my brother? These were questions that were never answered until much later in my life, and, even then, various family members had a different story to tell.

At this particular family meeting, I think all were ticked off with my Aunt Maude for telling Peter he had a sister who was living five minutes away from her. When I think about it, I can't believe my mother's sister lived just down the road – yes, literally a few minutes' walk from the Brisleys' home – yet I never saw her, never even knew she existed, and there was still no answer as to why Peter's father was alive and yet I had been told that mine was dead, and yet he was my brother! How difficult is that for a young child to try to understand? To say that I was in a state of complete and utter confusion was an understatement.

On that afternoon, it was explained to me I had now been legally adopted by the Brisleys, and from now on, I would be called by my first name, which was Wendy. I remember them showing me a piece of paper some time previously; it had truly meant nothing to me, but now to be told that it was legal made me sick at heart. Did this mean they really *were* my parents? Also, I now had to face the fact that Marie was my second name, and I must now be called by my first name. I found everything so confusing. I really began to wonder who I was. I desperately needed to hold on to the fact they weren't anything to do with me. I didn't know what *adopted* parents meant. The more they used the word parents, the more agitated I became. *She* had told me she was not my mother; now my grandmother was telling me she was my adopted mother. What did this mean? Maybe when one had a change of parents your name was changed too? As was my usual practice when I didn't understand, I completely zoned out and went into a world of my own. It was moments like those when the real world became too much for me to cope with.

It was very strange to go back to school, where, the previous term, I had been called Marie, but in this new term I would be called Wendy. Not one adult at the school ever mentioned the fact my name had been changed. However my school friends thought it hilarious, all wanting to change their names, and wondering what my new name would be at the beginning of the next term. It took a very long time for me to accept the change. It was as if a completely new person had invaded my body but still to the outside world I was the same.

It was around this time that I was allowed to have the occasional visit with my Aunt Maude, though I think that the Brisleys fought hard to stop it. The first time I was taken to her home by *the woman* and, as usual, I was schooled in what I would say and what I would not say. Although I was always lectured when meeting any new people, they needn't have bothered, for I was so indoctrinated by them that I would never have said anything to a single soul, even if my very life depended on it. I sat mute in her sitting room, wondering whether Peter was there. I was extremely disappointed when I learned that he had already returned home. Later, I was introduced to her husband, who was called Len Fletcher; he turned out to be my godfather. What a joke that was.

***

During those school summer holidays, when the Brisleys were at work, I would walk along the back road to my aunt's home. Considering how shy I was, I think it was exceedingly brave of me. But at the time, I desperately wanted to find out anything I could about my parents and Peter. On the first couple of visits, I said hardly anything to her. I would sit drinking lemonade, munching biscuits or cake and stare at her. She was a very pretty woman, and I often wondered whether she looked like my mother. On about the fourth visit, she sat me down on the settee next to her. "You are allowed to talk, you know," she said, and as usual, I burst into tears.

"I was told I mustn't talk to you. I had to behave myself and not let *them* down."

"And do you often let *them* down?"

"No. I'm not allowed to."

She smiled, telling me I could say anything I wanted and she would never tell a soul. From then on we became very close. Sadly, I knew even then that she was a very sick woman. When she was having a bad day, her husband would stay at home to look after her. Over the months, if Uncle Len was at home, we hardly ever spoke to each other. It wasn't that he didn't like me; he was a bit like Ken and didn't know how to talk to me. They didn't have any children of their own, and I never knew if it was because of her illness, or a mutual decision to remain childless.

On her good days, when we were alone, Aunt Maude would often try to prompt me into telling her about my day-to-day life at home. I always ended up talking about school instead. I knew only too well to steer clear on the subject of my home life. It was very dangerous territory. Now, looking back, I think she was suspicious about the Brisleys. Whenever they were all together, which wasn't often, there wasn't much rapport between the two couples. If indeed she was worried about me, she certainly didn't do anything about it. But then maybe, poor woman, she had far more important things to worry about.

***

I was now truly settled into my new school; I loved it, but always hated Friday afternoons when I would have to pack up and leave for home. I wanted to be with the other boarders, because I knew that they were having wonderful weekends, whereas the outcomes of my weekends were always horrendous to say the least.

When I returned home on one particular Friday evening, Chris Brisley was not at home and I realized that Ken was quite agitated. He kept staring out of the window, then phoned various friends they knew. He also had a long conversation with our next door neighbour. She had a daughter called Valerie, who was a year older than me, and every Saturday morning, if I'd finished all my chores, I was allowed out to play spin the top with her. We had become quite good friends, and she certainly made my weekends more bearable.

The woman had gone out early in the morning, on some pretext or another. I know it wasn't for the weekly shopping, as that was usually my chore. I never found out why Ken was so upset, but I learned that they'd had a mighty row before she went. She had probably left to cool off, but whatever had happened, he was certainly extremely jittery. The evening turned into night. I sat with him in the sitting room while he again rang certain friends to find out whether she was with them. The more negative the phone calls were, the more excited I became. When it was well past my bedtime, with me still not in bed, I realized for the first time that without *her*, Ken would probably be a different person. I began to wonder what it would be like living with him alone. Apart from knocking me off a chair, or giving me a cuff round the ear every so often, he had only been verbally abusive to me when she pushed his buttons. I was someone who came into his life without his having any say in the matter. In a way, we were alike. We were thrown together by a much stronger will than ours. I sat there watching him getting more and more disturbed and couldn't understand why he wasn't as excited as I was. I don't know what the time was, but I do know that it was very late when he suddenly realized that I was still sitting there. He told me not to worry, but I had better go to bed because if I was *not* in bed when *she* came home, there would be hell to pay; but I couldn't sleep. I was consumed with dark thoughts. Maybe she'd had an accident, or maybe she'd left and wasn't coming back. I didn't really care what the reason was, I prayed I would never have to see her again. Saturday morning dawned, and I could hear someone in the kitchen. I crept down stairs and saw Ken making tea and toast. It was obvious that she still hadn't returned. We sat in silence munching hot buttered toast, each deep in our own thoughts. By this time I was completely ecstatic, certain in the knowledge that, whatever the reason, she would not return: nobody ever stayed out all night. In my young world, staying away for a night was the end: there were no two ways about it. The morning turned into afternoon with still no sign of her. However, my ecstasy was soon to be cut short when I heard a car come up the drive and stop outside the house. Ken went to the front door, leaving me still sitting at the kitchen table, waiting for my cloud to burst.

The first thing she said as she came into the kitchen was that Ken should pay for the taxi and then that I should go to my room and stay there until I was called. With a very heavy heart, I dragged myself upstairs too devastated to even cry. I stayed in my bedroom for the rest of the day without being called and without any dinner. I could hear them talking and knew that, whatever it was it was quite serious. Something happened on that weekend which brought them closer together, not in love but in unity and misery. I stayed in my room until it was time to leave for school on Monday morning. This tiny glimpse into a world without *her* made me realize how dreadfully unhappy and alone I was.

I never did find out *why* she had left and stayed away for all those hours, and was too young to think of all the possible scenarios to this mystery. I do know that, at the time, our next door neighbors stopped talking to *the woman*, and any communication I had with their daughter was banned by *her*, and, presumably, the girl's mother. Whenever we bumped into one another, it was so embarrassing, not knowing why we weren't allowed to play together any more. After a while we stopped talking altogether and soon it was as though we had never known each other.

Now my only carefree moments were when I was at school. A quiet little mouse at home, yet, at the convent, I was becoming the clown of my class. I wasn't beautiful, like two of my classmates, Camilla Brockhurst and Linnet Berrisford. I was the funny skinny little girl who always had Frizzy Lizzie in tow, and *always* made my fellow students laugh, not to mention a few teachers along the way.

I had developed a crazy sense of humour, which had been crushed and stayed dormant before it even got started, yet being in a wonderful friendly environment brought it out and once out there was no stopping me. I would go to great lengths to be funny and make my school friends laugh. I would also listen to any problems the girls in my class had, and try to sort them out. I even had girls from other classes come to me for advice. It was quite ridiculous and I don't remember how it started but I became the regular soothsayer. I also started to read palms. Now don't laugh at this, but actually I was very good at it. I was a child who always listened. I also learned very quickly about other people in my life, whether they were child or adult. I had such a queue of classmates who were simply dying to know what they would be doing next week that it eventually came to the attention of the headmistress, a most feared nun, who was nicknamed Bonzo by the whole school. Inevitably. I was duly summoned to her study and told to sit down, which, under the circumstances, was a good thing, as my legs were about to give way. She smiled at me telling me my palm reading sessions were over, and only God could predict the future. I nodded vigorously at her, but it didn't stop the eager hands thrust in my direction; it only made us far more careful in the future.

It was during this period in my life that the school became deeply involved with missionary work, especially in some of the remotest areas of Africa. We would have special evening classes once a week where this topic would be discussed at great length. We were all made to give some of our weekly pocket money for the cause, and seeing that I didn't get any, I never gave any. I was never quite sure if anyone noticed that I would put my empty hand into the collection bowl and rattle the coins around. But if it was noticed, nothing was ever said.

One afternoon we were told that a missionary nun was coming to the school to give a talk about her experiences in some of the most poverty stricken areas of the world. The school was duly summoned into the assembly hall to sit and wait for the arrival of the said nun. She arrived and appeared on stage for her introduction to us by Bonzo. She was very thin and quite old, she was also dressed completely in a white habit, which I thought matched perfectly with her complexion, and from where I was sitting she looked like a rather frail ghost. I *knew* this was going to be a completely mind-numbingly boring afternoon. I was correct. As the talk rambled on, I could see some girls starting to fidget, while others yawned loudly.

Well, I hit on a brainwave. I would *faint* and would then be carried out of the assembly hall into the loving arms of Matron and away from this extremely dull talk on the political and religious problems of Africa. As an adult I certainly don't feel that way now, but at my very young age it all went completely over my head. Now, as I sat waiting for my dramatic exit, my very real concern was… when one faints does one still breathe? Or does one stop breathing altogether? I sat mulling this huge problem over while the nun kept droning on. If I was to do this properly, I had to get it right first time; Bonzo was sitting too close for comfort for me to make any mistakes. I decided that I would hold my breath for as long as possible, and hope that I would be rushed out of the hall quickly, before anyone discovered that I was indeed still breathing. The white nun was now in full swing, and it was obvious that she wasn't going to stop for quite a few hours.

I suddenly dropped to the floor, taking the chair with me and making as much noise as I could. I was clever, and fell face down so that, hopefully, in the confusion, if I had to take a quick breath, it would not be noticed. I was lifted up by a sturdy sixth former, rushed from the hall and into the anxious arms of Matron who then carried me into her room. As I snuggled under a soft blanket, she sat looking at me and said, "Well, that was some exhibition. The talk couldn't have been so boring surely?" I opened my eyes and told her it was the most boring talk I had ever had to listen to. She actually laughed at this, and replied that I was a little rascal and what was she going to do with me? I then got a mug of hot chocolate plus a huge piece of Cherry cake. At that moment, life could not get any better. In between munching and sipping, I asked her if one could still breathe when one fainted. Her answer was. "Oh no you don't breathe at all. So you see you were very lucky to get away with your plan. Our venerable head mistress will probably have words to say about this." I spent the next few days anxiously waiting for the axe to fall but I was never summoned to the Lion's den, so I guess I got away with it.

***

I was about eight when I started playing hockey. I loved it, but, like most sports, except tennis, I never really understood it. I loved racing up and down the field whacking the ball whenever it came my way. Being out in the open with the wind blowing in my face made me feel wonderful. In my mind, I was a champion hockey player with the world completely enthralled by this young athlete. During one of these games, I was hit across my right foot so hard that I passed out, and later, could hardly bear to put my foot on the ground. It was thought a cold compress and a good night's sleep would see me fit the next day. Sadly, it was not to be. The next day, my foot had swollen to grotesque proportions. I was driven to St. Martin's hospital by one of the school staff. *The woman* was informed, and met me in the outpatients department.

After an X-ray, and various talks with doctors and a surgeon, *she* was told that I had a tumour growing across the top of my foot, and that it had been growing there for some time. It had now surrounded the metatarsal bones, and the surgeon was very worried about removing it without damaging my foot. However, I knew nothing of this at the time, and as long as I didn't put any weight on it, there was no pain. It was decided that I should have an operation as soon as possible.

It was my first experience of hospitals, so I didn't quite know what to expect. As the operation was deemed an emergency, I was put into an adult ward, because the children's ward was full. I was the centre of attention for the patients, some of whom were quite elderly. I arrived the day before the operation, and was installed into my hospital bed. My foot was yet again inspected by the surgeon and another doctor. They prodded and whispered to each other, as if I was a piece of wood. The whole procedure made me very nervous. I didn't know that a patient was put to sleep during the operation, so I had visions of my foot being cut open with me writhing about on the operating table. I lay awake all through the night, worrying about how I was going to react when the first cut was made. Early the next morning, I was wheeled down to the operating theatre with a raging headache, and almost catatonic with fear. When I awoke, I was back in my bed with a huge cage over my foot and being clucked over by the mother hens in the ward. It was over, and I didn't feel a thing.

The next couple of weeks were a blur. My foot was extremely painful, keeping me awake most nights. I would simply long for the morning, waiting for any distraction to take my mind off the pain.

The post was always delivered to the ward each morning, around eleven. A nurse would bring the mail to each bed along with the various pills to be taken by the patients. As I carefully put all my pills into my bedside cabinet I would watch enviously as other patients opened letters and parcels from friends and relations. Since I lived not far from the hospital, I didn't get any mail, and each day I would bemoan the fact to anyone who would listen. One morning during my second week, the staff nurse stopped by my bed with a bundle of letters and a couple of parcels. I couldn't believe my eyes. Every person in the ward, including the nursing staff had written me a letter. How wonderful! I felt so important, and wanted to stay in hospital forever. On the third week, one of the nurses opened my bedside cabinet to retrieve my hair brush and all the pills I'd stacked up came spilling out in an avalanche onto the floor. From then on, I was watched until I swallowed my daily dose, something I hate doing even today.

I can now say that the operation was successful, though it took a very long time for me to have complete mobilization of my foot. For the first two months, I was confined to a wheelchair. For most children this would have been a catastrophe, but during all those horrendous years of living with this couple, it was the only time *she* ever seemed concerned by my progress; maybe she was worried that I wouldn't be able to continue my housewifery duties soon enough. Also, Aunt Maude was always visiting and taking me out for walks in my wheelchair and afternoon tea at her home. It was not something *the woman* liked, but there was nothing she could do about it without sounding the alarm bells. For years after the operation, I had dreadful cramps that would start at my toes, travel up through my foot, and then into my calf muscle. The pain was mind-numbing, lasting from five minutes to half an hour. It still happens to this day if I get overtired, or wear high heels for too long, though luckily not so fierce.

After the operation, I was told by a jovial nurse that I would never be able to wear high-heeled shoes when I grew up. Was the woman out of her *mind*? I remember looking at her as if she had flown in from another planet. Of course, when I was all grown up, I was going to wear this most coveted foot apparel. I couldn't imagine going through my whole adult life without them. Needless to say, I have a thing about shoes, the higher the heel the better. I guess you could call me a shoe-aholic!

HOT CHOCOLATE AND MATRON

When I turned nine, *the woman* became even more unbalanced. It was around this age that other people began to notice me. I could never understand why, because I was still a gawky child, but my face had started to change. The contours were becoming more defined. I would get comments as I walked into a room. The worst comments were, "Oh she's going to be a real heart-breaker when she grows up. Just look at her face," or "How lovely it is to be so young and such a pretty child!"

Those black eyes would turn to slits, and, like radar, hone in on me. The minute we were alone, she would attack, verbally and physically. I was becoming a slut, as well as a liar. At the time, I was quite fascinated by this new word *slut*. I lay in bed at night saying it quietly to myself and wondered whether it was the reason why people had begun to notice me. I made a mental note that, when I went back to school, I would ask one of the nuns what the word meant. In those days children were children until their mid teens. The use of bad language by most adults just didn't happen.

The first person I saw and felt I could ask was Madam Mary. She had taken me under her wing, and each Monday morning, when I arrived back at school, she would check me over to make sure I was still in one piece. She never said anything, but I knew what she was doing. She always asked me about my weekends, and I always gave her a bright smile and told her it had been wonderful. Sometimes I would make up imaginary places and parties I had been to. She used to listen and smile. Even then, I knew she didn't believe me. I also knew that if I said one word about what really happened behind closed doors, all hell might break out, and I could never take the chance; the ramifications were too horrendous to even contemplate.

While I was unpacking my weekend bag, I casually asked her what the word *slut* meant. You can imagine the reaction I got. She suddenly sat down on my bed and stared up at me. "Where on earth did you hear such a word?"

I was totally confused, and tried to explain. I now knew I had made a terrible mistake. I said I thought it was a compliment because I was growing up. She kept asking me who had called me that dreadful name.

"Was it someone in your family?" I shook my head vigorously, and she knew I would never tell.

She left me to finish unpacking, whilst no doubt she went off to discuss this latest piece of information with someone more knowledgeable. In the next few minutes, I was whisked off to Matron's room and given my usual mug of hot chocolate, her panacea for all childhood ailments. An hour later, and missing the first lesson of the day, I was still sitting with Matron, eating hot buttered crumpets and on my second mug of chocolate while she tried to wheedle out of me where I had heard the word. I think by mid morning she had realized that wild horses wouldn't drag anything out of me, though I'm sure she had a pretty good idea where the word had originated from. I also think she was sensible enough to know that, if she went any further with the enquiry, I would be in deep trouble. It must have been a difficult situation for them. I'm quite sure they knew I was being ill-treated; they didn't know how bad it was, or what to do about it. I firmly think they felt five days of freedom at school against two days of hell at home were passable. Again, in those days, even nuns didn't like to get involved in family situations.

Looking back, I wish that someone, *anybody*, had come to my rescue, but at the time I was so indoctrinated by this woman that if they *had* tried to intervene, I simply dread to think of the consequences. The beatings were so harsh, and not a week went by without me being punched or having my head smacked against a wall. I'm always amazed I got through my childhood without being brain-damaged, or even killed. There certainly were a few times when I was taken to the hospital and was told to say that I had fallen off my bicycle. Again, this woman could be so charismatic; who would ever believe that she could hurt a fly, let alone a child. In later years, I would often watch her working her charm on various people, and knew I never stood a chance; no one would believe me, I would be the ungrateful child who obviously had some sort of mental problem.

When I was nearly ten years old, we started going for summer holidays at a seaside resort called Severn Beach. We always booked the same rental chalet, a short distance from the small beach cove. There were about twenty small chalets rented out as holiday homes, in an area attached to a local farm. They were very basic but always clean and prettily decorated. When I was there, I felt a sense of freedom very rarely achieved at any other time with the Brisleys. Each morning, I would run to the farmhouse to buy fresh eggs, milk and home-baked bread. On the way back to the chalet, I'd cross the fields and pick huge mushrooms for breakfast. Though the beach and sea area wasn't much to write home about, I always so enjoyed those holidays.

One morning, a woman knocked on our chalet door in a complete panic. Her daughter had fallen and had severely cut the palm of her hand on some broken glass, and the child's hand was bleeding profusely. The woman had heard that Chris Brisley was a nurse and asked for her help. *The woman* was so thrilled to be singled out, I could almost see her puff up with pride. Off she went to minister to the poor child. Apparently the cut was deep and very jagged. The girl should have been sent straight to the hospital, but for the next week Chris Brisley went every morning to re-bandage the wound, telling the parents the hand would soon heal. Also, during this holiday, I had two abscesses on the side of my knee. I think that *the woman* was completely into her nursing mode, for she decided she would lance the abscesses herself with a red hot needle. It was an horrendous experience but Chris Brisley was on a roll, and nothing would stop her. Over the next week, my leg swelled to a frightening size but each morning the woman would squeeze and cut at the infected area. It was during one of these medical sessions that the girl's parents came to our chalet. The father was in a terrible state, threatening to sue Chris Brisley for medical malpractice as his daughter had been rushed off to the emergency department at the local hospital, and they had found out that she still had two jagged pieces of glass in her hand, which had caused a really bad infection. I remember a lot of screaming and shouting going on while I sat with my very swollen leg up on a stool. Apparently they had come back from the hospital where their daughter was undergoing an operation to try to save her hand which had turned septic. The man then noticed me, and was simply horrified at the state of my leg. I think he put the fear of God into the Brisleys, for I, too, was rushed off to the same hospital where I stayed for a week, until my leg, after proper medical care, got better.

A short while afterwards, we returned home. Chris Brisley received a solicitor's letter requiring her to appear in court on a certain date. As young as I was, I now knew that this woman had no nursing qualifications whatsoever, though she did have a badge which all state registered nurses wore at that time. Where she had acquired it was a mystery. Her nursing jobs were always either in private nursing establishments or private homes. Most of the time she did night duty. My guess is that, some time during one of her jobs, she had stolen the pin, and, unlike what would happen today, nobody ever asked her for her credentials.

The thought of the impending court date scared the hell out of both the Brisleys. They knew that, if the truth came out, she could go to prison for impersonating a nurse. Ken went to see the parents, and I'm quite sure that money changed hands, for the court hearing was dropped, and for a while, Chris Brisley left the nursing profession.

***

It was at around this time that I started to develop a family of my own. On a recent visit to my grandmother's, I'd been shown a photograph of my mother. I sat looking at it for a very long time. I thought she was extremely beautiful, almost ethereal. I guess that a photograph of any female would have been beautiful to me, but now, as an adult, I look at the same picture, and yes, to me she was, is beautiful. I didn't have any reference of my father until much later in life, but in my mind, he was tall and handsome. We made a happy family. Each night, when I was at home, I would go to bed at seven p.m. either battered and bruised, either physically or verbally, I would close the door to the outside world, tuck myself in bed and start my day over again. It would always begin with my loving parents calling me for breakfast, and then the day's events would unravel; whether at school or at home, my life was perfect. They were mine, and nobody else could take them away from me. I was much loved and wanted, and felt very secure. I was quite strict with myself, and would usually wait until my bedroom door was closed and I was safe; but when life got really bad, I would let them come into my world during the day. When the Brisleys were either screaming at me or between themselves, I would often escape to somewhere safe and have long conversations with my parents and they would help me through whatever crisis was happening at that particular moment in time. Soon the Brisleys became the fantasy. I would look at them, see them, but they weren't really there at all. At last I had developed a shield, and I could always hide behind it.

I certainly didn't have any sort of syndrome, at least I don't think I had. I needed my family to get me through those terrible years. I firmly believe that without them, I would never have made it. With them, I was not alone, and when I was being ill-treated, I would stand staring ahead of me, with no expression, just a shell, standing before my tormentor, wondering what I had ever done to deserve such cruel treatment. My mind would wander through those precious hours awaiting me where all the love I needed was mine. My mother's face would float before me, telling me to be strong and soon I would be with them to enjoy my life as it would be if they were still alive. Only they were still with me. I could see them, feel them and almost smell the perfume that I thought she would wear. At the time, they were more real than any other people on this earth.

***

For some unknown reason, the Brisleys suddenly decided to buy a piano. As neither of them was the slightest bit musical, I realized that it was for me. It duly arrived, and was placed in the front room. I was told by *the woman* that, as I had no talent whatsoever, it would be interesting to see whether I had one redeeming quality where they would not be ashamed of me and about which they could tell their friends; even though I was a sullen, plain child, I was at least musical. I hated that piano! Every Saturday morning, I was sent for music lessons, and then, when at home, made to practice for two hours each day. She would often stand listening outside the door, and any time I played a wrong note, she would enter and rap my knuckles with a wooden spoon, sometimes until they bled, often telling me what a completely useless idiot I was. It was true that I didn't have a flair for playing, but out of desperation I learned to play pieces without making any mistakes. But for me there wasn't any flow to my music. For although I have always loved music, I was never even going to be a talented amateur. I did go the Royal Academy of Music in London on three occasions to take my exams and passed each time. I am very happy to say that, one very cold winter's day, the paraffin heater that was heating the room caught fire, sending up plumes of smoke, covering every nook and cranny of the room, and destroying the piano. It was decided that it would be a complete waste of money to buy another piano, and for once in my young life, I thankfully and totally agreed with them.

There were many nights when I went to bed, and I could hear Chris and Ken Brisley's voices downstairs. I would often creep to the landing to listen. More often than not it was about me. *She* would complain there was something not quite right about me, that I was not like other children, a solitary child, with no emotions whatsoever; and he would answer that maybe if she hadn't bashed me around so much I might be more normal. Oh, if only she had known that it was she who had turned me into this emotionless creature! The fear of the *look*, of the constant terror of the hand or fist as it came toward me, hitting or punching! In those instances, I don't think I will ever forget the overbearing power of her domination and brutality.

Once, when I was quite young, she told me that I was a puppet, and she pulled the strings. There was total satisfaction in her voice when she said this. She had another human being completely under her control, and she loved it. It made up for the utter bleakness of her life. Her youth had disappeared, along with her looks and her figure. Now here she was, married to a man she hated, with a child she didn't want. She had to hang on to the marriage as long as possible, for in those days women were certainly not treated as equals. So, in a word, she was truly screwed. But the one thing she could do was to completely control me, and she revelled in it. If I was at home, I would wake up each morning wondering what the day held for me. As always, I knew her mood by the tone of her voice as she called from her bedroom. If she used the name *Wen*, I knew she was in a fairly good mood. If she yelled for me to get out of bed, then I knew it would be a bad day. To this day, I have *never* allowed anyone ever to call me *Wen*.

I would often sit looking at her, trying to scrape up some feeling for her. But in all the years I knew her, never once did I even like being in her company, not once. Whenever she went out, I always hoped and even prayed that she wouldn't return; but like the proverbial bad penny, she always did.

I must write, for the record, that I was a very obedient child. Whenever I was told to do something, it was done to the best of my ability. I didn't speak until I was spoken to, had excellent table manners, and could clean a house better than most adults. But there was no joy in my heart, no childish laughter ringing through the house, and certainly no tactile interplay between us. It was a barren life, without hope, and without an ending.

I don't often mention Ken. Although he was in my daily life when I was at home, he didn't have much to do with it. He was an impatient man. Everything *always* had to be spotless. I was forever making sure that the house would be to his liking when he returned from work. If the housework wasn't done, it was me who got into trouble, not his wife. I think he had given up on her a long time ago. He had absolutely no idea how to treat me, and, I'm sure, looked on me more as a housekeeper than a child. He was the shadowy figure who was stuck in a life with a woman he no longer loved, *if indeed he ever had*. There was no doubt she brought out the worst in him.

She knew what to do or say, which she did on a daily basis. She turned him into a violent man, with their fierce arguments usually ending in a screaming brawl. When I was around him, he would tolerate me. He must have often wondered how the hell he had got himself into this mess. Growing up with this hatred all around me left me feeling completely hopeless, and sad to say, I often thought it would be so lovely to go to sleep and never wake up again.

I would retreat more and more into my own private world, and at times, could barely separate reality from imagination. The strange thing is that I knew I was doing it, but I couldn't stop; no, I had no intention of stopping. It saved my sanity, and most probably, my life. I would take all the abuse and beatings and still be cushioned, knowing that I had my own wonderful family waiting for me.

As I said before I had excellent table manners. It had been drummed into me from a very early age as both the Brisleys' were insanely strict about good etiquette at the table at all times, and they watched for any lapse in their rules. One lunchtime I had forgotten one of their golden rules and put my elbows on the table. She picked up a knife which Ken had used to carve the meat. Then, pulling my chair away from the table, she sliced a two inch cut across my right leg just above the knee. It was so deep that the flesh on each side lay open. I was in such complete shock I didn't even cry out but when I looked across at her, she was smiling with those dead black eyes glinting with satisfaction. "Maybe from now on you'll remember your table manners. If not you'll have the same punishment every time." The cut bled profusely but she stuck a wad of cotton wool on it and then made me clean up the blood from the floor. There was no reaction from Ken, he got up and left the room. Each morning she would rip the cotton wool off the wound watching for my reaction. But I knew I must not cry. I mustn't let her see how much it hurt. I would look up at her and see that sick smile of shear pleasure spread across her face. I was shocked by her sheer brutality. I still have the scar, but I never put my elbows on the table again.

SONIA

I was nearly eleven years old when I found out that Ken Brisley had a sister called, Avis. She lived in London with a very much older husband, and a daughter named, Sonia. Apparently it was she who contacted Ken saying that they should put past differences behind them and visit each other, especially as she was now married, with a daughter around the same age as me. It was decided that they would come down to Bath, and would spend Christmas with us. I found this exciting, as it would mean that I wouldn't have to spend the holiday alone with the Brisleys. Also, much to Chris Brisley's irritation, they would now have to buy a tree, plus decorations and presents, which she had stopped doing years ago. Nearer the date, I was sent on my usual weekly shopping trip, along with a huge shopping list, only this time it was for all the wonderful Christmas day fare, such as a turkey, and all the other food that goes to make the holiday season what it is.

They duly arrived a couple of days before Christmas, and when they trooped into the sitting room, staring at this motley trio, I found myself in a state of what can only be called shock. If it was at all possible, Avis was even more ugly than Ken. She was a short, dumpy woman with grey, wiry hair, a flat, rather coarse face, huge nose *and* very hairy legs. During her stay, I was simply mesmerized by those legs, and couldn't imagine why she did nothing about this huge flaw. Mind you, I guess even smooth, silky and hairless legs wouldn't have made much difference. She was one very ugly woman. It was also the first time that I realized Ken must be Jewish, for there was no doubt in my mind that his sister Avis was, and I had just learned about the extermination of the Jews during the war in a history class at school and had seen many photographs of them. Avis threw her arms around me, and I was immediately overwhelmed by her perfume. It smelled of dead flowers, and I think she must have literally thrown the bottle over herself with the hope of masking the rather musty odour permeating the room whenever she entered.

Jim, her husband, was thirty years older than Avis, a fat man with a florid face, pale blue watery eyes and wearing clothes that had certainly seen better years. He was definitely one of the laziest men I have ever met. Once sitting down, he rarely moved, except to visit the bathroom. It was also the first time I had ever seen cartons of beer brought into the house, for neither Ken or Chris Brisley drank beer. Jim, on the other hand, started drinking around mid-morning, and carried on throughout the day.

Then there was Sonia? Where, oh where, had she come from? I couldn't believe this small, dainty little creature, with a rather elfin face, could possibly be their daughter. She looked somewhat incongruous standing beside them. I was to find out the answer later when we were told that, like me, she too had been adopted. I instantly felt very relieved for Sonia.

During her stay, Sonia and I became good friends. She was sharing my bedroom, so I helped her unpack. She was two years younger than me, which, I guess, brought out the mothering instinct in me. She was very shy, and at first, was aghast that we had to share a room, let alone a bed. After we had spent most of the first night whispering under the bedclothes, she became much more relaxed, and during that Christmas and throughout their stay, Sonia hardly left my side.

Chris Brisley did not like Avis, and the feeling was obviously mutual. One could cut through the animosity like a knife. Ken, on the other hand, seemed to come to life and would spend hours talking avidly with Avis about their rather puritanical upbringing. Apparently their mother had been a very cold and distant woman, who had rarely smiled and had been fanatical about cleanliness. Well, now I knew where Ken got that trait from, and I now have him to thank for being such a neat freak!

On Christmas Eve, Sonia and I were in bed by seven p.m., and for the first time in a long while, I was really looking forward to the next day.

As Sonia snuggled down under the bed clothes, she turned and said, "Is there really a Father Christmas? Only the girls at school told me he doesn't exist, and that I was stupid to believe in him."

Chris Brisley had long ago burst my balloon for me, and with the mothering instinct coming to the fore again, I assured her that there really *was* a Father Christmas, and right now he was out delivering presents all over the world. I could see by her look that she completely believed me, and it gave me a warm feeling knowing that, at least this year, anyway, she would believe in this wonderful fairy tale.

Whilst living with Ken and Chris Brisley, it was the one and only time when I truly had a lovely Christmas day. The Brisleys had even bought me some presents. What were they thinking of?

***

The next time Sonia and her parents came to stay, it was summer. They decided to join us for a couple of weeks; the first week was spent at Severn Beach. This year would be the last time we stayed at the chalet, with my daily runs to the farm for produce. It was nice having someone to play with, and many happy hours were spent at the small cove; and more importantly, we were allowed to go there by ourselves each day. This was the first time we had been back to the area since Chris Brisley had played at being nurse, with such dire consequences. Luckily we didn't meet anyone who remembered us, so the week went off without a hitch. As usual, Sonia never left my side, only this time, she started to admire some of my possessions, few though they were. The last time I saw my grandmother she had given me a very beautiful gold bracelet. I immediately put it on and never took it off again. Sonia loved it and asked if she could try it on. I shook my head explaining that from the minute my grandmother gave it to me I had never taken it off. She accepted my answer with a slight shrug and it was not mentioned again.

At the end of the week we packed up and returned home. Halfway through the second week, the Brisleys took Avis and Jim out for the day, saying that we girls could look after ourselves for a few hours. I will never know why it happened, or what *really* precipitated it, but suddenly Sonia and I got into an argument which became heated and out of control. I suddenly slapped her across her face. The minute it happened I was absolutely mortified and also very scared. She started to cry, and no matter what I said or how much I apologized she wouldn't stop crying. I had *never* hit anyone before *or* since. It's one of those awful moments when you have no idea what makes you do such a dreadful thing. I just sat looking at her. At last she stopped crying. I knew the next important thing was to somehow stop her from telling either her parents or the Brisleys; if she did, then my life wouldn't be worth living. I guess it's self preservation, but by then, that was uppermost in my mind. When I first asked her not to say anything, she was adamant she was going to tell her mother; I shook with fear. Why, oh why, had I done this terrible thing? We were supposed to be friends, and now I felt I'd forever lost her friendship, and in her eyes, I was tainted. Then I started to cry. I cried because I had done something awful, and I also cried because I knew I would get a most serious beating when Sonia told her mother what I'd done. I think the crying helped, because, eventually, Sonia relented and said that, if I gave her my gold bracelet, she would never tell. At first I thought she wasn't serious, but she was deadly serious. A very high price to pay! But it was one that couldn't be ignored, so I undid the clasp and reluctantly handed over my precious bracelet. The incident was never mentioned again. Strangely enough neither Sonia's parents nor the Brisleys ever acknowledged the fact that the bracelet was now being worn by Sonia and not me. It took me a very long time to get over slapping Sonia and losing the bracelet. It made me realize that when you do something bad, bad things happen.

I only ever saw Sonia one more time, and she was still wearing my bracelet. We went up to London to stay with them for a long weekend. It turned out to be a very uncomfortable visit, for the animosity between Chris Brisley and Avis had reached a boiling point, and also, I think that the feelings Ken had had for his sister had again waned somewhat. It was quite a few years later that I heard that Sonia had got pregnant at a very early age, and had been railroaded into marrying the father. I hope, for her sake, that it was a happy marriage.

IT'S ALWAYS FRIDAY

It was a Friday once again. And at the time, *she* was again working as a nurse in a retirement place, and wouldn't be home until late. Ken was away on BLESMA business. (British Limbless Ex-Service Men's Association.) He was one of the leading lights in this organization. I left the convent at four p.m., and decided, on the spur of the moment, that I would go to visit my grandmother, something which I never did without an invitation. As I walked across the Parade Gardens to catch the bus, I saw a young boy who looked like Peter. It was some time before I realized that it *was* Peter. It had been years since I'd seen him, but I knew instantly it was him, and I knew he was going to visit my grandmother. I sat behind him on the bus and was simply trembling with excitement. Apart from our very first meeting, this was the only time I would be with him without some sort of chaperoning. When we left the bus, I walked behind him all the way to my grandmother's house, not daring to speak to him, just so happy to be following him. At that time in my life, I think I would have followed him to the ends of the earth, I was so enamoured with him. When we reached her house he turned and grinned at me as I croaked out a squeaky hello.

"I wondered how long it would take for you to talk to me."

I was surprised and it must have showed. "Did you know it was me?" I asked.

"Of course. Can't be anyone else walking around Bath looking as skinny as you do."

At first I was both embarrassed and heartbroken that my brother thought I was so skinny. But then he laughed, giving me a bear hug and telling me that he was only joking. He didn't know what a complex I had, and I don't think he ever did. I've managed to hide it from most people throughout my life.

It was a magical afternoon. My grandmother seemed delighted

to see us both, and we had afternoon tea in the garden. I remember looking at Peter and thinking, "We all sat out here when I was a very young baby." So happy, with me in my mother's arms while Peter ran wildly around the garden then coming back to tease me. Now, years later, here we were once again, both very different; and I wondered whether Peter had a better life than me? Somehow, I sensed that he did. Years later, I saw Peter for one last time, so it's sad to say that I never really knew him at all.

I never thought about it at the time, but my grandmother must have been so lonely, living all by herself. She married young, and had five children, all close in age. It must have been such a busy life. Noisy young children running around, and a loving husband at her side. She didn't talk about him very often, but when she did there was a wistfulness in her voice and a sad look in her eyes. It was obvious that they had been very deeply in love. I can't imagine how it felt to have your husband away at war for so long, then to have him eventually return home and die soon after of tuberculosis. Sadly, he passed it on to his daughters. The saying goes that they were the ones who would sit on his lap and cuddled him. The boys thought it too sissy, and so avoided the deadly disease. My grandmother's youngest daughter, Vere, died at twenty-one, and then my mother, at twenty-four. Maude, the eldest daughter, lived until she was in her early thirties. My grandmother's sons married young, and moved out to start their new lives. Now this woman sat alone with only her memories to keep her company. Life can be such a bitch at times.

***

While I was boarding at school I was a very different child. I was learning fast what it was like to be normal. I was also learning how to interact with the other girls in my class and in the dormitory. I had fun and was very mischievous at times; in fact, looking back on those halcyon days, I think I must have been rather a handful.

I dreaded going home at the weekends. It was as if a black cloud descended upon me the minute I left the school grounds. I could almost feel myself changing back into this sombre other child.

One Friday, *she* came to the school to pick me up for the usual weekend at home. While waiting for me, she met and started talking to another woman who was also there to take her child home. It turned out to be a dreadful meeting, at least for me. The minute I saw her I knew that something was terribly wrong. Her face was like thunder, and those black eyes seemed to be on fire.

"So, you're the class clown?" was her opening remark as she gripped my arm so tightly I could literally feel the bruises pop out. At first I didn't understand what she was talking about, but then I saw Sara Middleton waving at me as she and her mother exited the building. I think I almost threw up on the spot. I literally shook with fear, knowing what lay ahead for me when I got home. As it turned out, my fears were completely justified. To say I had eight bells bashed out of me was an understatement. I think the fact that I was such a quiet, monosyllabic girl at home, yet the life and soul of my friends at school, *actually* got to her; even Ken had something to say about the revelation. As usual, I stood staring at them not saying a word. I don't think they ever realized that at those times I *couldn't* say anything. It was as if my voice box had been removed. I would try to let the insults hurled at me go over my head. I felt so small and insignificant during those battles. It was as if nobody in the world cared what happened to me; and I was correct, no one did. How could I ever be spontaneous and happy in their company? One had to have some sort of feedback for that to happen, and I don't think there was even one occasion, in all the years I lived with them, when they brought any laughter into the house. As I stood before her, that evening, she kept hitting me, trying to get any sort of reaction. When no reaction came, she punched me hard in my stomach, and I literally threw up on the floor. *The woman* grabbed my hair, pulling me down to the floor, rubbing my face in my vomit. My only satisfaction was that I immediately threw up again all over her shoes. On the Monday, when I returned to school, it was quite obvious I had been in some sort of altercation. Before class started I was summoned into the Reverend Mother's study. I hadn't seen her for some time so watching her, once again, gliding into the room, sitting at her desk and staring closely at my bruised face, made me feel as if I was in some sort of dream. I was always completely mesmerized by her, because, to me, she was so beautiful. She asked me how I received the bruises on my face, and like the programmed robot I was, I said I had fallen off my bicycle. I knew she didn't believe me, but wild horses wouldn't drag the truth from me. Later on, I was allowed to go to my class, but somehow I knew that it was not the end of the situation. I felt a deep foreboding inside me, and expected at any moment to see *the woman* appear to spirit me away from this wonderful safe haven.

Toward the end of the afternoon, I was again summoned to the Reverend Mother's study. I was correct: there was more to come. I ran straight to the toilet and threw up. I did a lot of throwing up in those days. I then walked with leaden feet toward her room, and was surprised to see my grandmother sitting there instead of *the woman*. I almost cried out in relief. Again the Reverend Mother asked me how my face became so bruised and swollen and again I gave her the same answer. The two women looked at each other, and my grandmother shook her head.

"You must have been travelling like the wind to cause so much damage to your face," the Reverend Mother said. I stared back at her and nodded dumbly.

Unbeknown to me there was another family meeting. As far as the law was concerned, I was now the property of the Brisleys, so under the law, my family had relinquished all rights to me; but apparently my grandmother took a great interest in my schooling.

The Brisleys had another meeting with my grandmother and it was decided, for the time being, that I should become a full boarder at the convent. Only for a while, nothing was set in stone. I was told later that my grandmother got around this by saying that since both the Brisleys were working full time, it would be better if I only went home for holidays. I'm sure my family must have known I was in dire trouble, yet no one lifted a finger to get me out of the situation. I am quite sure that, if it had been brought to the attention of the authorities, I would have been removed from that evil environment altogether; but no one lifted a finger to help me.

By the time all the arrangements were settled, there were only four weeks before the school Spring break. It was determined that I should stay a weekly boarder until the start of the new term. That decision almost cost me my life.

HAPPY SUSAN

For whatever reason *she* had, it was obvious she truly hated me. I could never understand why. I would often catch her looking at me with those oh so black, empty eyes, and as young as I still was, I was in no doubt there wasn't an ounce of love for me in her whole body. Even as I look back on those dreadful years, I still cannot fathom what made this woman into the person she was.

As far as I know, she had a normal childhood, with parents who loved her. She had an elder brother, who, in later years, would have nothing to do with her. So whatever problem she had, it started way before I came onto the scene. She was a strange, many-faceted human being, very intelligent, with a minimal academic education. I sincerely think that if she'd had a better start in life as far as her schooling was concerned, she could have done almost anything. Sadly, when she was a child it was deemed more important for the male of the family to have the education. It was always thought that the female would get married, have babies and look after the home. Her brother had the education, and ended up working for an aeronautics company. I met him only once, and it was quite obvious that he disliked his sister. No, not 'disliked': he absolutely *detested* her. God knows what had happened in *their* past.

***

It was around this time that the Brisleys became friendly with a couple who lived in Midsomer Norton. They had a really beautiful house, set in extensive gardens. To this day when I smell new mown grass and am walking around my garden, here in Virginia, I can almost transport myself back to that time, remembering the feeling of absolute pure joy whenever I was there. Considering how short the time span was which was spent in those beautiful surroundings, it still amazes me that those few months remain so clear to me. Their gardens were incredibly beautiful, typically English, with herbaceous borders, rose beds and many specimen trees.

They had a daughter named, Susan, who was my age. We liked each other from the beginning, and many happy hours were spent roaming their estate with her pet Labrador. Often, at weekends, after a lunch or dinner, Susan and I would play outside, sometimes until the sun went down. We would disappear into the wooded part of the estate, climb trees and, like monkeys, swing from branch to branch. No one came looking for us. We were children, playing at being just that. It was a wonderful interlude in my life, which, for me, only happened when the Brisleys were busy enjoying themselves with other people, which sadly, wasn't very often.

Susan was the girl who told me I must *never* sit on a stone wall or I would get hemorrhoids. She wasn't too sure what they were but said that, apparently, they were extremely painful and most adults were afflicted with them. I was quite fascinated by this piece of medical information and dreaded the thought of getting this awful disease; so for many years, I heeded her warning and was always very careful not to sit on stone walls or anything cold.

During my brief friendship with Susan we became very adept at climbing trees. Some of the trees on the estate were huge and extremely old. We were like monkeys swinging up through the branches until we reached the heady heights. It was wonderfully exhilarating reaching the top and then looking out over the gardens, knowing that no adult would ever think of looking for us up at our lofty summit. I was always exceedingly good at climbing up, but not as sure-footed when coming down. Susan always reached the bottom before me. One day, while we were sitting at the top of a particular tall oak tree, Susan decided that we should have a race to see who could get to the bottom first. Needless to say, my agile friend made it down first, and then started taunting my very un-athletic descent. I made the mistake of looking down at her while letting go of the branch I was holding on to. The outcome was that I swung out and started to fall; the result could have been quite devastating. I was saved by my school-issue navy blue knickers. A small branch found its way up the knicker leg, but left me hanging out of the tree, with no way of getting a grip on any of the larger branches. Susan thought it was the most hysterical thing she had ever witnessed, as she watched me swaying helplessly, but with every movement, I could feel the thin branch bending, and had visions of it snapping, sending me hurtling to the ground. After some fairly futile attempts at rescuing me, Susan decided she should go for help. I was left dangling almost at the top of the tree, wondering what kind of reception I would have when the Brisleys found out what we got up to. All four adults trooped into the woods, walking around the tree, wondering how the hell they were going to get me down. It was certainly much too high for a ladder so, in the end, they decided to call the fire brigade. It was a most embarrassing incident, and even made the local news. I think it was headed *Girl saved by her knickers*. Amazingly, the Brisleys didn't have too much to say about it. Luckily, at the time, they were too interested in their new friends to worry about me. All I can say is, thank God for heavy-duty navy school knickers, and also thank God it never stopped us climbing trees.

Susan also taught me some of the latest songs of the day, and we would sing at the top of our voices, elated in the knowledge that, at some time in the future, we would both become famous singers. Oh, how I wish the friendship had lasted! But, as always, for some unknown reason, the Brisleys fell out of favour with Susan's parents, and I never saw her again. Still, while it lasted, life was so good.

For a very brief period, I was privy to a child's wonderfully secure and happy life, and it was then that I realized that not all children had unbearable lives.

There were so many nights when I lay in my bed thinking about Susan, and wondered what had gone wrong between the adults. Maybe Susan's parents saw through the facade, and thought it better to end the friendship. It was sad, but came as no surprise. Very few friendships lasted with the Brisleys. I often wondered why this couple were so screwed up. And why, oh why, did I always bear the brunt of their moods? Sometimes, instead of having my imaginary mother and father, I tried to envisage what it would be like to have at least one real life parent who loved me beyond all else, and whether, in this dark world, that was truly possible. At this stage in my life, I questioned everything I saw, especially relationships between a child and their parents. Sadly, for me, there was something rather creepy about watching a small boy or girl being embraced by an adult. I felt there must be some ulterior motive. I was so sure that it was just an act, and I would always watch very closely to see the reaction of the child. Did they cringe away? Did they show any emotion? Or even fear? Or did they genuinely love being made a fuss of by the adult? It was strange, but I only had to look at a boy or girl to know whether they were being ill-treated; I could see it in their eyes.

I could never bear to have any physical contact with either Ken or Chris Brisley. On very rare occasions, and usually for the benefit of another adult, they would force themselves to put an arm around me, or try to hold my hand. It was not a natural or fluid motion, and the arm or hand was removed as quickly as possible once the wanted impression had been achieved. It was a long time before I could bear to have contact with anyone, and in later years, any mention or show of affection often brought a very quick demise to the relationship.

***

With the school term now over, I was back home for the Spring holidays. *The woman* seemed to be more hyper than normal, and as usual, I could do nothing right. It was as if she was waiting for me to make a mistake. On this particular day, she had a friend come for tea. The friend was a Spiritualist, named Jean, a very nice person. I think she must have been in her middle to late forties. While they were having afternoon tea, I was asked to come in and sit with them. Jean seemed to take an unusual interest in me, telling me that she could see many people around me, with arms outstretched to guard and protect me. Chris Brisley sneered at this; but Jean insisted that they were all around me. From then on, whenever Jean came to visit, I kept well out of her way as much as possible. Spiritualism was the latest fad in Chris Brisley's life, and she was completely besotted with it.

One afternoon it was my duty to make tea, and bring it into the sitting room at a set time. I watched the kitchen clock, and when the chimes announced it was four p.m., I punctually took the tray and entered the room. I remember locking eyes with Jean, and sensed a strange feeling wash over me. Whoever she was, and whatever she believed in, there was no doubt she was a very powerful woman. As I poured the tea, I could feel her eyes watching my every move.

Suddenly she said, "You are a very beautiful child."

I almost turned around to see who she was talking to, certainly not to me. I looked up at her, willing her to stop praising me, for I knew I did not deserve this accolade, and it certainly would not go down well with *the woman.*

She smiled at me and said, "One day, you will get married, and it will be an extremely happy marriage. Your husband will love you like you've never been loved before, but you will have to wait for quite a few years before this happens. There will be many avenues for you to follow before you meet your future husband." How prophetic her words turned out to be, though at the time she made me feel extremely sad. Certainly marriage had no real meaning for me, it was just a word; but the thought of having to stay with *the woman* for many years to come was almost too terrifying to contemplate, for it was what *not* being married meant to me.

I am never sure whether Jean noticed the frosty air now suddenly permeating the room. I certainly felt it, and I shivered, and try as I might, I could not stop myself from looking across at *her*, and into those coal black eyes. They were on fire; they spat venom out at me, and I knew that the evening would not be a happy one. As I washed up the tea cups, I thought, *why couldn't the world leave me alone?* There were so many times when I thought that.

Well, the world wasn't going to do that, and as soon as Jean left the house, I was called into the sitting room, and told to sit before her. The look on her face was almost maniacal. The tirade of words spewing from her mouth really meant nothing to me. I'd heard them all before and was so used to them. I was waiting for what would come after she had finished yet again telling me that I was destined to become a complete slut, and how happy she was that my mother had not lived to see the day. In the next second, she was upon me, hitting me around the head, blocking my small body with her ample one, as I attempted to get away from her. She then pulled me off the chair and onto the floor. I tried to protect my head from the brutal beating and got kicked in my stomach. I remember her hitting me across my right ear *and then nothing*. She had, yet again, knocked me out. I must have been unconscious for quite some time, because the next thing I remember was lying in my bed with her hovering at the door. The awful thing is that I was still a very young child, but even then I knew what fear smelled like, whether it was my own, or someone else's fear. This time it emanated from *the woman*, filling the room up with its warm sickly aroma as she stood in the doorway intently watching me.

I sat up slowly, and was immediately sick over the bed sheet. My eyes darted across the room toward her, knowing that she would be furious, but there was no reaction at all. She stood there staring back at me. Eventually, she changed the sheet and brought me a hot drink. Not a word was spoken between us. The light was turned off, and I drifted off to sleep. I heard a car in the drive, and knew that Ken had returned from a BLESMA meeting. During the night, I woke and felt sick again. I managed to make it to the bathroom in time. Being sick in bed twice in one night would have had dire consequences. The pain in my stomach was now so bad that I collapsed on the way back to my room and lay drifting, in a semi-conscious state. *The woman* was either still awake, or must have heard me fall. As always, Ken was nowhere in sight. The next thing I remember was the anger in her voice as she pulled me to my feet, dragging me back to my bed. She told me that I was malingering, and that she wasn't going to keep running after me. I remember her stamping out of the room. Her footsteps echoed as I now started to hallucinate, feeling my body floating toward the ceiling and back to the bed again. Each time I floated toward the ceiling, I thought I would hit it, but then I would float back down again, trying not to scream out loud as the pain got worse. I was quite convinced that I was going to die. I thought this time that the beating must have gone too far. Strangely, the thought of dying comforted me, and as I started to float again, I wondered if this was how dying felt, as I somehow got through the night. The next day I drifted in and out of sleep, curling my body up to try to stop the pain in my stomach. *She* brought me up some warm milk in the morning, and I didn't see her until later on in the evening. During the day I managed to crawl to the bathroom a couple of times to be sick and remembered yet again being so thankful that I had not been sick in my bed again. During the second night I listened to the clock in the hall strike each hour and wondered if pain could get any worse. On the following Saturday morning the woman came to my room and hurled abuse at me telling me to stop being a lazy cow and get the hell out of bed, as I had the weekly shopping to do; then she left. I heard her walk halfway down the stairs, then nothing. I listened hoping and praying she wouldn't return, but she did. The change in her was quite incredible. She was obviously very frightened about something. She patted me on my head, saying that everything would be all right, then she left again only this time she *ran* down the stairs.

I remember the doctor coming to examine me, and then hearing the ambulance as it pulled into the drive. I arrived at the Royal United Hospital, always known as the RUH for short, to the clanging of bells, but was in no state to enjoy the attention I was getting. In a matter of hours I was in surgery having an operation. Apparently I was not in hospital because of the beating, but my appendix burst and I had peritonitis; I was very near to death. At some point during my stay, a hospital doctor examined me and asked both Ken and Chris Brisley, who were visiting me at the time, about the bruises around my head and on my body. Their reply was that on the night I was rushed to the hospital, I had collapsed and had fallen down stairs which was their main reason for calling the local doctor. The explanation was immediately accepted, and was never mentioned again. Looking back I'm amazed at how irresponsible the hospital staff were, for I know that, with a more thorough inspection of my body, they surely would have seen quite a few old scars. Some I still have to this day.

Although I was not a Catholic at the time, I did have the last rites twice during my stay in the hospital. Since I was a convent girl, I guess they thought better safe than sorry. Luckily, I pulled through, and after three weeks, I was again back at home. During my stay at the RUH, I often wondered what had caused the sudden change in *the woman* when she had returned to my bedroom that day. From openly hostile to scared witless in a matter of seconds was dramatic to say the least. I knew that I would have to assuage my curiosity and ask her.

After a week back at home, I plucked up courage and asked her why she had looked so frightened when she came back into my bedroom on the night when I had gone into hospital. Remember this woman was now deep into spiritualism, so one could indeed take what she then said as complete nonsense, but this was not a fanciful individual by any means. She looked at me and said that my mother had been standing in the middle of the stairs blocking her way, and had told her I was dying. Actually the words my mother apparently had said were, "My child is dying, you must do something to save her." I am not a deeply religious person, but I do believe there is a higher being and that we are here for a purpose. To this day I *do* believe that my mother was there, and the fact is that she saved my life. The only sad thought is that she never appeared when I was being beaten, and never told Chris Brisley to stop abusing her child. Maybe spirits only appear under very extreme circumstances!

While I was recuperating, and missing school in more ways than one, I was treated fairly well by both the Brisleys. Though it would be silly of me to say there was any affection shown, for a few weeks I was excused from washing up and housework. To me, that meant being treated fairly well.

***

Nothing lasted in the Brisleys' lives for very long. They would get excited about people who would drift in and then out of their lives, then move on to new people. Around this time, Ken started visiting a very badly disabled young man who was living in a nursing home. On this particular Sunday afternoon, it was decided to bring the young patient to the Parade Gardens, a park situated in the centre of the City, to listen to the band. Though the young man didn't say much, I could tell he was enjoying himself. It made me very aware that there were people far worse off than me. Some of the nursing home staff joined us, and we all sat on blankets, listening to the music. During the interval, one of the doctors looked across at me, and nudging Chris Brisley, he said, "I guess she's the fruit of your loins then?" She didn't say anything, just nodded, winked and then smiled at him. I certainly had no idea what he meant, but at the time, it seared into my brain, and made me feel dirty. I was not the fruit of her anything, and I wanted to scream out to let him know I was nothing to do with her. The saying stayed with me for years and when I eventually learned what it meant I found it utterly disgusting. Even more disgusting was the fact she'd misled him into thinking I was her child.

While I was still recuperating from the operation, and when they were both at work, unknown to them, I would again walk along the back lane to my Aunt Maude's home, where she pampered me with interesting lunches and homemade cakes. She never talked about my mother even though I would ask her to tell me about her. Aunt Maude got terribly upset, and the only thing she did say was that I looked so much like my mother that, at times, it almost left her speechless. It was a small crumb, but something I held close to my heart, and another picture I could add to my long and often sleepless nights where I could now almost see her as I imagined what she looked like. A sort of grown-up version of me. In my imagination, Eric, my father, was always the mysterious, good-looking man who doted on me and my mother, and brought much love and laughter into my lonely life. It was strange, but at the time, no one ever talked about my father; it was as if he never existed. I would often ask my grandmother or Aunt Maude about him, but would always get strange looks. Once I asked my aunt why Peter lived with his father and I didn't. She sat very still, not saying a word, just shaking her head, but I could feel the atmosphere tense between us and I knew I mustn't ask her again.

However during one of these visits I found out that all my family were Catholics, but I had not been baptized into the faith, and had been brought up as a Protestant. I made up my mind that I wanted to have closer ties with my mother and decided that, when I went back to school, I would ask Madam Mary how one went about becoming a Catholic. The thought of it excited me, though, I must confess, not really for any religious reasons. I desperately wanted to belong. Although non-Catholics were never pressured into the convent's beliefs, as boarders we always went to mass on Sundays. If, at any time, a pupil expressed a desire to become a Catholic, the school certainly didn't hold back.

On my return to school, and after I'd spoken to Madam Mary, the wheels were set in motion fairly quickly. The school had to have consent from either parents or a legal guardian. I knew that the Reverend Mother still kept in touch with my grandmother, so instead of asking the Brisleys she contacted her instead. She was delighted to hear it had been my decision, and readily gave her consent. Boy, did that open a can of worms! The Brisleys were not informed for quite some time, and when they heard, you would have thought that I'd asked to take up Satanism. Also, given the fact they were my legal adopted parents, they were incensed that this very important decision had been taken out of their hands.

On my first home weekend, which we full boarders had every few months, I was given an icy welcome and told in no uncertain words I would *not* be a Catholic, I would *never* be a Catholic. I think the jargon went something like, *over their dead bodies, or mine*. There were no beatings, just silence whenever I entered a room. I was informed there was to be a meeting at my grandmother's home on the Sunday, and I would return to school from her home. I now knew why there were no beatings. I thanked my new God for that.

The afternoon tea at my grandmother's home was not a happy experience. It was the first time I ever saw her lose her temper. The Brisleys informed her she had no right to interfere in what I should or should not do. I guess that, under the law, they had a point, in so far as they were now my legal parents, but my grandmother dug her heels in. She reminded them that all my family were Catholics, and only the tragic death of my mother had stopped me being baptized as a baby into the Catholic faith. She also felt that, as a blood relative, she had every right to agree to my wishes. I remember at the time I did not look at the Brisleys, and had the terrible feeling if I'd gone home with them that night, I might never have left.

The next few weeks were taken up with extra religious classes, mostly in the evening. At the time the mass was conducted in Latin, and as I took Latin in my school curriculum and already went to Sunday mass, the nuns thought I was well-versed in the weekly ceremony. I wasn't, and always made sure I stood either in the middle or at the back of the church or chapel; then I could stand, kneel, or sit in all the correct parts of the mass. This was a very exciting period in my life, and I was made to feel very special. I didn't always feel closer to God but I *did* feel so much closer to my dead parents. For I was now fairly certain, though nothing had ever been said, that Eric Wilton was not my father. No father would let one child go, yet keep the other.

All the wheels were set in motion, but there was one dark cloud on the horizon. Before I could be baptized I had to go to my first confession. It was to be at a church near my home and it was to be between the priest and me. Sadly, I can't remember the priest's name, but he used to come to the Convent once a week, to go over my religious studies. He was always very friendly and I liked him a lot, until I realized that it would be him who would hear my first confession. I lay awake for nights, thinking about the awful moment when I had to walk into the confessional and tell him all the dreadful sins I'd committed during my young life. I kept remembering the time when I stole the Christmas fairy from the school tree. And the time I hit poor Sonia. What would he think of me after that revelation? I was even supposed to confess all my bad thoughts. How could I tell this man that there were quite a few times when I wished Chris Brisley dead, or that she would vanish, never to be seen again. I wouldn't be able to look at him after *that* particular confession. I agonized for many hours over this monumental problem. Maybe I wouldn't tell him the really bad things I'd done or thought. Or *maybe* I could make up some lesser sins that would satisfy him, and not make me squirm the next time I saw him. I realized this was not a very good way to commence practicing my new faith. In one of the classes I was told after the first confession all my sins would be absolved and I would start out with a clean soul. I very much wanted this, so when the dreaded day came I poured out my heart to him hoping it was true about a clean soul, and I would not see a look of disgust on his face as I left the confessional. I smile when I think of him now. I'm well aware that he must have heard some really bad things during his duties as a priest, but my confession weighed heavily on my mind for a very long time. These were huge milestones for a child about to reach her tenth year.

BECOMING A CATHOLIC

The battle may have been won over my religious desires, but the battle to continue with the rituals of being a Catholic had only just begun. When I was at school at the weekend, going to mass was the normal Sunday routine. As always, I felt very holy, especially at communion. I would sit in the church, letting the whole atmosphere wash over me. Then, along with all the girls, I would go back to the refectory and tuck into a splendid Sunday breakfast. It was colourful, fun and, above all, it was safe.

When I had to go home for the odd weekend, it was a different matter altogether. I was still determined to go to mass on the Sunday, and would creep out of the house very early, hoping not to wake anyone. I would run across the fields to the local Catholic church where I was baptized.

On my first Sunday mass there, I met a lovely family who took me under their wing, and, after the service, asked me to have breakfast at their home. They had two boys who were within a year or two of my own age, and were easy to talk to. It was wonderful being in their warm and happy home. The kitchen table was always laid, and soon we were all sitting down to eggs and bacon, with toast to follow. The babble of excited conversation, laughter and the warm family atmosphere would leave me, though happy to be in their company, with a deep longing to belong to them and be loved, as their children were. After breakfast, I would reluctantly say goodbye, and promise that I would see them on my next weekend home. I would then run back across the fields, hoping that the Brisleys were still asleep. Of course I was never lucky, and again, according to her mood of the day, I was either ignored or set upon the minute I walked through the door.

On the last time I went to Sunday mass from home I stayed longer with my church family than I should have, and knew I was in trouble. I flew back home across those fields with heart pumping and stomach knotted. The minute I entered the house she was waiting for me. She had one of Ken's trouser belts wrapped around her hand, and she struck me the minute I closed the front door. She lashed out with such fury and the only thing I could do was to huddle down in a fetal position while she rained blow after blow across my body. Then she pulled me up by my hair, something she did regularly, and dragged me up the stairs, screaming that I was never to go to church again, or my punishment would be even more severe. From that Sunday on when at home I was much too frightened to ever disobey this command, so I never saw my lovely church family again.

Now, at that time, to miss mass on a Sunday, unless one was too ill to go, was a mortal sin. So, every Monday morning, each day pupil, or boarders spending their weekend at home, were asked if they had attended mass the day before. On those dreaded Mondays when I had been home, I would sit in class knowing I was going to lie, and therefore have not one but two mortal sins on my soul. How could I sit there and tell the world that, if I went to Sunday mass, I would be beaten each time I returned home? I was still very young, and this new faith was the most important thing in my life, yet already I was weighed down with so many sins that I was quite certain hell awaited me when I died. I used to pray by my bed each evening, and ask God to forgive me my two sins for that particular week. Any other sin I may have committed during the week was carefully overlooked.

I dreaded going home for those weekends more and more. Not only was the church out of bounds, but now *the woman* took great delight in serving me meat on the Fridays when I arrived home. Again, at the time, it was a rule in the Catholic church that eating meat on a Friday was a mortal sin. So now my Monday morning questioning included the Friday dinner. I clocked up three mortal sins every time I went home. I now knew, without a doubt there would be no place in heaven for me.

That year Christmas came and went without any feeling of excitement. No tree to trim. No presents from them, though as usual, my grandmother sent me some books which I loved, and, as there was no church, I had a religious calendar hidden under my bed, and would cross the days off until I went back to school.

THE PARTY

For some strange reason, on my tenth birthday, Chris Brisley decided to give me a party. As usual, Ken was away on business at the time. Needless to say, I was very excited. I had never had a party before and never been allowed to attend any of my school friends' parties either.

She told me I could ask six friends to come for tea on the 5th of January. I was very careful in choosing who I would ask. Four of the girls I knew quite well, but the two most important ones were two girls I had hardly spoken to, but hero-worshipped from afar. I thought them both so beautiful, and to me, they seemed to be perfection personified. Everything about them was what I wanted to be. Linnet Berrisford was a petite girl with a very pretty face and dark auburn wavy hair reaching her shoulders, and looked glorious. She had a bubbly personality, and was always in demand for whatever was going on at school. Her father had some important job abroad, but would often visit her when he was in England. The affection between them was obvious, and for me, extremely painful. I wanted so much to be a part of her life, but I don't think she ever really noticed me. Camilla Brockhurst was very tall for her young age, or so it seemed to me. She had blonde hair and pale skin, she excelled at everything she did. Camilla had a very light pink tube of lipstick she had squirreled away in her tuck box. She would wear it in the common room, during the evenings, when we were quite sure none of the nuns were on the prowl. I was so impressed with her that, at times, I could hardly breathe when she was around, for even then I could appreciate beauty. Camilla's face was beautiful, with the brightest blue eyes I'd ever seen. She didn't have to do anything to get noticed. I'm sure she grew into a very attractive woman. I was quite sure that if I invited them to my party they would become instant friends. Above all, they would at least acknowledge my existence.

I was allowed to buy a pack of party invitations, and on returning to school after the Christmas break, duly handed them out to the chosen six. I could hardly believe it when all accepted. I told Madam Mary that I was having a birthday party and asked if I would be allowed home for the special occasion. Being a boarder at a Convent was a bit like being in the Army; you had to have permission for everything. It was agreed I could stay home for two nights, but three of the girls who were also boarding had to be back at school after the party. Their transport was organized, and I was ecstatic. I was going to have my very first birthday party.

Around this time Chris Brisley was quite friendly with a woman who had a teenage boy named, Brian. He played the piano accordion rather well and was invited to come and play for my birthday. It all seemed too good to be true, and as usual, it was. On the morning of the 5th *the woman* woke in a black, black mood and by mid-morning, for no reason at all, she was screaming at me telling me there would be no party for me that day. I was commanded to go to Brian's home and tell him that he would not be needed to play for us that afternoon. It was a cold wintery day and I remember running and crying all the way to his house, wondering what I had done to make her cancel my party. By the time I arrived I was almost incoherent as I attempted to explain the party was canceled. I tried not to think of what excuse could be made to my school friends. I wanted to curl up in a tiny ball somewhere and hide. How was I ever going to face everyone when I returned to school. It was too humiliating to even contemplate. When I arrived back home *she* was at the front door waiting for me, demanding to know where I'd been. I timidly reminded her that she'd told me to cancel the music for the afternoon. Now, as an adult, I realize the woman definitely had some sort of mental problem. No one could be in their right mind and behave as she did, but on my tenth birthday, I was just a skinny little child who desperately wanted nothing more than a promised party. Once again those black empty eyes were on fire and I thought she was going to hit me so I huddled in the corner of the kitchen waiting for the first blow. She then did an about turn, and told me she'd said no such thing and I was to go back immediately and explain I'd made a mistake. I think the trip back to Brian telling him I'd made a mistake was even more colder and mortifying than the first one.

So the party went ahead. All the girls brought presents. We had little sandwiches, fruit jelly, and a birthday cake. I blew out the candles. We then listened to the piano accordion being played by what must have been, by now, a very confused young boy. My school friends thoroughly enjoyed everything and I could tell they were very impressed by the event, but for me the whole experience was a complete nightmare. The day is seared into my brain and even now when I think about it how I ache for the little girl who ran crying and heartbroken to tell the boy her party was off.

Though Linnet and Camilla did not become my close friends, and I was never truly invited into their inner circle, they were always very nice to me and I thanked God that the humiliation of that day did not extend to them, or the other four girls.

On that birthday, my grandmother sent me a most beautiful present; in fact it was the best present I'd ever had. It was an almost life-sized baby doll, whom I called Shirley. She came with a beautiful cot, plus sheets and blankets, along with lots of baby clothes. This was my first real doll, so she became my most treasured possession. Most of my presents were usually books, or school stuff like a geometry set, or sports gear. Shirley became a big part of my life. When I was doing my given chores around the house, I would always make sure that Shirley was either up and dressed, or put to bed for the night. I think it was the only time in my life that I felt any mothering instinct. I was not allowed to take Shirley to school, and this was the only downside to returning to the convent after the Christmas holidays.

Still, it was good to be back. I could let my wild side come to the fore once again. As a child, I had a passion for practical jokes, I think I got this from my grandmother, who had a devilish sense of humor. I would spend hours sewing up bed sheets, changing the rota for weekend duties and switching uniforms around. Remember, we all had a strict uniform code, so all the clothes look identical. I found it simply hilarious watching one of my skinny dormitory friends looking ridiculous in a rather large girl's uniform and visa versa. It was not always appreciated by the others, who had to put up with my pranks, but at least they never had to look very far to find the culprit. On the other hand, they always forgave me my sins against them, for I was also the one who would go down to the kitchen after the lights went out, when we knew the nuns were in their own private house, and only one senior supervisor left to make sure all was quiet. Well, quiet it was, and I always knew how to circumnavigate the supervisor. Many a night I would stealthily sneak along the corridor and down the stairs, through the refectory and into the kitchen. I always had two empty gym bags with me, and would carry them crammed to overflowing back up to the dormitory where hungry and eager mouths would be waiting for our midnight feast. I never got caught once, and, to my knowledge, no kitchen staff ever queried the missing food.

I was keen on playing all sports, and would play netball like I used to play hockey, with gusto, doing nothing more than running up and down the court, never learning a single thing about the game. But it was such fun. I loved being out in the open. Since my foot operation, hockey was out for me but the one sport activity I was really good at was tennis. I think that if I had taken the game more seriously, I would have become an excellent player but at ten years old, and when away from home, I didn't take anything too seriously.

Academically, I was a quick learner. Very good at most subjects but hopeless at maths, I would scrape through the maths exams with written notes from my teacher saying things like, *must try harder* or *obviously lacks interest in this subject.* Forget algebra! I hated it with a passion, and my mind would go completely blank even thinking about an impending lesson on the dreaded subject. It was quite incredible, but for one whole term I never once presented a single sheet of class work or homework on algebra and was never asked why. Big slip-up there, but as long as it lasted I was one happy puppy. I was not quite so fortunate during my next term.

In the Spring, as a belated birthday present, Ken allotted me a part of the back garden. It was given to me on the understanding that I looked after it. He said that I could choose whatever plants or flowers I liked, and he would buy them for me. My little square of garden got me through many sad and lonely hours of my young life. I first asked Ken for some paving stones. He had never been to Grandpa Lewis's allotment, and I know he was mystified by my request, but they were purchased and stacked ready for my start. I was given a small fork and spade, and spent the Easter holidays digging and laying out my paving stones. I think it was the first time that I saw a glimmer of admiration in Ken's eyes, as he looked at my well prepared garden. I planted vegetables in one half of the garden, and flowers in the other half. My main concern was that, when I went back to school I would not be able to tend my new project. Ken, who because of his disability couldn't do much outside work, assured me our weekly gardener would take care of it while I was at school. As usual, during the Spring term boarding pupils were allowed to go home for the odd weekend every now and only then if they wanted to. I had never requested a home weekend, but now that I had Shirley and a garden to look after, I went home once a month. It was one of the only times Ken kept his promise, and when I returned home on those weekends, though my garden was not up to my high standard, I knew it wouldn't take me too long to get it back into shape. I was at my happiest when digging and tending my plants, like a mother hen with her chicks. It was a great day when I presented the *woman* with my very first vegetable produce, puny though it was. A bunch of strange looking carrots and some very small lettuce. Grandpa Lewis would have been proud of me.

Thankfully, my garden took up most days in my home life, but I was happiest when away from *the woman* and in the school environment. I was now well and truly fitting in with my school mates. I was one of the leading lights of my classroom. Having a great need to be noticed and loved, I was ready to get up to almost any prank that would amuse my friends. One Friday evening, I, along with six other girls in my dormitory, decided that it was time that we all climbed over the wall into the forbidden garden, to see exactly where the nuns lived. I've never worked out why we all decided to climb over the wall instead of going through the unlocked gate, but climb over the wall we did. I guess it was a far more exciting way of gaining entry into prohibited territory. It was absolutely off limits to any school child, and this was made completely clear to all new girls. Only God knew what would happen if any errant child decided to stray. We were soon to find out.

The nuns had a separate building from the main school. At one time it must have been a private house, and it was quite large, with a beautiful garden attached. It was where they retreated at the end of their working day: their secluded world where they could relax, have their meals and do whatever nuns did when they were not praying or looking after demanding school children.

It was a dangerous mission and very important that all the girls listened to their leader, which, of course was me, seeing it had been my idea in the first place. When I think about it now, we must have looked liked Ninja warriors in our pyjamas, as we all successfully scaled not only the hedge but the wall as well. Although it was quite late in the evening, it was the beginning of summer, so still light. The gardens were absolutely beautiful, full of blooming shrubs, colourful plants, and a myriad of flowers. As far as I knew, only the nuns looked after the garden, so certainly, some had very green fingers. I was impressed, and wanted to sit on the lawn and enjoy the view. But the most important part of this adventure was to find out as much as we could about the interior of the house. There was nothing around the building that would conceal seven girls, so we made a mad dash to one side, hoping that we wouldn't be spotted. Little did we know that we had been spotted when the first head had appeared over the wall, and apparently the head mistress, (Bonzo) had been summoned to witness the extraordinary scene.

Oblivious, we carefully made our way around the house, stealthily peering into each window. I'm not sure what we expected to find, but the rooms looked very normal, just like any other country home, except that they were completely deserted, and we wondered hopefully whether the nuns had a small private chapel where they might be having evening services, or maybe they went to bed very early. As we made it to the back door we were extremely pleased to see that it was mostly glass, and we could see into the kitchen, which was small and again, thankfully, empty. We crowded around the door, and I knew all six girls were now looking at me waiting for my next move. I had no idea what I was going to do once we got over the wall but I now knew they all expected me to enter the kitchen. I hoped and prayed the door would be locked but it wasn't. I thought that if I walked in, opened a couple of drawers, then beat a hasty retreat, we could say we had been where no other pupil had dared to go. I remember being scared, but I was the leader, so in I went. I reached the end of the kitchen and was about to open the pantry when the light went on, and the six girls disappeared in a puff of smoke. I stood alone, shivering and shaking, looking up at none other than the feared Bonzo. I was completely doomed.

I was ordered to go back to my dormitory and told to report to her study before class in the morning. When I arrived back, all the girls were in their beds pretending to be asleep until they were quite sure that I was alone, and not accompanied with a posse of irate nuns. They apologized profusely, all saying they should have stayed to face the music. Talk about rats and a sinking ship! I put their minds to rest by telling them I wouldn't snitch on them. It wasn't that I was being such a noble child. It didn't make any difference how many of us were involved. It was going to be me who was expelled, or the whole six of us. Either way, I would still have to face the wrath of Chris Brisley sometime in the near future. Needless to say, I didn't get any sleep that night.

At eight thirty a.m. I was standing outside the headmistress's study, waiting to be summoned. My bony knees were shaking so much that they actually made a noise. I *knew* I was going to be expelled, and the thought of going home and explaining why to *the woman* made me feel sick. The voice of the headmistress boomed out and I slunk miserably into her study.

She sat staring at me for what seemed an eternity, then very quietly said. "You know quite well you are forbidden to come into our private dwelling. Whether by gate *or* over the wall."

I nodded, not daring to look at her in case I was turned into stone.

"And yet you blatantly broke the rules."

Again I nodded, as I now carefully inspected my highly polished shoes. "I'd like to know the names of the other girls who were with you."

I looked up at her and shook my head. "It was my idea and I don't think they really wanted to come."

"And so you threatened them with fire and brimstone if they didn't do as they were told?" There was a suspicion of a smile hovering around her mouth.

Of course the tears then came and I broke down. "I'm still waiting."

I absolutely knew I would never tell. I would not be able to face my friends if I did and they would probably never speak to me again. So I shook my head and let the tears flow. Her next words were like manna from heaven.

"You obviously have a very strong influence over your fellow students. So I am going to suggest that you and *all* of the other perpetrators spend next Saturday thoroughly cleaning the refectory, and I do mean *thoroughly*. I shall expect *all* to be there." She tapped a notepad as she leaned over the desk and said. "I have the names of the six girls who were with you, and when you have finished, I will inspect the refectory. If I am pleased with the result I will give you all a pass."

I was completely stunned. "Does this mean I won't be expelled?" I blurted out.

"Oh I'm sorry, was that what you wanted?" Her face now broke into a broad smile.

I remember shaking my head so violently I gave myself a headache. Needless to say, we girls cleaned the refectory as it had never been cleaned before.

Bonzo had always been a formidable figure, but from that moment on, I worshipped the ground she walked on.

AUNT MAUDE

It was a few weeks after this episode that, in the middle of a French lesson, I was once again called into the headmistress's study. I wasn't particularly worried, as I had been on my best behaviour since my last meeting with her. She pointed to the chair in front of her desk, and I duly sat. She had a sad expression on her face as she quietly told me my Aunt Maude had died and I was to go home and be with my family. I didn't say anything; I couldn't. My Aunt Maude had been a wonderful, if all too fleeting, an oasis in my young life, someone I could go to during the long lonely holidays when I was away from school and left to fend for myself. Now where would I go? Uncle Len, her husband, was a nice but distant man, and even though he was my godfather I hardly saw or knew him. In fact, after that day, I never saw him again. Why did she have to die? The question pounded through my head. At the time, though I knew she was ill, I didn't know that she had *always* been very ill and had not expected to have a long life. I didn't know that she was only in her late thirties. I knew she had gone, and I had lost another most precious connection to my mother. I was feeling very sorry for myself. I remember sobbing dry wracking sobs as I bent double holding onto my knees for support. Bonzo gently lifted me up and cradled me in her arms as she tried to comfort me. No one would ever know what the loss of this woman meant to me. I was truly devastated.

It was obvious I would never make the journey home by bus, so a taxi was ordered and the Brisleys were informed that I was on my way.

I arrived home to a flurry of activity, and was immediately bundled off with the Brisleys to my aunt's home. On the way, I was told she had died the week before, and the funeral had been that day. Again, I was stunned. She had been dead for a week, and I didn't know, and even the funeral was over. Apparently, the only reason I had been summoned from school was that the whole family was gathered at my aunt's home, and my two uncles had asked to see me. It would be the first time they had set eyes on me since I had been a baby, and at the time, I didn't even know they existed.

I walked into my aunt's sitting room, and stared at the crowd of faces looking back at me. Peter was there, and for a second, I hated that, because it meant he had been to the funeral, whereas I had not. I guess they thought mc too young for funerals. Little did they know how old I was inside my young body. I stood like a statue, gazing across at my grandmother, who had aged dramatically since my last meeting with her. Death of a child will do that to a person, and this was the third child she'd buried. I wanted to run to her, do what I usually did, bury my head in her lap and stay there forever; but I knew nothing would change, and I felt lonelier than ever. As my grandmother started to introduce me to my two uncles, there was a gasp from a rather handsome man sitting across the room by the window.

"My God, for a second I thought Eileen had walked through the door." It was Uncle Cyril, who stood and came over to me. He tilted my face up to his. "It's incredible. You're the spitting image of your mother." He kissed my forehead then went back to his chair.

I'll never forget that moment. To this day, I can still hear him, and will always hold those words close to my heart, and I can see the room as if it were yesterday.

Uncle Bob introduced himself, and told me that the woman sitting next to him was his wife, my Aunt Olive. I don't remember Cyril's wife's name. But anyway, I never saw her again, so it doesn't really matter.

Everyone started talking at once, and I was left standing like a block of wood, feeling awkward and out of place. Luckily, Peter came to my rescue and took me into the garden, where we sat together on a bench and a very nice woman brought us some sandwiches and lemonade.

He started to say that he was sorry that I had not been included for the funeral, but I cut him short.

"It doesn't matter. It's too late to be upset about it, and I'm sure she understands," I replied curtly. Peter gave me an offbeat look but said nothing.

On the way home, the two Brisleys were talking about the events of the day as if I wasn't there.

"Well that's another one out of the way. At least she won't be sticking her nose in our business any more."

I looked at *the woman* and couldn't believe what I had heard. I was still very young, but not too young to know who they were talking about.

"Yes, and I can see the two men are pleased we have the child. It's quite obvious they couldn't care less about her," Ken replied.

Chris Brisley nodded. "The old lady looked dreadful. In my opinion, she doesn't look long for this world."

I followed them down the back lane in abject misery.

One Saturday afternoon, around a month after my Aunt Maude's death, I asked Madam Mary if I could go to see my grandmother for tea. Amazingly she said yes, with the proviso that I return to school no later than five p.m. I was ecstatic. It didn't even cross my mind that my grandmother might be out. I ran all the way to the bus stop, wondering whether she would be pleased to see me. She was at home, and as usual, in her sitting room, reading; she was an avid reader. If my grandmother was surprised to see me, it didn't show. After that, I regularly went to see her, and it was on those precious Saturdays that I started to learn about my family.

My grandmother told me that the years spent with her husband, my grandfather, had been happy and busy. Bringing up five children had been quite a task. But she'd loved every minute of it. Her eyes twinkled when she told me she was born to be a mother. I think it was around that time in my young life I knew I would definitely not be one. It wasn't that I didn't like children. It was because I never imagined being adult enough to have the responsibility of being a mother. Strange thoughts for a young girl to have, but they never really left me, and it was to be many years before I felt like an adult, and accepted being treated as one. By that time it was too late to think of having children.

At last, my grandmother started to talk to me about Eileen, my mother. She was the middle daughter, a gentle child who brought sunshine into each room she entered. She became a tall, slim, leggy teenager, with a beautiful face and a ready smile. When it was warm, she loved to spend hours tucked away at the bottom of the garden reading. She had a good education, and then she met my father. At the time my grandmother thought her much too young to get involved with an older man. That was the sum total conversation about my father. My mother was always devoted to her younger sister Vere. Apparently, when Vere became sick, Eileen nursed her until, tragically, Vere, at the age of twenty-one, eventually died. My mother, like her mother, never got over Vere's death. She was the first of the three girls to die so young.

I loved hearing all the stories about my family. It made me feel as though I still belonged to them, and not to the two outsiders who had so successfully swallowed me up, and had then spat me out into a dark and terrifying world. I never told my grandmother how lonely and frightened I was, and how I longed to be living with her once again. I never told her, because by now, I realized I would never come home; and maybe she wouldn't want to know anyway.

I could not bring myself to blame my grandmother in any way. I'm quite sure she thought she had done the very best she could under the circumstances. And I think she was either oblivious or maybe turned a blind eye to the rumours that must have circulated where I was concerned, and indeed, certainly did get back to her much later on. However, I do blame my two healthy uncles. They truly threw me to the wolves, without giving me a second glance. I don't think either of them lost a single night's sleep over me. It wasn't until a good few years had passed and I was almost out of my teens that a warm loving woman called Mabel Redwood went to see my grandmother and told her she must make me leave Chris Brisley before it was too late.

***

The summer holidays were looming once again, and, as always, I dreaded the weeks ahead. No school, no friends, and sadly, no more secret Saturday visits to my grandmother until the start of the next term. I arrived home at the start of the holiday, and dutifully went to my bedroom to unpack my school uniform and other clothes. It was then that I saw the empty space where the cot and Shirley had been. I feverishly searched the room, but they were gone. I couldn't believe it. She must have put them in another room. I ran down the stairs and into the kitchen where she was preparing the dinner. Now, if I think about it the answer to my question still rings in my ears, even after all this time.

"I have given everything away. You are much too old to be playing with dolls."

I stared at *the woman*. I couldn't believe what I was hearing, and I wanted my Shirley back. She was the most beautiful possession I had, and oh, how I loved her! I continued to stare at the woman, hating her and simply numb with grief. I turned and ran back to my bedroom and cried until I couldn't cry anymore. Some time later I heard her on the stairs, and knew I was in trouble. I scrubbed at my face, hoping that she wouldn't notice the swollen eyes and the tear-stained cheeks.

"Look at you, crying over a silly toy. It's about time you grew up. I'm sick to death of you, and now I'll give you something to cry about." And then the beating came.

Once she started, it was as if she couldn't stop. It was always bad, but this time it seemed to be much worse. My legs, arms, and head were all battering targets. Yet again she was completely out of control. She threw me on to the bed and continued to beat me. I remember turning to face her, trying to ward off some of the blows and she caught me across my windpipe and nearly choked me. I started to cough and splutter and gasp for air. I then heard Ken clomping up the stairs. He almost flew into the bedroom.

"For God's sake, one of these days you're going to kill the child. What the hell has she done this time?"

"Nothing," I croaked. "She gave Shirley away, with the cot and all the clothes." I buried my head in the pillow and started to cry again.

"You're a mean bitch!" he screamed at her. "She's just a child, for Christ's sake!" Then they started on each other while I crept out of the room and into the bathroom to see what damage had been done to me. This time it was a really *bad* beating, but it was the first time I had ever heard Ken stand up for me.

In the morning, I could hardly get out of bed. My whole body was bruised. My face was so grotesquely swollen that I didn't recognize myself. Both eyes were half-closed, with one cheek completely puffed up; I looked like something out of a horror movie. I crawled back into bed and sobbed. This was a living hell, and I just wanted to go to sleep and never wake up again. It was the very first time that I actually started to think of ways I could kill myself, but at the time I was in too much pain to devise any plan. I drifted off to sleep, hoping that she would leave me alone, for I knew that, if she started on me again, I would not make it through another day. If I was going to die, I wanted it to be quick and easy, only I was too young to know how.

Later on in the morning, I heard Ken coming to my bedroom. I cowered in the bed. He entered carrying a tray with my breakfast of toast and hot chocolate. He helped me sit up and then sat on the edge of the bed watching me as I tried to eat the toast. I remember looking across at him and actually saw tears in his eyes. This was something completely new to me.

"I'm so sorry," he whispered. "I tried to get Shirley back for you, but I don't know who she gave her to, and she won't tell me." He began to cut the toast into small pieces, then held the mug to my lips. My lovely doll was never mentioned again.

***

One morning during my school holiday I went into Bath with *the woman* to do some shopping. As we passed a toy shop, I saw a most beautiful doll sitting in the window. She was smaller than Shirley but she was simply exquisite; I fell in love with her. Chris Brisley saw me looking at her and for some reason she took me into the shop.

Maybe she was feeling guilty about giving Shirley away. Anyway, she asked the assistant if we could look at the doll in the window. I was so excited I could hardly contain myself as I held her in my arms. I thought I was going to walk out of the shop with her, but instead Chris Brisley asked the assistant if she could pay so much a week until the doll was paid for. Not what I wanted but certainly better than nothing. Maybe *the woman* was going to give the doll to me as a Christmas present. It would be a long time until Christmas but she was worth waiting for, and I had already decided to call her Jane. For a change, I couldn't wait for the Christmas school holiday, which seemed a lifetime away.

***

Now the Summer holidays were nearly over, and once again, I was getting garbed out with my Autumn and Winter uniform. The blue dresses with their white collars and short sleeves were put away along with the straw boaters, which I hated with a passion. I preferred the maroon gymslip, white blouse with maroon and gold tie, plus the heavy maroon winter coat and velour hat; I thought it much more stylish.

It was wonderful to be back at school, and now a confirmed full boarder, with no temporary sign hanging over my head.

Because a lot of my friends had read the now famous, or infamous, newspaper article, about my escapade from the tree, they thought it high time that I showed them my tree-climbing prowess. Late one evening, when we were all tucked up in bed, it was decided unanimously that I should climb down the tree which was close to our dormitory window. Since I had neglected to tell the girls why I'd fallen out of the tree, I saw no reason now why I should pass on to them this small defect in my climbing prowess. Still, on looking out of the window and seeing that the tree was almost touching our window, and also not too far up from the ground, I thought it would be a piece of cake; and anyway, who was I to disappoint such an enthusiastic group? I managed to get out and on to the tree with most of the girls now hanging out of the window cheering me on. I was halfway down before I realized, much too late, I had forgotten that the room under our dormitory was Bonzo's study. Suddenly there I was, gripping on to the tree, looking straight into her study and Bonzo sitting at her desk, looking straight out at *me*. Needless to say, I was so surprised that I let go, and fell the rest of the way. As I lay there looking up at the dormitory window, I noticed that not one girl was in sight. What was the saying about rats leaving a sinking ship again?

By the time Bonzo arrived I was standing up, and none the worse for this latest exploit. She said not a word just beckoned me to follow her back into her study. Her first words were "The door is a much safer way to exit the dormitory, or was there a reason you were thinking of making a quicker getaway?" Yet again, I could see a slight quirk of her lips. "Thankfully, I can see you are still in one piece, so at least I didn't have to call out the fire brigade to extricate you again." She could see I was surprised. She nodded and said, "I try to keep up with all my students activities even when they are away from school." She then looked me over, to make sure I really was in one piece, and then said, "You know, we had a really quiet holiday without you." I promised her that I wouldn't climb either up or down any more trees. She smiled, shaking her head, and said, "This truly would be a blessing indeed."

WAITING FOR JANE

At the start of the next term, I was moved up into a new class. The lessons were now becoming more challenging, and I realized that I had to knuckle down. For a few months, I went through a phase of sitting in class and completely zoning out, as I did at home. Usually, I could sail through each lesson, but now my quick grasp of anything the teachers put forth seemed to drift completely over my head. I missed the friends who hadn't moved with me, and as most of them were day girls, I hardly ever saw them. I still had my dormitory friends, but I only saw them at night or weekends. I felt disorientated, again as if I didn't belong. When asked a question I would sit and stare at the teacher, wondering what she was talking about and why she was talking to me. It was a strange time, which, thankfully, didn't last too long. But my end of term report stated that, through this school period, it had been noted that I lacked concentration, and that most of the teaching staff were quite worried by the change in me. After *the woman* read the report she, as usual, slapped me across my face, splitting my mouth with her ring. She kept hitting me until I promised never to bring a report home like that again.

I had been home for a couple of days when Chris Brisley made a point of saying she was going into town, and that, if I hurried with my chores, I could go with her. She said that she had some last-minute Christmas shopping to do. I was absolutely certain this would be the day when Jane would be coming home with me. I was right; we arrived at the toy shop, and I was told to wait outside. I saw money being exchanged and was trembling with expectation. What I didn't realize was that the shop assistant was *returning* money to *the woman*. Eventually she left the shop, minus any package. In a small voice I asked her when she would be getting the doll.

She turned to me and coldly said, "I asked for the deposit back. I was quite correct when I said you were too old to have dolls. You need to stop walking around with your head in the clouds and grow up." With that she walked on. I was completely heartbroken. I had wanted my new doll so much. She was to be a replacement for Shirley, and I desperately needed something to love, even if it was only a toy. Oh, how I wanted that fantastic doll! It's so sad that a young child should know what emptiness felt like, but I truly did, and detested her on that day. I was so cold with misery that I shivered uncontrollably. I was suddenly awkward and uncoordinated as I lurched along beside her, not quite knowing how I was going to get through the day. She never missed a moment to squash me as one would an insect, and for the moment, she was again one happy woman.

I'm now quite certain that she had no intention of ever getting the doll. For whatever reason, she truly enjoyed making my life hell. I am told that we must forgive those who sin against us. I still find it very difficult to forgive this woman who so viciously stole my childhood and teens from me.

Over the years, I have often been asked why I didn't leave home sooner. If you have never been controlled in mind, body and soul by another person, especially from a very young age, you simply have no idea how much fear you live with. Also, freedom is just a word, it means nothing to the controlled. To be frequently told that I was her puppet, and that she pulled the strings, was an apt description. When she said "Jump!" I jumped as high as I could. I don't think I ever heard her say *anything* nice to me. If she had, I think I would have gone into shock. I often thought she must be a demon sent from hell to torment me. Christmas came and went as it always did, a day to be got through: no joy, no religion, no presents.

TWO RABBITS

One day, during the Easter holiday, Ken arrived home with two baby rabbits and a small hutch. I fell in love as soon as I set eyes on them. One was pure white, and the other was black. I named them Snow White and Black Beauty. Not very original, but they were mine. The holiday had started off well. I spent endless hours grooming and feeding them. The only concern I had was *the woman*. From the first moment she saw them, she hated them, and would cringe if ever I brought them near her. I eventually took the hutch to the bottom of the garden, well out of her way. Unlike my school friends, I didn't have any close friends at home, so Snow White and Black Beauty were my little companions during the holiday. They became very tame, and would follow me around the garden. I would spend endless hours talking to them as if they were human. But all too soon the day came when the holiday was over and I was to return to school. What to do with my little creatures? I knew I couldn't leave them at home. I was quite sure they would receive the same fate Shirley had. Ken saved the day and my sanity. He knew a co-worker at his office with a large family. They were willing to look after the rabbits while I was away at school. Problem solved! And with a much easier mind, I returned to the Convent, knowing that my pets would be safe. During the summer break, they were returned to me, and again at the Christmas holiday.

I remember it being an exceptionally cold winter, and running to and from the rabbit hutch each day was not quite so much fun. I decided to bring the hutch nearer to the house. By now the rabbits were fully grown and very pretty. I was responsible for them. They gave me something else to think about, apart from Chris Brisley and her continual screaming along with the usual beatings. I had two little friends to care for. I stayed away from the house and her as much as possible.

One Saturday, a week before Christmas, I was allowed to visit my grandmother alone. For Chris Brisley this was a first. As usual, I was primed in what and what not to say, and luckily she still did not know of my Saturday visits when I was at school. It was a lovely afternoon, with a tea party fit for a princess. It was also the very last time, as a child, I had my grandmother all to myself. It was dark when I returned home, and I knew my pet rabbits would probably be asleep. I would get up early in the morning and give them a special feed to make up for leaving them the day before.

I rose early, to a very cold day, with a heavy frost. I was exceedingly glad I didn't have to walk to the bottom of the garden to feed the rabbits. I took some food from the kitchen and went outside to the hutch. The hutch latch was undone, and there was no sign of the rabbits. I frantically scoured the garden, calling out their names but still no rabbits. I was hysterical. I couldn't believe they had run away; they were so tame, and always came when I called. Neither Ken nor *the woman* seemed unduly perturbed by this catastrophic happening. I spent the whole day hunting for them to no avail; they had simply vanished.

Dinner time came and by then I knew I would probably never see them again, I was inconsolable. As the meal was being served I suddenly saw a look of sheer malice on the woman's face. She watched me as I ate the first piece of meat, then pointed at my plate, saying, "Here are your rabbits, they were getting much too big for the hutch, and, anyway, rabbits are made to be eaten."

I looked across at Ken, praying that this was another one of her sick jokes; but I could see by the expression on his face that it was no joke. *They had killed my rabbits and cooked them.* I ran from the table and managed to make it to the bathroom. I locked the door, and stayed huddled on the floor until it was time to go to bed. For the next few days, Chris Brisley was extremely happy; she had got rid of the rabbits and was now enjoying my abject misery. Ken kept out of my way, for I think he was ashamed of the blatant cruelty of his actions. Somehow, I knew that it would have been him who had actually killed them. I could always accept her cruelty, and although

Ken was a distant, and often cold and violent person, he didn't have her perverted streak, so, to this day, I will never understand why he killed them. In later years, when we met up again, I would often look at him and want to ask him why he did such a terrible thing, but I never did; and now, looking back, I'm glad I didn't.

PADDY

Paddy was a female black Springer Spaniel who came into my life as a small furry creature with soulful eyes and a very wet tongue. I have no idea why *she* called the female dog Paddy, but somehow it suited her. On a whim, Chris Brisley bought her at a local kennel, and naturally thought of Paddy as her dog. But as soon as I set eyes on this little bundle, it was love at first sight, and no matter how much coaxing or sweet talk *the woman* did, Paddy was my dog from day one. As soon as she could get up the stairs Paddy would come into my bedroom and sit by my bed, willing me to lift her up where she would spend the night sleeping next to me. As she grew, she would wait for me to go to bed, then up she came. She would put her front paws on the bed, look at me and then do a funny sort of hop with her back legs until she was firmly on top. After giving me a serious licking she would settle herself at the foot of the bed, and not move until the next morning.

It was the first time another animal had come into my life since the demise of my two rabbits. Having a dog made my life much more bearable when I was at home. During any holiday and home weekends, I would take her for long walks, which was considered a chore to the Brisleys, for neither of them were outdoor people, and the infatuation of owning a dog had soon worn off. When Paddy and I were let out of the house, we would run across the road and down a small lane leading to the fields, which seemed to go on for miles. Sometimes I would sneak food for Paddy and me, and after racing across the first field we would then sit quietly together and eat whatever strange concoction I managed to find in the kitchen. I must say that, for a dog, Paddy had a very eclectic taste. She loved chocolate, marmalade sandwiches, sausages, cold rice pudding and hard boiled eggs, though her favorite was jam sponge cake. Well, what dog wouldn't like all those goodies? Paddy grew up to be quite a large dog, and so full of life that she got into everything. No food was safe if it was left out on the kitchen table or counter top, and when she shook her body her black fur would fly simply everywhere; but when I was at home I was quick to clean up after her.

*** *

One memorable day at school we were informed that there was to be a film show in the hall for the whole school. I was not allowed to go to the cinema when at home, so, sick with excitement, I could hardly wait until the next afternoon. It was a film called "Rose Marie" starring Jeanette Macdonald and Nelson Eddie, and considered a classic. The afternoon came, and we all filed into the hall. I sat absolutely mesmerized by the beauty of the singing and wonderful story of romance between the actors; of course, they were absolutely real to me and when it was over I left the hall in a trance-like state, suddenly realizing that there was a magical world out there.

The next time Paddy and I went flying across our fields, it was with an added purpose; for by now, I had learned most of the love songs from the film by heart, and for my next few weekends at home Paddy would sit by me, and, I felt, watched in awe as I played both leading characters, singing as loud as I could, and imagining I was Jeanette Macdonald being wooed by Nelson Eddie.

Whenever there was a row at home, whether it was my turn, or the Brisleys tearing each other to pieces, Paddy would *always* come and sit as close to me as she could. She would stare up at me with her lovely brown eyes, as if telling me that everything would be all right, and soon we would be together, running across those fields. If an animal can be called a soul mate then that's what she was to me.

One Saturday morning, while I was doing my chores, Chris Brisley came down the stairs dressed ready for an outing. She called to Paddy and clipped the lead onto her collar. I was surprised, because, in the previous two years she had *never* taken Paddy out any further than the back garden. I asked her if I could go with her and she shook her head saying, "You might as well say goodbye to the dog, because I'm taking her to be put down. I can't stand having her around any longer." For a moment I couldn't take her words in. It was as if she had physically punched me in the stomach, taking all the breath out of my body. I ran to Paddy. Kneeling down I put my arms around her and we rocked together as if in mutual disbelief of what was about to happen.

"I'll take care of her," I whimpered. "I'll even keep her in my bedroom, so you won't ever have to see her."

"And what happens when you're away at school? Who's going to clean up after her then?"

"I'll take her with me." I was now clutching at straws, but I didn't care. I would have done anything to keep Paddy with me. My sobs came out in great bursts of abject misery as I looked at this precious animal, not more than two years old. "Surely they won't let you kill such a young dog?" I whispered as I clung onto to my soul mate as if not only hers but *my* life depended on it.

The woman kicked me out of the way and opened the front door. "Don't be such a stupid bitch! As if you can take a dog to school."

It was obvious Paddy knew that there was something dreadfully wrong, for she had to be dragged out into the driveway with me now lying prostrate on the hall floor.

It seemed I laid there for hours as vivid pictures crammed unwanted into my head of Paddy being taken into some awful place without me being there to save her. I wondered if she thought I'd abandoned her, and at that moment, I knew what heartbroken meant. I can still see her face, and those soulful eyes, looking at me as if asking me to rescue her. What an empty life lay ahead of me without my beautiful Paddy!

Whenever I could, I would still run to those fields and lie in the long grass thinking of her, and how much I missed her. I often used to dream of her at night, licking my face, and I would wake up in the night thinking she had come back to me; but she would never come back and I would look into those empty black eyes and wonder why this woman was still alive and Paddy wasn't.

JOHN STRAFFEN

In July of 1951, John Straffen murdered five-year-old Brenda Goddard, who lived with her foster parents in Camden Terrace, Bath. Straffen saw Brenda picking flowers, and offered to show her a better place. Later, he told the police that he lifted her over a fence and into a copse where he said the child fell and hit her head. While she was unconscious, he strangled her. In August of that year, Straffen murdered another child, a nine-year-old girl named Cicely Batstone, in a meadow near Bath.

At the same time, Ken and Chris Brisley were very friendly with Brenda's foster parents, and I had once met the little girl when she came to tea. I remember being so shocked by her violent death, and would try to stay awake at night, in case I dreamed of her being killed.

Her murder became the topic of conversation for the next few weeks, and sadly put an end to any hope I had of the few precious hours I spent playing in the fields where I used to take Paddy, for those fields were very near to where Brenda was murdered; and it seemed that Straffen liked to kill in the open countryside. From then on, Chris Brisley would watch me like a hawk. I was only allowed out to do the usual errands and then I was given a precise time when I would have to report home or take the consequences. Sadly it wasn't because they so adored me; they thought it would look bad if anything happened to me. I'm sure that, under any other circumstances, they would have been exceedingly glad to get rid of me. As I got older, I was under no illusion as to how my grandmother felt about Chris Brisley. But she'd made the monumental mistake of handing me over to this couple, and it was something which I, not she, had to live with.

Every so often, Brenda's foster parents would come to our home for tea, and once I heard *the woman* tell them how she understood what they were going through. I remember thinking *how could she possibly know?* She was a woman without a heart, and had no idea what it was like to love a child let alone lose one. She told them they had to stick together, as only special people took on other people's unwanted children! When Straffen was caught in August of that year and eventually tried for the two girls' murders, the visits from Brenda's foster parents slowed down, and eventually stopped all together. I'm sure that, by then, the thin veneer of friendship had worn off on both sides.

Well, the murderer had been caught; so I thought that I would be able to escape once again to those wonderful green fields where I could pretend Paddy was still with me and we could sit together eating stolen goodies, and feel free and happy, if only for an hour or so. How wrong I was. When I asked *the woman* if it would now be all right for me to go and play in the fields, the answer was an emphatic *no*. It was also made very clear that if she ever found out that I had disobeyed her, I would be thrashed long and hard. Her logic was that there was no dog to exercise; and if I felt *I* needed exercising, then there was plenty of work to do around the house. There were times later on when I would leave school early on a Friday evening for the dreaded weekend stay. I would walk all the way home up through those fields. It gave me a feeling of empowerment, and the fact I'd put one over on her as I got ready for the dreadful time ahead.

In April of 1952, John Straffen escaped from Broadmoor, and that afternoon killed another little girl called Linda Bowyer. He was recaptured that day, and remained in prison until he died in 2007 at the age of seventy-seven.

MY WORLD
CAME TUMBLING DOWN

I was eleven when Ken Brisley was asked if he would be interested in running the BLESMA home for Disabled Veterans. Because of her so-called nursing credentials, Chris Brisley was asked if she would be Matron of the home. Apparently, Ken was very interested, being a disabled veteran himself. *The woman* was not quite so sure. It meant leaving Bath and moving to a place called Blackpool, where the veterans' home was situated. Unknown to me, the negotiations went on for quite a few months.

As usual, when anything of importance had to be discussed, or I had blotted my copybook, I would be summoned into the study and asked to sit before them. And as usual, my tummy was churning. Had I done something wrong? Was I going to be punished for a crime I didn't even remember committing? Well the request for my presence on that particular morning was no different. The routine formalities were adhered to, only this time I was not to be reprimanded. I was to be informed of cataclysmic events that, yet again, changed my life.

Eventually, Ken said that he would be taking a new job which was running a home for wounded war veterans. At the time, I wondered why they were bothering to tell me. They never bothered with matters which they thought didn't concern me. Then the bomb dropped. I was told I would be leaving the Convent and going to a new Convent in the north of England, called Layton Hill. This time I would not be a boarder. I was completely stupefied by this news. The last few months had been relatively quiet and as the majority of my life was now spent at school, I was leading a fairly normal and happy life away from them. Now it was over. I was on the move again. I thought of all my school friends, the teachers, and the nuns who had kept me sane, and, to a certain extent, safely away from the brutal tongue lashing and beatings I got from home. I went into a deep depression. I think nowadays it would be called a clinical depression. I was always a fairly upbeat child, even though I was living in hell, and I think this quality, or God-given gift, kept me going. But this news completely floored me. I was going into the abyss again, and without a safety harness. I had a school atlas book, and found that Blackpool was in the North of England. For me, it was another world away. I was leaving absolutely everyone I knew. I tried not to think of my grandmother and our secret Saturday afternoon tea parties. I also feared that, with her continuing bad health, once I left, I might never see her again. A sense of foreboding descended upon me, and wouldn't go away.

During the next few weeks, I was swept along by the tide of events, and could do absolutely nothing about it. Once the wheels were in motion, the furniture was loaded into a removal van and cases packed; there was no turning back.

One of the most painful episodes in my memory was my last day at the convent in Bath. All my friends, for I now had quite a few, were wishing me good luck, and saying they were going to miss me. We all cried together and I knew I would miss them far more than they would ever know. I was then summoned into Bonzo's office for her official farewell. I sat mute before her, wanting to tell her not to let me go but I knew it would be useless.

Her last words to me were. "We are all going to miss you. I think we will have a much quieter life, but I know it won't be half so much fun."

Of course the tears flowed yet again. I wanted to say so much but I couldn't speak. The pain in my heart completely overwhelmed me. I was then shown into the famous inner sanctum to say goodbye to the Reverend Mother. It all seemed like a bad dream and soon I would awake to find that nothing had changed. But sadly, this was no dream, and everything had changed.

For the last couple of weeks in Bath, we moved back in with the Chalkers. I was also taken to say goodbye to my grandmother, and for the first time, I felt that a chasm had opened up between us. I remember looking at her, waiting for her familiar warm smile; but it seemed to me, even then, that she had written me off. There was almost a look of relief on her face. Was it me she was glad to see the back of? Or was it *the woman*? Either way, the hurt seared into me like a naked flame; even my adored grandmother had now cast me aside.

I had one final Saturday trip with Grandpa Lewis to his allotment. It was a bittersweet occasion. And I remember sitting idly on a bench aimlessly swinging my legs watching him work, wondering if this was to be the last time I saw *him*.

After he'd finished packing his weekly vegetables into his basket, he came and sat next to me. He told me that whatever happened I must stay strong. He smiled rather sadly at me. "You know you won't be a child forever and there will come a day when you will spread your wings and, like a bird, you will fly away."

I nodded gravely, knowing I would never have the courage to ever leave her. I was so frightened of this woman, and so controlled by her. Even a look could turn me to jelly and ready to throw up with fear. I couldn't imagine I would feel any braver when I was older. I smiled at him, but I know that he could see through my smile, for I remember him shaking his head as he squeezed my hand.

We walked very slowly back to the house, each knowing this would never happen again. Just before we reached the back gate, he stopped. "If ever you need me you must write."

I looked at him. "Grandpa, I don't have your postal address."

"I will give it to you before you leave."

Bless him, he never did give me the address, and I knew, anyway, that I would never have the courage to write.

For me, suddenly it was *déjà vu*. I looked up at Grandpa Lewis, and there I was, back at my grandmother's home, as a small child, crying with the old gardener on the day I was told about the Brisleys. Here was a man who had shielded me through some of my most treacherous times, bathing my wounds and creeping up to my bedroom with forbidden food. Why did these people who all said they loved me abandon me, and always in my hour of need? I wanted to run to him, cling to him, as I had my grandmother, plead with him to keep me safe, but the moment slipped away as we continued walking toward his home. I remember the feeling of utter desolation, a loneliness and isolation that seeped into my body as I looked up at his weathered face. No one could help me; I was beyond help. I was tied to her with invisible shackles so strong with the people around me mere shadows that would only confuse me, with a useless hope, never to be fulfilled. How is it that one remembers these milestones in one's life? I don't know; but for me every one of those milestones is still burned into my being, and I can remember almost word for word the conversations that were directed to me and about me at those significant times.

BLACKPOOL

The journey to Blackpool and my new home was even worse than the journey to London, all those years before. It took forever, and if my spirits could sink any lower they most certainly did as I watched the rolling hills of Somerset disappear.

Even though I say it myself, this new life and my survival through the next few years is a testament to my will power. Or maybe it was a testament to my dead parents who were still very much in my bedtime life. For no matter how awful the days were, I still had the nights, where I would transform myself into this most beloved child; and although I didn't sleep much, their devotion for me kept me going.

Now to the reader this may sound very strange, but if you think about it, most human beings need to have something in their lives that will get them through the rough passages. Well, I had my imaginary life, and it enveloped me with some sort of inner strength. When times were really bad, my dead parents were far more real to me than any other living person on earth, even *the woman*. When she was screaming at me I could completely zone out and not even hear her. The only time she could get through to me was when she hit me, which sadly, was even more frequent now because I was at home most of the time.

BLESMA

BLESMA Home was a beautiful old house turned into a nursing home for the ex-service limbless men. It was set in about three acres of very pretty gardens. The Brisleys had a flat in the house, with all the usual rooms, bathroom, sitting room and two bedrooms. Though one great thing about the flat was that it didn't have a kitchen; Chris Brisley was a terrible cook. The home had its own cook, and a huge kitchen. It was where I first learned to love cooking, and many a happy hour was spent with the resident cook, Mrs Briggs, who would let me help her make apple pies, cakes and wonderful desserts. Often, in the mornings, I would watch her fry thirty eggs at a time on a huge griddle.

Mrs Briggs was a sweet, funny little lady, no more than five feet tall, with bandy legs and a broad Lancashire accent. I remember that one day in early Spring two little baby geese arrived at the BLESMA home, and I was given the task of looking after them. They were adorable and soon would follow me around the gardens. Sadly I soon learned that they were not bought as pets but were to be fattened up for Christmas; memories of my two rabbits flashed through my mind. When the geese were almost fully grown, each morning they would wait for Mrs Briggs to walk down the drive, and, seemingly from nowhere, those birds would fly at her and chase her along the drive, right to the kitchen door. I'm afraid I used to watch for this regular occurrence to happen with some glee, for it was an extremely hilarious vision. It used to scare the hell out of her but she always made it to the kitchen door in one piece. I'm quite sure those birds knew she was going to cook them for Christmas dinner. After a few weeks, Mrs Briggs took over the role of Grandpa Lewis and when I was being punished for being *me,* she would creep up the backstairs to our flat and bring me food when the coast was clear.

It was still a well kept secret, and although I know that most of the adults in my life knew exactly what was happening to me, nobody ever came forward to any authority to let them know I was being so abused, or more than likely beaten repeatedly to a pulp. It just wasn't done.

About a week after we moved into the BLESMA home, I was taken to my new school, called Layton Hill Convent. It was situated just outside Blackpool. The building was impressive, and, to me, quite forbidding. The exterior certainly lacked the charm of my old and much loved school in Bath. To me it was a dark grey structure, and I feared that I would not be happy there.

As with my first visit to my school in Bath, I was shown into a small room, and given a written test. I remember it being easy, but I did wonder what would happen if I gave the wrong answers to the questions. Would they deny me a place? I answered the questions in record time, and apparently impressed my new headmistress. *The woman* was told that I could start as soon as I had acquired the uniform. The next few days were spent going to various shops to be equipped with my new green school uniform.

On the morning of my first school day I was told by *the woman* that I would be going to school by myself. I was to follow the same route we had taken a few weeks earlier. At first I thought she was joking, but soon realized that I was completely on my own, *literally*. To get to Layton Hill I had to catch two buses. Getting on the first bus was easy; it was almost outside the BLESMA home. Getting off at the correct stop and knowing which second bus to get was not quite so easy. Now, to this day I am *very* directionally challenged, so I had absolutely no idea how I was going to achieve this immense task. I was a very shy child, and the thought of having to ask strangers to help me find my school seemed insurmountable. I got on the first bus in my new school uniform, which felt so uncomfortable and was slightly too big for me. Thank God the bus conductor was a nice, friendly man. In a timid voice I explained the dilemma, giving him the name of my school. He told me not to worry; he would let me know when to get off and what bus to catch next. Somehow I managed to get to school, trying not to think of how I would make it home at the end of the day.

I was starting a new school in the middle of term, so, yet again, was presented to my class rather as one would exhibit a strange bug. I was the centre of attention, and once again stood before a sea of faces, feeling silly and very self-conscious. Luckily this time, there was a desk waiting for me, and I slipped on to the chair behind it, wishing that the floor would open and swallow me up.

However, settling into this school was fairly easy, though I missed all my friends at La Sainte Union and hated the fact I had to go home each evening. When you live at a convent, you become part of a large family. As a day pupil, one is considered an outsider, though, and more or less only becomes friendly with other day pupils. The borders were always very clannish, and how I envied them!

All schools have their own customs and daily routines. At Layton Hill, every day after morning prayers in the great hall, each pupil, starting with the sixth form, would file out and give a bob courtesy to the headmistress who was standing by the entrance. From the very start, I couldn't get this courtesy right. There would be this perfect line all doing their perfect courtesy rather like a chorus line in a theater, then along came me with my spastic bob, and from then on, the whole line would be broken and disconnected. I would agonize all through the service, praying that this time I would get it right. This new headmistress noticed me, and I rather liked that. She would give a rueful smile as it came to my turn and it was not too long before she was taking a personal interest in me and my school activities. I very soon learned how to bob courtesy correctly, but on certain mornings, when I was feeling a wee bit mischievous, I would fall into my old habit, and send the line behind me into disarray. She would look at me and wag her finger, for she knew; but there was always a smile on her face. At that age, I was so desperate for adult acceptance that I would do almost anything to be at the centre of attention. Luckily, then, being the centre of attention did not include drugs, boys, or killing your school friends or teachers. I needed validation, someone to let me know I was worthy. Someone to let me know I was *real*.

One day, when we were all gathered in the hall, waiting for a visit from yet another missionary Nun who was again to give a talk on her travels in some far-off place, teaching the Catholic religion to children living in abject poverty, and who were yet again probably not too interested in God saving their souls, I remembered my successful fainting tactic at La Sainte Union and thought I'd try it again, only this time I completely mistimed the fall, and hit my head on the chair in front of me almost knocking myself out and thus disrupting the talk which was terminated almost before it had begun, to the soft ripples of applause as I was carried out of the hall with a huge lump on my forehead and a raging headache to go with it. As it was a Friday, I was sent home early with a note explaining what had happened and hoping I would feel better by Monday. When I returned to school at the beginning of the next week the lump on my forehead was still very visible, but I was a shining star as the school filed into the hall for the morning prayers, and to listen to the headmistress's usual Monday morning talk. I don't know when it happened, but around this time, I had taken to sucking my small finger when I was nervous. It then became a habit. The headmistress walked along the rows of girls until she came to my row. She touched her forehead giving me a questioning look and I nodded back that it was much better, still with my finger in my mouth, she then mimicked me, putting her little finger into her mouth. I couldn't believe she'd singled me out. From that moment on I sought out her attention in any way I could. Yet again she was a creature from another world, at least to me. Unlike Bonzo she had an incredibly beautiful face and as I was always much taken by physical beauty, she became an angel in my eyes. Above all, she was always so kind to me, and I believe from that day on, she took a genuine interest in me. Whatever the reason, it was always a sad day if I didn't get a glimpse of her.

She was the headmistress for my first three terms at Layton Hill, and during that time, we became very close. She would often make a point of telling me how well I was doing and how pleased she was that I had settled in so quickly. I simply adored her, for at this stage in my life, she was the only person who ever took an interest in me. Whenever she came into a room I would feel a glow of self-worth and would will her to look at me, will her to acknowledge me in some way, and she never let me down. There were many times when I would arrive at school with either my arms or legs badly bruised, and would be questioned by the teachers and school friends but my excuse to any inquisitive person was yet again that I was learning to ride my bicycle, and was still not very good at it. *The woman* was now very careful to keep any punishment away from my face. but sometimes forgot about my other extremities. If I had ever been undressed at school my body would have told a far different story.

I was now twelve years old and starting the new Winter term at Layton Hill. I couldn't wait to see my headmistress, for I had missed her so much over the holidays. The school assembled as usual in the great hall. An unknown nun walked to the centre of the stage, and informed us that she was to be our new headmistress. She told us our last headmistress had been transferred to another school. I stood very still, completely dazed, and unable to take this news in. I couldn't believe I would never see her again, and I have to say that, for the rest of my time spent at Layton Hill, I never quite got over it. I was now, yet again, abandoned, at school as well as home. How frightening that one human being could make such a difference in a child's life. Sadly, I can't remember her name, but to me she was a very special person.

I don't know if it was a blessing or a curse, but I always found my school work very easy. I think the Convent in Bath was a little further ahead with their scholastic achievements than Layton Hill, so I was usually one step further on from the rest of my class, and after a couple of terms, I was moved to the next class where some of the pupils were at least two years older than me. I soon became a star pupil, and the darling of various teachers. I'm not too sure whether any the girls felt the same way though.

In my new class I made one fairly close friend, a girl called Sylvia. At the beginning, I think I felt rather sorry for her. She was a pretty child but was born with a lazy eye which, at times, made her look quite strange. One weekend *the woman* suddenly announced that I would be allowed to ask a school friend to tea. I told her that I didn't really know anyone very well yet, but she insisted. I don't know why she suddenly decided to play the mother, but then I never knew why she did anything. So, with some reluctance, I extended the invitation to Sylvia, hoping that she'd turn me down. She was delighted, and immediately accepted. I wasn't looking forward to this tea party; maybe my gut feelings started to kick in. Anyway, the whole event was a complete disaster. Sylvia arrived on a Saturday afternoon wearing a very short tight skirt and an extremely skimpy sweater over her well developed breasts and with more than a touch of make-up on her face, though only a little older than me. I had never seen her out of uniform and I must say it came as a shock even to me. She looked very grown up, and her outfit was certainly *not* appreciated by Chris Brisley. The tea was stilted and awkward. I couldn't wait for it to be over, and yet dreaded the time when Sylvia would leave and I had to face *her* wrath. It took only a couple of seconds from my saying goodbye to then being dragged into my bedroom, where she beat me unmercifully. I was accused of bringing a cheap and common girl home for tea. It was then that she first said "You can always stoop and pick up nothing, and that's what you'll be doing for the rest of your life." She must have liked the phrase, for it was to be used time and again over the years to come, along with the usual saying: *thank God your mother is dead, at least she can't see how you've turned out.*

As I was leaving for school on the following Monday, I was instructed to stay away from *the common piece of trash* and concentrate on my school work. Sylvia was waiting for me, unaware of the storm she'd created at home. Again, I was still only a child and had not yet learned the phrase a *still tongue makes a wise head,* also I was certainly not schooled in the art of letting someone down gently. She could see I was upset and kept asking why. I knew I had to stop seeing her, so I thought it best to get it over with and tell her I could not talk to her any more. I then made the terrible mistake of telling her what *the woman* had said. *Boy,* did that set the wheels in motion. Early that evening there was an irate mother, with Sylvia in tow, shouting at the BLESMA home entrance, demanding to see Chris Brisley. *Of course* I took the blame. How could anyone think Chris Brisley would say anything so hurtful and untrue about such a sweet child. I was made to apologize to Sylvia and they were told I would be severely punished for having such a wicked tongue. Mother and daughter left somewhat mollified. Needless to say I *was* severely punished, and Sylvia never spoke to me again.

I hated Blackpool with a passion. To me, it was an ugly place. No rolling Somerset hills, no historic Roman City. It was a holiday resort where vacationers came to see the Blackpool lights and eat fish and chips along a concrete promenade which was bleak and usually extremely cold and windy. I know it was horrid of me, but I also hated the Lancashire accent, which was hard and grating to the ear. I felt as though I had been beamed up on to another planet with no way of getting back to earth.

DONALD LORD

The first time I saw Donald Lord was in Ken's office at the BLESMA home. Donald was one of the amputees sent to BLESMA for rehabilitation and vacation. I never knew his exact age, but at a guess, I would say he was in his early twenties. As most of the men, either living at the Blesma home permanently, or for short periods, were well into their later years, Donald was a refreshing change. He was a serviceman, had obviously been wounded on some mission, and had lost an arm. So here he was, looking like something out of a glamour magazine, and I was just a child; but it was the very first time I noticed how very attractive a man could be, and I definitely had a crush on him.

At first, whenever I saw him, I would smile and say hello, hoping I didn't sound like a tongue tied idiot. Then, one morning, as I passed him on the main stairs he asked me if I wanted to have my photograph taken. Apparently he was either a professional photographer or an avid amateur. I nodded, almost sick with excitement. We agreed to meet in the afternoon at the summerhouse, which was situated behind a small copse in the back gardens of the house. To this day I still have the photograph, and whenever I look at it, I always think of my very first puppy love.

After that day, and as it was my summer holidays, we spent many a happy hour walking in the gardens talking and laughing about nothing in particular. I knew absolutely zero about Donald on the first day I met him, and precious little more on the last. I didn't even know how he lost his arm. I never asked him and he never told me, it wasn't important. The fact was that whenever we were together, we enjoyed each other's company; he made me feel so happy at a very vulnerable time in my life.

The BLESMA gardens were large and beautifully kept. Sadly, when I visited the home some years later, the gardens were almost gone. The house itself had been enlarged and another building now stood where the copse used to be. I guess they call it progress.

Personally, I loved the wooded area, because I could disappear and climb favorite trees without ever being seen. Often, Donald and I would make for those trees and sit on the grass to eat the packed lunch Mrs Briggs had made for us. It was perhaps rather silly but we always felt as though we were having a picnic out in the country, far away from any other living person. The fact that we were in a garden in a fairly populated part of Blackpool didn't cross our minds. It was exciting spending time with a grown man, someone who found me good company and fun to be with. At the time I didn't think of him as a man, he was a wonderful person to be with. He didn't treat me as some insignificant child. I was Wendy and he listened to what I said and, above all, I made him laugh. It hadn't been long since he lost his arm so the *high life* of Blackpool wasn't for him. I could see that he was still very fragile emotionally as well as physically. And me being the only person around who was anywhere near his age didn't cross my mind. I got up each morning and raced through any chores I was required to do, then off into the garden where I knew Donald would be waiting. I once asked him why he never went into town. He smiled rather sadly and said it wasn't time to face the world yet. The inevitable day came when I was summoned into the Brisleys' office and told in no uncertain words that I was not to see or speak to Donald Lord *ever* again. I was simply shattered and couldn't think what I'd done that was so wrong. As commanded, I had stayed on the property, done all the things I was asked to do and yet I was not even allowed to have a friend of my own. I was so incensed I asked *why?* The answer was, he was a grown man and I was still a child. They couldn't understand why he would want to spend all his waking hours keeping company with me. They thought it was very unnatural.

Looking back now, I guess I can understand, but at the time it was yet another devastating blow. I still had another month of my school holidays, and I knew Donald had three more weeks stay at BLESMA. What harm would there have been for us in spending those last weeks together? I remember running out to the copse, hoping that he would be there. As I made my way to the summer house, I saw him sitting on the grass. He looked so sad and I wanted to cry. He patted the grass next to him and for a long while we sat there not saying a word, each wrapped up in our own thoughts.

At last Donald spoke. "They told me I'm not allowed to see you anymore." I nodded my head miserably. "They think because I'm a few years older than you I might either molest you or make you think you have feelings for me."

"Well, they're right. You are my very best friend," I cried. He looked startled but said nothing. "They have to spoil everything that's good in my life. Why can't they just leave me alone?"

"The trouble is," Donald said. "I *do* have feelings for you, but not what they are thinking. To me you're untouched by this crazy world we live in and it was such a wonderful interlude to get away from the harsh reality of my future life."

"Does this mean we won't ever talk or see each other again?" I asked, for to me I was losing a playmate.

I remember his smile as he said. "We will always have had this time together and I won't forget you. And you still have the photograph. Whenever you feel sad, look at it and remember that there is someone in the world who thinks you're smashing." He got up and walked back to the house.

We never spoke again, just the odd stilted hello if we happened to see each other. I couldn't wait for him to leave. It was so painful knowing he was at the home, so near and yet so far.

KEN AND BEDTIME

I was now twelve and like most girls of that age, *especially convent girls*, knew absolutely nothing about sex. Ken and Chris Brisley were going through another very rocky patch in their pathetic marriage, and it was obviously having an extremely bad effect on both of them. They could hardly keep a civil tongue in their heads whenever they had the misfortune to cross paths.

On this particular evening, I went to bed at the usual given time. The Brisleys were out at a BLESMA charity meeting. The organization was not subsidized by the government, so there were many events held throughout each year in order to keep the home going. For some reason, Ken came back early while she stayed on. I could only imagine that, as per usual, they'd had an argument, and had gone their separate ways.

I was in my safe room with the door firmly closed, where, for a few precious hours, no one could get at me. Suddenly the door opened and Ken walked in. First I kept my eyes tightly closed hoping he would think I was asleep and go away. Hoping he would not wake me, not want to intrude on my private world. Until much later in life, I never quite knew what to say to him, and even as a child, I know that he felt the same way. We were complete strangers, even though we'd been part of each others' lives for so long. *So*, what could be that important, making him want to have any conversation with me *now*? He didn't go away; instead he came over and sat on the edge of my bed. I could smell the drink on him, as he leaned over and started stroking my hair. It was so unlike Ken to have any contact with me, physically or otherwise. I lay in the bed, my body now as stiff as a board, still hoping he would think I was asleep. He kept softly calling my name and asking me if I was awake. Eventually I opened my eyes and stared up at him. It was the first and last time I have ever seen him the worse for drink. Such an ugly man, and sadly, someone who didn't and never would fit into my existence imaginary or otherwise. I almost felt sorry for him. I dumbly nodded my head wishing he wasn't quite so close to me.

Then the unthinkable happened. He slipped his hand under the sheet, and started to undo my pyjama top. I simply froze. At twelve, I was still as flat as a pancake, not even the slightest suggestion of breasts, very much a child. I remember staring up at him in terror. He was touching me, feeling my nipples, then running his hands over my tummy and back up again. I was living through some dreadful nightmare, but I was awake and he wasn't stopping; it simply went on for what seemed like an eternity. His voice, though still soft, had now become raspy and his breathing had quickened alarmingly. He leaned in closer and said. "I think it's time you learned about the world and what it means to be a woman. If a man does this to you, you must stop him unless you want him to go on. Do you want me to go on?" As he asked this question his hand started to travel down to my pyjama pants. He pulled at the cord and I knew that if he went any further and touched me *there* I would die. He stopped and his hand travelled back up to my chest. I felt sick, I mean *really* sick, and had the terrible feeling that I was going to throw up all over him. He turned his head toward my face, and put his lips over mine. Again, this had never happened to me before. Not only was I never kissed, I was *never* kissed on my lips. His lips were wet and over large. They seemed to cover the best part of my face, I literally gagged as once again his hand traveled to my pyjama pants, and he started to pull them down. By now I was completely terrified and was suddenly galvanized into action, almost catapulting my body out of the bed. I laid crouching on the floor, shivering and shaking like someone having a fit. I was so frightened and so repulsed by what had happened. I couldn't look or talk to him. I just wanted him to go away. I just wanted him to go far away, and never have to look at him again.

Thank God my actions brought him to his senses. Suddenly, he was stone cold sober, and he stood in the corner of the room with his hands covering his face. How close he had come to doing something so dreadful. I was still too young to know how devastating his actions could have been that night. But what he did do stayed with me for a very long time and from then on I couldn't bear to be alone with him.

It was an incident that coloured my adult life for many years, and probably a good reason why I could never get too close to anyone, and did not want any physical contact with men. They could look at me, say nice things to me, then go home. It was enough to know that they thought I was attractive, and it was enough to know they wanted me, but more than once, Ken's face would loom over me, as it had done on that night, and any feeling of passion would fade into the night like a dark cloud covering the brightest moon.

POCKET MONEY

It was a very long time before Ken would stay in a room alone with me, and I was thankful for that. We tried never to make eye contact with each other, but later, when I was thirteen, he decided I was old enough to have pocket money. He gave me a new post office savings book, and said I should start to save some of the money; that way I would learn to be sensible where finances were concerned. I was to be given five shillings, two shiny half-crown pieces, each week and could choose how much to save. At the end of six months, Ken said he would double whatever I had put into the post office. I was excited, and felt very grown up. For the next two weeks, I paid two shillings into the post office and spent the rest on sweets. On the third Saturday morning, Ken gave me my pocket money as usual, and then left for a BLESMA meeting. *The woman* walked into my bedroom, smiling at me as she sat on the edge of the bed. "So, I hear you are getting money from Ken each week."

I nodded dumbly. She held out her hand and like a robot I put the two pieces of silver into her palm. She then left the room without another word. From then on, each Saturday, after Ken had given me my weekly pocket money she would hold out her hand and I would give her my precious coins.

On a Saturday morning at the end of the six months Ken asked to see my post office book. I had dreaded this moment and handed it over knowing he would be so displeased with me. I waited for his chilling response to the measly four shillings in the saving book. To my astonishment he didn't say a word. He handed me my pocket money and left. Within five minutes, Chris Brisley slithered into the room, hand outstretched. As usual, I gave her the money, and *she* left. What I didn't know was that Ken had come back into the hall and watched the whole procedure. I've never seen him quite so angry. Apparently, he felt sure he knew exactly where my pocket money was going. He twisted her arm sharply making her drop the money, then he slapped her hard across her face. It was a strange scene. So many times in the past he'd walked away while she hit and screamed at me without lifting a finger to help. This obviously was the last straw. I shut my door and crawled under the bed, *literally under the bed!* The episode was definitely a contributing factor toward the inevitable breakdown of their marriage.

From then on it was open war between the two of them with me bang in the middle. She blamed me for everything, saying that if it hadn't been for me, their marriage would not have broken down. For some time I thought and hoped yet again that I might be sent back to my grandmother, for I was ever the optimist where that was concerned, but no such luck. I was simply used as a punching bag; even Ken lashed out at me if I got in his way. The talk of divorce was about the only conversation they had, but neither one would actually set the wheels in motion. In the end, it got so bad that *the woman* decided she could no longer sleep in the same bedroom as Ken. I came home from school one afternoon to find that she had moved into *my* bedroom. I was absolutely horrified. My room was a safe haven for me. I could shut the door and pretend, at least for a few precious hours, that *they* were no longer in my life. The realization of her sleeping next to me night after night made me almost freak out. Apart from the frequent beatings throughout the years, there had never ever been any physical contact between the three of us. I could never bear for either one to touch me. Now I was to share a bed with her each night. In recent years she had an increasing weight problem, and was now quite a large woman. There was no way we could share my small bed and not come into contact with each other. I shuddered at the thought of her flesh touching mine, *and what about my family? How could I go to them at night with her in my bed?*

The first night I lay awake waiting for her to come to bed. I pretended to be asleep but watched her undress through half closed eyes. To me she was gross, a mass of flesh that had grown into unflattering proportions. I positioned my body as far away from her as possible, gripping on to the side of the bed to stop myself falling off. I stayed in the same position until she was asleep, then I slipped out of bed and laid on the floor using my dressing gown as a cover. I tried so very hard to bring my own family to life and drown myself in my imaginary world, as I did every other night, but it was no good; my world had been violated, so I laid shivering on the floor until morning, then I slipped back into bed before she woke up. This went on for a what seemed like an eternity. Each night I would wait for her to come to bed and fall asleep, then I would lie on the floor until morning. By the end of the fourth week, I was suffering from sleep deprivation. It became so bad that I couldn't concentrate on anything. My school work was non-existent and because I was usually a good student my teachers began to notice my almost trance-like state and eventually phoned the Brisleys to say they thought I might be sick.

Luckily, Ken came to the rescue; even if she couldn't, or didn't care, Ken could see I was walking around like a Zombie. He told the BLESMA staff to put a single bed in their room as he was having trouble with phantom pains in his limb, and felt it unfair to keep his wife awake at night. I'm quite sure they all knew what was going on but were too discreet to say anything. The bed was duly set up in the master bedroom, and I had my precious room to myself once again. I still suffered from insomnia, but at least I could have my night hours in my own world and alone in my own bed.

The rows got so bad they were told by the board of trustees that if their private lives continued to invade their work they would be asked to leave the BLESMA home. It took almost one more year before the staff and board realized that the running of the home was suffering due to their continuing preoccupation with personal problems. They were eventually given three months' notice from the BLESMA home. But luckily for Ken, he got his job back once they were divorced. No one wanted to know about her.

The divorce papers were finally drawn up and then the battle started as to who would have me. Amazingly, Ken said he thought

I'd be better off with him, and I silently agreed, but she dug her toes in.

I was nearly fifteen when one morning I was yet again summoned to the sitting room where I sat before her and told I was to be a witness for her at the divorce hearing. I was to tell the judge Ken was physically and mentally cruel to both of us and that I wanted to live with her. I was completely dumbfounded. Although Ken had never been a loving person, I wanted to stand up and tell the world he had never been as cruel to me as she had been, and still was. I wanted them to know how frightened and lonely I was, but who would listen? It's crazy to think that, today, some girls are getting married and having babies well before they are eighteen; but when I was in my early and middle teens, we were still considered children and were legally not adults until the age of twenty-one. Becoming twenty-one was a lifetime away and I couldn't see my life changing even then; the yoke was tied too tightly around my neck for a mere date on the calendar to change anything.

The day arrived, and I was dressed in my convent school uniform as Chris Brisley thought that would impress the judge. On the way to the court, she kept repeating over and over again what I was to say and what a terrible life we both had with Ken. I had lain awake for nights on end wondering what I *would* say in court. I decided to tell the judge that I thought I would be better off going back to live with my grandmother. I felt sure under the circumstances he would readily agree. How wrong I was.

We filed into the courtroom and I listened to the judge prattling on about the sanctity of marriage, and how divorce was not to be taken lightly. He then spent the next few minutes going over papers concerning the breakdown of their marriage and asking them if there was any way a reconciliation could be reached. Both parties shook their heads. He then looked at me and said he knew I had been asked to choose which adopted parent I wanted to live with. Then after a pause he said "As you are an adopted child, the court has no option but to give you to the adopted mother. The adopted father is not related to you in any way, and as you are still under age he can have no legal right to a minor female living under his roof." He looked across at me and smiled. I was completely devastated and now knew I had to tread very carefully. I could not ask to be sent back to my grandmother for I now legally belonged to *the woman* and no one else. I was just an object to be given to another person by the say of the court.

Who knows, if I *had* stood up in court and told the judge I was regularly beaten to a pulp by Chris Brisley, he might have listened, but, on the other hand, he might not have. He might have thought I was lying, and now I *knew* that I was going home with her, I stood no chance of any outside help. When it was my turn to speak, I stood up in court and, like a parrot, repeated her words. She was granted the divorce and Ken had to pay the court costs. Before Ken walked out of my life, he put his arms around me and said he totally understood my dilemma. He also wished me luck, he probably knew I would need it. Suddenly he looked ten years younger as he left the court. It was a black day for me, for now I was completely alone, and at her mercy.

***

Chris Brisley was overjoyed with her newfound freedom. For me, the only good thing to come out of the chaos was that she decided that we should go back to live in Bath. She phoned her parents, and asked them whether she could stay with them until she found somewhere to live. I thought I would be going back with her, and was so looking forward to seeing Grandpa Lewis once again. But as I was in the middle of a term at Layton Hill, it was decided that I should stay on there as a boarder and finish the term. It was a small respite, and one I enjoyed to the full, not wanting to think of the future and *her*. During that time, I worked extra hard, determined to pass my end of term exams and have a good start at yet another school, when I eventually returned to Bath.

Chris Brisley had found a small furnished flat on the outskirts of Bath. It was a hideous flat with roaches that would come out at night and run along the hall to the various rooms, which scared the hell out of me. *The woman* went back to work at a private nursing home as a night sister; yet again, obviously, no real credentials were ever asked for, and so, for a few precious nights a week, I was left alone in the roach-infested flat to fend for myself.

For nearly nine months I did not go to school. I had simply been lost in the system; but while it lasted, I was quite content to be on my own. Although I was not too far away from my grandmother's home, I simply had no way of either getting to her or contacting her. I didn't know until much later that she already knew I was back in Bath. Apparently, Ken got in touch with her, maybe hoping she would come to my rescue. Eventually, I think again through Ken, a letter arrived at the flat requesting that Chris Brisley attend a meeting with the school council, or whatever it was called then. I wondered if I would be sent back to the Convent, but no such luck. Still, a place was found for me at a college just outside of Bath, and as I had a very good report from Layton Hill, I was welcomed with open arms. Yet again, I had to face new pupils who were well established in their school life. I always seemed to be the outsider trying to fit in with everyone else. After a couple of weeks, I settled in, but as this college was a day school I had no respite from *the woman*. I was alone with *her*, tumbling through life trying to make the best of it and not think too much of the future.

My new school was an all girls' college with no uniforms required, a mixed blessing as we had no money to buy any required attire; on my first day I must have looked rather like a refugee with mixed match clothes consisting of some of my old convent uniform, plus a coat having seen better days, and shoes that were now becoming too small. I settled in fairly well, and even though I had lost nearly a year of schooling, I was again way ahead of my new class. I was now coming up to sixteen, and although I had not missed the routine of school during those fallow months, I was starting to realize that my only chance in this world was to do well; so, against all odds, I spent as much time as she would allow finishing all my homework each evening and excelling at my school work. I don't remember making any specific friends at this time, and don't remember much about the college either. By now I had *truly* become a loner, content to do my school work, keep the flat as clean as possible, and most of all, keep out of her way when she wasn't working.

There was one horrific Saturday while I was doing the usual housework when I dropped a glass ornament and it smashed to pieces on the floor. For a few seconds, I stood staring down at the remains, then all hell broke loose. Before I had time to even realize she was in the room, and I was suddenly hit from behind falling face down on to the jagged glass. I didn't have time to cover my face and felt shards of glass cut into my chin and forehead as she dragged me to my feet and started punching me as if she were some prize boxer. I put my left hand up to ward off the blows and felt a sharp crack in my wrist. I remember screaming out in pain trying to ward off more attacks while holding my arm. Eventually she ran out of steam, and left the room, while I stood looking at spots of blood from my face splash on to the broken pieces of glass on the floor. I will never know how I managed to clear up the mess, but, like the well-trained robot, clear it up I did; then I cleaned the cuts on my chin and across my forehead, before curling up on my bed in a foetal position in excruciating pain. I wasn't called for lunch or dinner, but food was the last thing on my mind. I lay on the bed all night, not daring to move, not wanting the pain to get any worse.

I think *the woman* usually had a sixth sense as to when she had gone too far, because early on the Sunday morning, she came into the bedroom and carefully looked me over to see what sort of damage had been inflicted upon me. My wrist had turned blue, with mottled red marks around the joint. The cuts on my face had crusted with blood through the night. It was decided that I should be taken to the hospital, and I was told to change my clothes and tidy myself up. This was no mean feat, as any movement of my wrist sent spasms of white hot pain through my body. We eventually got a taxi to St Martin's hospital outpatient ward. The journey was taken up with me trying not to be sick and her telling me exactly what I would say when we arrived. It was the very first time *ever* that there had been an in-depth discussion by the doctor about my injuries and questions as to how I had acquired them. I was somewhat excited about this, thinking that maybe, at last, this would be the time when someone would do something about me. I don't truly remember what she told them, and I could see the doctor wasn't too placated by her answers, but eventually the questions ceased, for he was either happy with her account, or was too busy to take it any further. Either way, I was now in so much pain that I didn't care what was said; I just wanted to go to sleep and wake up somewhere, far away from her. My wrist was X-rayed and plastered. I had a couple of stitches above my eyebrow, and then was duly released from the hospital, with the medical staff obviously accepting the woman's account of my accident, *which was the age old story concerning a bicycle and my falling off onto a broken bottle, even though I didn't possess a bicycle at the time.* On the way back to the flat, she happily told me it was so good it was the left wrist as it wouldn't stop me from going to school on the Monday. Her comments didn't even surprise me; so what else was new? Everyone at the college accepted my explanation without comment, and life went on.

One morning *the woman* received a letter from my grandmother. She was furious, turning on me, absolutely convinced that somehow I had contacted her, which was quite untrue, for by this time, I had completely given up on any love or help coming from any of my family. The years of utter devotion were at last being replaced with the sad realization that my family didn't really care about me, and were happy to continue their lives without *the Albatross* hovering over them. Still, the letter sent a surge of adrenalin through me, for it seemed my grandmother wanted to see me. I was older now, and I so wanted to visit her and tell her that since she had given me to this woman my life had been hell. I wanted her to know that the things done to me had sealed my past and future forever. I wanted to tell her she had been so wrong to hand me over to the Brisleys; but I knew I wouldn't. Even then, I knew it was too late for there to be any change in my life now. Too much had happened to me for me to start living a normal life, I was now old enough to realize that there was no one out there to help or save me; I was truly on my own.

Even if I had found the courage to tell her about my terrible existence, it wouldn't have happened. Chris Brisley certainly wasn't going to let me visit my grandmother alone. After the usual preparation as to how I was to conduct myself, we duly arrived on a Sunday afternoon, to have tea. I was amazed that my grandmother didn't even raise an eyebrow at me still in a plaster cast and stitches on my face but it seemed she accepted I was truly a klutz when it came to bicycles. I was now so different from the child who would so enjoy the secret visits with her when a boarder at the convent. I remember sitting like a stone, hardly looking at her, saying nothing, while Chris Brisley prattled on about how hard life was now she was on her own. It was one of the very few times when I felt no love for my grandmother. Gone was the childlike optimism that eventually she would heal all ailments. The thin thread of hope and belief that, in the end, I would be saved, had been well and truly severed. It was with a very heavy heart that I left her home on that day, wondering whether I would ever see her again, and for the very first time, not really caring if I did.

Around this time, Chris Brisley was offered a house to rent just off Camden Crescent. It was the second house in a row which was called *Perfect View*. Though the house was small, the view was certainly perfect. It was at this time Ken agreed to halve the contents of their marital home, and on a cold Winter's day we moved into the house, and waited for the container to arrive at Perfect View. When it arrived, she went out to lunch, while I tried to organize where the furniture should go. The house hadn't been lived in for a few months, and was in desperate need of a good clean. So I set to work cleaning kitchen cupboards, unpacking boxes and sorting out clothes etc, while she made sure she was out long enough for everything to be done by the time she arrived home. I remember that nothing was said; it was as if we had lived there for ever. She looked around, then reprimanded me because I hadn't prepared any dinner for her.

***

One Friday, after I left school, I knew Chris Brisley would be spending the evening singing in her church choir. How ridiculous was that? Having saved some money from my many joints to buy the weekend groceries, on an impulse I decided to take the bus to my grandmother's, and see whether there was any reaction to my visit. As always, she was impeccably dressed in her afternoon attire, and sitting in her favorite chair. It was very strange, but it was as if the years had fallen away, and we were grandmother and child again. She was still a lovely woman, but now looked a little frail. We had tea and crumpets and then we talked.

I had waited a very long time to hear her say it, but it was on that day that she told me of the dreadful mistake she felt she'd made all those years ago, when she sent me away to live with the Brisleys. She said that she wished so very much she'd kept me with her, then she leaned across and asked me if I had been happy with them and if I was all right with the way things had turned out. As I sat there munching hot buttered crumpets I realized I was looking at a very lonely woman who had so much of family life taken away from her. How could I now tell her that, yes, indeed it had been the *biggest* mistake she'd ever made. I knew I couldn't destroy this woman. Also, what could she do now? It was too late; the cast was set. I felt absolutely certain – *at least I fervently hoped* – that she didn't know what sort of woman Chris Brisley really was. I wondered what would happen if I told her what my life was like, if I told her what my non-existent childhood had been like? No, I couldn't do it. We had all paid the price for her fateful decision. I then asked her how she knew I was living back in Bath.

She nodded, "Chris came to see me when she first returned. I was sad to hear about the divorce. I always thought them such a happy couple."

I almost choked on my last mouthful of crumpet. "They hated each other," I replied, looking straight into my grandmother's eyes. I saw her wince, but it was the only reaction I ever saw from her in all those long years. *Did* she know how unhappy and how very damaged I was? Or was she truly oblivious? Looking at her I realized that she lived in a completely different world. I was growing up in a new world, and she was staying in hers. We would never talk about it. We would keep up the facade. I would come and see her and have hot buttered crumpets and tea, and she would never know, at least not from my lips. Still, I had to know why she'd not contacted me. Her answer was that she knew, eventually, I would come to see her. Not the sort of answer I wanted; but I guess it was better than nothing.

Six months later, Chris Brisleys' mother died and I went with her to the funeral. It was such a very sad occasion, especially seeing Grandpa Lewis looking so frail and desolate. It was the first time I had seen him since leaving for Blackpool, and I was told on my return to Bath, in no uncertain terms, that I was never in any way to contact her family. I think there must have been a rift, for whenever I mentioned them her lips would become two thin hard lines, and she would hurl abuse that made no sense to me. As we entered the church, I was introduced to *the woman's* brother by Grandpa Lewis. He was a very tall man with a strong face like his sister, but there the similarity ended. His eyes were warm and welcoming as he solemnly shook my hand. A vast difference, though, as he turned to his sister, barely acknowledging her, sitting as far away as possible throughout the service. After the service, we all trooped back to Grandpa's home for the wake, and, as unbelievable as it may sound, Chris Brisley started to go around the house telling her father what furniture she wanted and how soon it should be delivered. Her brother almost physically set upon her, telling her to leave. It was the first time I have ever seen Grandpa Lewis cry. I literally ran to him and held on to him, for he had made some of the most unbearable moments in my life more tolerable for being Grandpa Lewis. This day I felt he needed my support and the knowledge that I loved him dearly. For me, the saddest thing was I never saw Grandpa Lewis again. A compassionate man with a gentle soul. I know that I was all the better for having had him in my life.

SIXTEEN

My sixteenth birthday came and went. I was still stick thin, and still excruciatingly shy. I always felt exceedingly plain, and while the other girls at college were beginning to notice the boys and be noticed by them, I was glad and very relieved they never took an ounce of notice of me. I was known as the bookworm, for I was never seen without at least a couple of books under my arm; they indeed, were my escape. The only ray of sunshine was that I did shine academically, and was told on many occasions there was nothing I couldn't do if I put my mind to it. I would come home and, at night, after I'd gone through the ritual with my dead parents, would wonder what the future held in store for me. I knew I could legally never be free of her until I was twenty-one and often thought I'd be extremely lucky to reach that age alive. Those five years stretched ahead like a prison sentence, for there was no one I could turn to. *The woman* was far too clever to ever let her guard down when in company with or without me. I know for sure most of her friends thought her a saint. If ever I met any of them, they would barely acknowledge me. In their eyes, I was an ungrateful child who had usurped the privilege of being with a loving woman who had taken me from the gutter. She loved saying that, and God knows where they thought I'd come from! She was truly Jekyll and Hyde. To go and try to tell any one of her friends of the violence and verbal abuse which I received on almost a daily basis would be like telling people that the Pope was a really bad person.

The weekends with the woman were now becoming a feat in survival. On looking back, I'm quite sure that she began to worry whether she might lose her grip on me. Here was a woman who hated being alone, and when she was not working, she would hardly let me out of her sight; but it would be a continual battle as she gnawed away at any self-worth I might have acquired while at college. She would love to make fun of me, always telling me how extremely ugly I was and that, for certain, I would remain an old maid; for what man in his right mind would even give me a second glance? This wasn't news to me. I had been told from the age of four that I was one of life's misfits, and by now, truly believed it.

On looking back, it's quite unbelievable that my physical and, yes, my mental state was never questioned, for I *always* had bruises on my body somewhere. There were only very few times when a classmate would either ask if I was accident-prone, or did I have some sort of sickness where I would bruise easily. I always opted for being accident-prone, and there the enquiries would cease, and life would go on.

THE CIRCUS CAME TO TOWN

Every year, the circus would come to Bath for a week. It was always a big event, and packed to the rafters for the whole time. As Chris Brisley was still doing night work at the local nursing home, on their second night I decided to go. It was the first time I'd seen animals perform, and I simply hated that. Such majestic creatures being made to act for the pleasure of us humans! But most of all, I hated the clowns. I remember watching the children laughing at them and couldn't understand why. I found them really scary and would close my eyes whenever they appeared. To this day I can't watch clowns perform; I don't even like to see them in pictures. Still, I have to say that the magic of the glitz and glamour absolutely enthralled me. All the people involved seemed so exotic, leading such exciting lives; to my mind, they all had to be extremely happy. As I sat there, watching the acts, I tried to imagine what it would be like never having to stay in one place, always travelling, beholden to no one. As the evening wore on, I thought what a wonderful way it would be to leave, with the certain knowledge *she* would *never* find me. After the show, trying not to think of the clowns, and as people were making their way home, I walked to the far end of the field where the caravans and trailers were parked. I wandered around for quite some time with no one taking much notice of me until eventually a rather handsome young boy asked me what I was doing there. I simply said "I'm looking for a job, and are there any available?" I think this tickled him until he realized I was quite serious. When the question of my age came up I said, with tongue in cheek, "I'm twenty-one." His look was incredulous, and one would have thought I'd told him the funniest joke.

"Get out of here, if you're twenty-one I'll eat my hat!" came his reply.

Quite suddenly the burning desire to leave town with the circus evaporated like a puff of smoke, and we both ended up sitting on the grass eating crisps and drinking lemonade. For the next five nights I went to the circus, and would end the day eating either fish and chips or cold curry with my new friend. During that time I met his family, and soon realized that a travelling circus was extremely hard work, with a nomadic lifestyle not nearly so romantic in the cold light of day. When I look back on those few days it always brings a smile to my face. What on earth was I thinking about? But as the saying goes, *it seemed like a good idea at the time.*

***

Christmas came around, and of all things, my grandmother invited us to her home for Christmas lunch. I was mildly excited, as this would be the first time any festivities would have been celebrated by me for a number of years. At first *the woman* said we would go, and I tried to imagine what it would be like to actually sit down at the dining table and eat a meal with my grandmother. It's strange, but I can't ever remember doing that and, sadly, I never did, for at the last minute, Chris Brisley sent a note saying she had to work on that day, and would be taking me to the nursing home to celebrate there. Of course, she didn't have to work and we stayed at home, with her in bed all day, and me doing the usual chores around the house. Just another day at Perfect View.

On my seventeenth birthday, my grandmother sent me two tickets for the pantomime at the Theatre Royal in Bath, and, as usual, the day started badly with Chris Brisley waking in a foul mood, telling me that I would not be allowed to go to the theatre that night as pantomimes were for children and not for the likes of me. Shades of another, still very much remembered birthday! I was becoming so immune to any and all adversities, having learned long ago never to expect the expected, until it actually happened. My day was spent waiting on her, when called to do so, and keeping out of her way for the rest of the time.

My last year at college would be busy, and hard work, as I had decided that I wanted to go to university. Of course, this was never mentioned, and at the time, I wasn't sure how I was going to achieve it. I decided that I wanted to get a degree in English History. It was a subject I excelled in, and I would read anything and everything I could get my hands on. I never really thought how this would help me in my adult world, but I did rather imagine I would end up teaching at some university somewhere in the future.

It was a difficult time, for I was now neither child or adult. I would lie in my bed at night, agonizing for hours about the future. It still amazes me that all through my childhood and teens, I could function on very few hours of sleep each night. There was always so much I had to do before I could even think of sleeping. I had to put the happenings of the day in order, and try to make sense of any adversities that might have happened. I still held on to my parents, but I knew the time would come when I would have to let them go. I knew I couldn't go through the rest of my life relying on two dead people who only came to me each night in my imagination. Though I still maintain to this day that if I hadn't had them, I would never have made it through my childhood.

Every day, Chris Brisley ranted on about my staying at college. She wanted me to get a job and, above all, start to pay her back for all the years she had sacrificed. I spent most of my nights wondering whether I would get into University, and if indeed it was possible, how on earth would I ever have the nerve to tell her. The verbal abuse was now an everyday occurrence. It seemed the older I got, the more venomous she got. She would pick away at me. My body, my face, my hair and most of all how incredibly *ugly* I was. Having been indoctrinated about my appearance from the time when I was a small child, I saw what she saw, and there were still many occasions where I could hardly put one foot in front of the other and would shrink away from the outside world. I wanted to be on my own *in my world*, where I was beautiful, accomplished and, above all, without her.

I passed my exams with flying colours, and was accepted into the University of Exeter. I was simply euphoric. I went to see my grandmother, and, with great excitement, showed her the letter I'd received. Her first words were, "What does Chris think of this?"

I looked long and hard at her, realizing that she did know something about my life. "I haven't told her yet, and I'm going to need your help there."

"I think before you tell her, we should have a meeting. That way you can tell us both at the same time."

The date was set, and like three puppets we all went through the motions of enjoying an overdue afternoon tea together. My adrenalin started pumping, and I was paralyzed with fear. I think this was the time when I started to say to myself just do it and to hell with the consequences. We were way through the tea, with my grandmother giving me looks before I plucked up the courage to tell Chris Brisley I had been accepted into Exeter University. Luckily the woman had no idea how one acquired a place at any university. She stared at me then said. "How nice! It's a pity you won't be able to go, but truly unbelievable that you were asked." My grandmother took over with seemingly great excitement, saying that it would be a travesty if I didn't go. During the rest of the afternoon, I sat back, letting them get on with it. In the end Chris Brisley didn't have a leg to stand on as my grandmother kept extolling how clever I was, and how she must be so proud of me.

We left my grandmother's, arriving home without either saying a word. I thought I was in for a massive beating, but, incredibly, nothing happened. She said she was very tired and we would talk in the morning. I didn't even go to bed that night. I sat in the kitchen drinking copious cups of tea wondering what the new day would bring.

We had breakfast in silence, while I watched for any sign that I might be in imminent danger. And then it started. She caught hold of my hand and laced her fingers with mine, then proceeded to squeeze and push them back as hard as she could. I wanted to scream out with the pain, but I sat there looking at her, trying to fill as much venom in my eyes as she had in hers. Surely she must know how much I hated her. I thought she would break my fingers, but still I showed no emotion at all. Eventually she let go, saying, quietly, "You think you've won but you'll have to go a long way before you get one over me." But I had won, and because my grandmother was now involved, all the necessary arrangements were made for me to go to university.

EXETER UNIVERSITY

Exeter seemed a long way from Bath, and to me, there was no way *the woman* could govern my time there. Again, how wrong was I? As soon as I had a start date, she set about finding a room to rent in Exeter, ensuring that I would be a day student and not live on Campus. As much as this woman hated me, it seemed she was determined to stick to me like glue. She had managed to buy a secondhand car, and would turn up unexpectedly, to make sure I was not out enjoying myself. She was also very against my furthering my education. She kept reminding me that the degree I was studying would not bring in a living wage for quite some time, if ever. She thought I should be put to work, so that I would be the one bringing money into the home. University had not been on her agenda, so, from the very beginning, she set about to sabotage my life there.

I loved university. There was a wonderful sense of freedom about it. I was now living in a semi-adult world, with other students who were ready to spread their wings and venture into the unknown of make-up, boyfriends, cheap restaurants and crazy clothes, all of which were prohibited to me. Some days, my whole body literally ached to join in with them and stand on the brink of life without this dreadful millstone around my neck. It seemed I was never to be free of her. I had long since given up on that luxury. Even now, at eighteen, I was still too brainwashed to fight the good fight. It was so much easier to give into her every whim, for she was still verbally abusive and physically violent if I ever disobeyed her.

On many weekends, during my stay in Exeter, Chris Brisley would often drag me back to Bath. She didn't like Exeter, and kept telling me that I should give up the high and mighty idea of getting a degree that wouldn't help me, or her, with any future earnings. It became a constant thorn in her side, and now, every time she was within shouting range, she would tell me I needed to get a job and start supporting myself and her.

One memorable weekend, Chris Brisleys' car broke down while she was in Exeter so we both took the train back to Bath. We had just got seated when *the woman* started screaming at me for no reason at all in front of a carriage full of people. She would take great delight in doing this as often as she could. She told me what a lazy lying little cow I was and she was sick and tired of me ruining her life. The traveling onlookers were obviously sympathetic with her and gave me dark looks, but all were very eager for the tirade to carry on. They need not have worried; there was no stopping her when she was on a roll. She reminded me of all the sacrifices she'd made over the years and how she'd given up her youth *and* marriage to give me a good start in life yet I had treated her like dirt. I sat like a stone, as always, listening to the abuse being hurled at me, *then suddenly* it was all too much, even for a brainwashed girl, I simply flipped. Something snapped in my head and I desperately wanted to physically hurt her like she'd hurt me for all those torturous years. I started screaming back at her, telling her what a cruel hateful person she was and how she had destroyed my childhood, and now was hellbent on destroying the rest of my life. The carriage was agog. It was a bit like the gladiators being led out into the forum, ready to fight for their lives. It was the first time I had ever stood up for myself, but I must have sounded as bad as her. We were still hurling abuse at each other as the train came into the station at Bath. Sadly, by then most of the fight had left me, and I was once again a very frightened little girl who had stepped over the line, and now must await my fate. We got a taxi from the station, and I sat as far away from her as possible, knowing what was to come as soon as the front door of our home was shut behind me.

She was so quick I didn't see the first blow. She hit the side of my face and I went down, smacking my shoulder into the banister rail. I felt something crunch in my ear. She kept on kicking me until I managed to get into a kneeling position then she literally grabbed me by my hair and dragged me up the stairs. She threw me into my bedroom, and slammed the door shut. My legs were bruised and bleeding from the stairs, the pain in my left my shoulder was so bad that I was certain I had broken it, and, yet again, my face looked like I'd been hit by a ten-ton truck. I think it was one of the lowest moments in my young life. I knew then that I would never have the strength to leave her. Wherever I went, she would track me down and probably kill me, as she had so often promised me. I sat on a chair in the corner of the room for what seemed like hours, watching the sun go down and knowing that I could not face any more beatings like this one.

I have read that people who contemplate suicide are usually not in their right mind; but for me, at that moment, this was not so. I was very calm, and everything I did from then on was deliberate and fully thought out. I remember hearing her go to her room and I waited well into the night when I knew she would be asleep. I then went downstairs to the kitchen and found a very sharp knife. I went back to my room, laid on the bed and very carefully cut each wrist.

When I look back on that day, I realize maybe it was a selfish thing to do; but who was there to mourn my dying? Certainly not my uncles. I could now pass them on the street and not recognize them, or them me. My grandmother didn't really know me, though she'd done what she thought was best for me. On that night I thought it would probably be a blessed relief for her. At least this way, she'd have *the woman* off her back for good. I can only say it was a very deliberate act. I was so incredibly tired. Not the sort of exhaustion one feels after a full working day, and knowing that a good night's sleep will revitalize one. No, I was so very, *very* tired of actually living. I realized I'd spent all of my life watching other people enjoying their friends and families, planning their futures and fulfilling those plans. Where had it gone wrong for me? I can honestly say that, in those moments, I didn't feel sorry for myself. I was simply too tired for any emotion. I desperately wanted to go to sleep and never wake up again. The thought of never having to see her or hear her voice again motivated me on that dark night. I tried not to think of the Catholic church, for I felt sure if indeed there was a God, he would forgive me. However, I guess I was lucky that the cuts weren't deep. I think when I saw the blood flowing, I thought I'd done enough for me to go to sleep and never wake up again.

I will never know why and I never asked her why she came to my room, for it was something she never did, but sometime during the early morning hours *the woman* literally ran into my bedroom. I can't say what would have happened if she hadn't come when she did. I only know that, for the first time ever, I scared the living daylights out of her. She was like a cyclone running up and down stairs with hot water and bandages. I lay there feeling woozy and was not sure if it was from the beating or my actions. She kept saying over and over again that I mustn't tell anyone about this. The bed was quickly stripped and changed and before I knew it I was back in it and given a sleeping tablet, which I didn't really need. I slept until late the following day.

When I eventually woke, she was there by my bed hovering like a dark cloud. I looked from my bound wrists to her. I could tell that she was extremely afraid.

"I've decided that, as a treat, I am going to take you to London tomorrow. We'll catch an early train. That way we'll have the whole day there. We can shop, have lunch and maybe see an afternoon matinee." She looked at me waiting for an answer.

I didn't know what to say to her. How on earth could I go anywhere? Unless by some miracle my face had healed while I was asleep. As if she read my mind she said. "If anyone asks what happened to you, I'll say you were in a car accident." I found it incredible that she would make such a ridiculous statement. It was like living through a black comedy, with me as the leading lady. I remember I started to laugh and couldn't stop. The woman was definitely deranged but as I've said before, when she was on a roll there was no stopping her. She wanted to take me to London, and London was where we were going to go, even if she had to carry me.

I knew why she was doing this. She was aware she'd gone too far. She was now dealing with someone who was beginning to fight back, if only in a most feeble way. If anyone found out what I had done, questions would be asked. I got up and went into the bathroom, trying not to look at my face. It hurt and I could not hear very well in my right ear. My shoulder and arm were almost immobile. I just hoped there was no major damage anywhere.

I was given another sleeping tablet, and slept for the rest of the day. During the night, I awoke, and sat on the edge of my bed trying to clear my head, but my thoughts were still a jumbled mess. I couldn't think straight, and I suddenly felt very scared. How easy it would have been to end my life, and, as I sit writing this, I can't imagine doing such a terrible thing; but now I have so much to live for, then I did not. Still, there was no excuse, and I made a solemn promise to myself and God that I would never do anything like that again. As the grey dawn crept up through my window, I could hear Chris Brisley moving around, a most unusual thing for her to do if she was not working, so I knew that we were London bound.

It was so strange to see *the woman* running around like a scalded cat, helping me to get dressed, and even making me breakfast. I knew from the past that if she'd gone too far, she would always suck up to me and *always* call me Wen – oh, how I hated that abbreviation! On this particular morning there were so many Wen's it made my head spin.

Somehow we got to the station, and caught the London train. I sat in a complete daze, wondering whether I would make it through the day. Dark stockings covered my legs, long sleeves covered my arms but my face was out there for all to see, and I did get some very strange glances. There was a perverse part of me that wanted to laugh out loud and tell everyone what had happened to me. I hadn't won the battle but I'd certainly got her running around in all directions, not knowing quite which way to turn. Oh I knew it wouldn't last and at the time I didn't really care.

The day seemed an eternity, it was as if the clock had stopped and I would forever be walking around the streets of London with this albatross on my back. Wherever we went the first thing she would say, to anyone who even glanced my way, that I'd been in a bad car accident. Everyone was extremely compassionate, and I felt completely stupid. I think it was then I knew that I needed help both mentally and physically. I needed someone else to lean on, someone who was much stronger than me but there wasn't a soul in my life who would come to my rescue; I was completely on my own.

Still that memorable day was the beginning of the end for Chris Brisley, even though I didn't know it at the time.

BREAD WINNER

Sadly, my university days came to an abrupt end. I knew there was no point in continuing, even though I was doing well. Chris Brisley had made it almost impossible for me to go back and have a normal life there.

So, at nineteen, I realized that I had no skills whatsoever for me to get a job with enough earning power to keep Chris Brisley happy and allow her to give up the job she had at the time, which was now looking after an elderly woman in her home during the day, a job Chris Brisley absolutely hated. God knows what the poor woman went through. Yet another huge crisis had arisen in my life and I was told in no uncertain terms to get out there and find a job.

I also realized I didn't really fit in with other teenagers; in fact I didn't seem to fit in with anyone. Though I was tall, I was still very skinny, not the graceful swan I always wanted to be. I was not allowed to wear any make-up, and my clothes were plain and dowdy, to say the least. Any shoe with a heel, no matter how small, was also not allowed. The foot operation was the said reason for my living in flat and unexciting footwear. In other words, I most certainly faded into *any* background.

I simply had no idea what I was going to do. The thought of becoming a shop assistant was a depressing and scary thought.

It was while out on the weekly shopping in Bath with my list for the usual groceries, and any other requirements *the woman* might need, that I had an exciting thought. I would become *a hairdresser*. I gritted my teeth and walked into a small salon just off Milsom street. It didn't look very up-to-date, but I thought it was worth a try. I was immediately asked what training I'd had, and when I answered, "None" the interest in me noticeably evaporated. I also learned that apprentice hairdressers earned almost nothing until they became fully qualified, which took years. The owner told me that I should have started at sixteen. I left the salon feeling dejected. Then I hit on another great idea. I would walk into a salon, say I was fully qualified, and ask for a job.

With great excitement I took the weekly shopping home, got out my hidden stash of makeup, put on the best of my drab and limited outfits and set forth to become a hairdresser. I decided I would visit every single salon in Bath until I got me a job.

At the top of Broad Street, opposite the York Hotel, there was a new salon about to open, called Bernard of Mayfair. It looked rather chic and very fancy. I was scared witless, but said to myself, "Nothing ventured, nothing gained." This attitude has stood me in great stead through the years. With my newly made-up face, I sailed into the salon, hoping they wouldn't laugh at my *very* short and rather lopsided haircut. Apart from being a dreadful cook, Chris Brisley was *really* bad at cutting hair. As I smiled at the receptionist who was busy setting up her allotted area, I kept telling myself the worst thing that could happen was I'd get thrown out on my ear. There are many times since then when I've sailed into situations with tongue in cheek and made other people, *and even myself,* believe I could do the job. Then I would do it for fun and adventure. This time, I needed to start earning money.

It worked like a charm, and they were looking for fully trained stylists. After a short interview with a rather obnoxious man called Mr Michael, who amazingly enough did not ask me if I was qualified, *I was hired.* I was told that my salary would be fairly modest to start with, though it was much more than I'd expected, but I was assured that as soon as I proved myself worthy of my position, I could expect my salary to rise considerably. *What a creep!* Anyway, I was to commence my new job, when the salon opened, in a month. I was euphoric as I left the salon, and stayed that way until I got home, then, as I very quickly scrubbed the make-up off of my face before *the woman* got home, I realized that I didn't know the first thing about hairdressing. I was then in a complete state of panic. I decided to say nothing to *the woman* until I'd checked this new venture of mine out with Mabel Redwood.

MABEL REDWOOD

Mabel Redwood had come into my life a few months before, and was like a guardian angel to me. Again, the common denominator was Chris Brisley. They met at a church choir meeting: yes, *the woman* belonged to the local church, and as far as I know, all thought she was a paragon of virtue. She had a fair singing voice and also enjoyed the social side of the church.

Mabel Redwood was mother to a daughter named Margaret, who was a few years younger than me, and still at school. I don't know whether Mabel was divorced or widowed, but Margaret's father was not around and was never talked about. Somehow, I knew instinctively it would not be appropriate to ask. I guess it seems strange that I gravitated to Mabel, and not to her daughter Margaret. Although I liked Margaret, I had nothing in common with her. We had what I would call a pleasant relationship. I think that, deep down, her mother was the mother I desperately wanted. I used to watch the pair of them together, and marvelled at the easy and relaxed way they had between them. I envied the fact that Margaret was free to pursue her out of school activities. It was a freedom I could only dream about, and could never ever imagine happening to me.

Mabel Redwood lived in a Georgian terrace house on one of the hills overlooking the City of Bath, about ten minutes from my home. Her house was typical of the grand old homes belonging to this historic City, though sadly, today, most of them have now been turned into flats. Mabel's home had four floors from basement to attic. It had a long walled front garden, which was beautifully kept by her. There was also a kitchen garden at the rear of the house, where she grew most of her vegetables.

I rather fancy that, at one time, Mabel must have been a very unusual young woman, for her approach to life was always rather

Bohemian. Even though she was only in her fifties, her face was extremely weather-beaten, making her look very much older, certainly a face that had not worn too well. But to me, she was one of the most beautiful women I knew. Whenever I unexpectedly turned up at her house, there was always a welcome. No questions were asked, and I never discussed any turmoil I might have been going through at the time. When I look back on those days, I now realize that she must have had a tough time making ends meet; but she always had a ready smile on her face. I remember her in her large, old-fashioned kitchen, either cleaning or cooking. She *always* wore an apron, and her unruly short greying hair was clipped back at each side with hair grips. Yes, she was definitely Mother Earth.

At the beginning of our relationship, she certainly had no idea what sort of person Chris Brisley was. Everyone thought *the woman* remarkable, and I suppose, in many ways, she was. *The woman* definitely had a split personality, and the side other people saw was a charming and charismatic person. When she was dressed up, she could still command attention from both the female and male population. I would watch her on many of those occasions and marvel at how a person could beat the living daylights out of me and then, a couple of hours later, walk out of the house and become a completely different woman. She hoodwinked many people, which made it all the harder for me. Who was ever going to believe a girl like me against this powerful and dominating force? It took Mabel Redwood only a couple of months to see through the facade, *but* she stayed friendly with *the woman* so that she could keep an eye on me. Yet again, as with so many people, it didn't enter her head to make a complaint to the authorities. It was very strange, because although Mabel knew my situation, it was never discussed until much later in our relationship. Still, she was the only living person who eventually went to my grandmother and told her that she must get me out of "*that woman's grip.*"

Mabel Redwood had rather a grand paying guest who lived on the third floor, and was a retired high court judge. His name was Mr Drake, and I was told many times by Chris Brisley that he could look at a person and immediately tell what sort of character they had.

Needless to say, her eyes were boring into mine at the time, as if to say that, if he met me, he would most certainly know I was a bad lot. It was ridiculous, but I always tried to steer clear of him in case she was right and he would meet me, and then instantly know that I harboured bad thoughts, especially where she was concerned. The day came when Mr Drake asked Mabel if, on my next visit, I would take tea with him in his sitting room. She had either told him about me, or he had watched me from his window. I was informed that he liked to observe people. I was simply beside myself with nerves. I knew I should look him straight in the eye, as I'd always been told to do at school. "Never avert your eyes when holding a conversation. It's bad manners, and shows a shifty disposition," Bonzo would frequently say, mainly when telling a frightened pupil that they'd strayed from the path of righteousness. So my dilemma was I had to eat cake, drink tea, and keep looking Mr Drake squarely in the eyes while answering a battery of questions which I felt sure would be asked, or risk a bad report to Mabel on my lack of moral character. Well, the outcome of our first meeting obviously went well, for I was to become a frequent guest of the rather imperious and very reclusive Mr Drake. From then on, I spent many a happy hour munching Mabel's delicious cakes and talking with this grand and probably lonely old man.

Mabel was definitely the proverbial mother hen, always baking bread or some wonderful fruit pie for Mr Drake to sample, either at afternoon tea or dinner. She looked after him as if he were a King, for he was her only means of support. He must have paid her well, for as far as I knew, she didn't have any other job, and it certainly was a very large house to maintain.

Much later, I was to learn from Mabel that he'd told her I was a chrysalis waiting to turn into a beautiful butterfly. One question Mabel did ask me was why had I left university? I explained that my qualifications wouldn't necessarily find me a job, and it was decided I should leave and enter the workforce. "And what sort of work had you in mind?" came her reply. And it was at that time I told her of my plan.

***

Well, I'd found myself a job, and now my problem was what on earth I was going to do about it. We sat at her kitchen table, drinking tea and eating hot buttered toast, while I told her of my earlier adventures in Bath. After I'd finished, Mabel laughed so hard she spilled her tea in her lap.

"It's not funny," I said. "It won't take them long to find out that I don't know the first thing about hairdressing."

She sat looking at me. "Have you ever had your hair done professionally?" I shook my head. "You have one month before you start. I suggest you go to other salons, have your hair done, and watch everyone and everything."

"What on earth can I learn in a month? And anyway, I haven't any money."

"I'll give you the money." She started laughing again. "What a fine fix you've got yourself into." I could see that she thought it very amusing. I made her promise she wouldn't breathe a word to *the woman,* and so the plan was hatched. I would have my hair done in one salon, a manicure at another and anything else any other salons had to offer. It was a hare-brained scheme, (excuse the pun) but it was the only thing we could come up with. At the time, Chris Brisley was now back working at a private nursing home, so thankfully, was out from early morning to late evening. I had to make sure all my house chores were done by the time she came home, and my daily visits to various salons would never be found out.

VERY FIRST KISS

One of the most frightening and saddest days in my young life was when Chris Brisley hit me harder than she had done for a few months. Her fist landed to the right side of my face, and at the time, I was certain that she had broken my jaw. A few days later, I was taken to the hospital, and yet again, they were told that I had fallen off my bicycle. My jaw wasn't broken, but it was pushed out of alignment, and has remained that way ever since. For a long time, it would click and stay in one position until I clicked it back.

It all started when I was invited to a birthday party by a neighbour who lived near us. I was hardly ever allowed out on my own, especially in the evenings. Actually, the neighbor asked *the woman* if I would like to go. It was her son's twentieth birthday. His name was Paul, and apparently he'd been wanting to ask me out. Most of the time he was away at university, and only came home for the odd weekend. When he was at home I'd see him riding his motorbike past my house, and he would give me a wave. I thought he was extremely handsome, and could hardly believe that I had been invited to his party. Chris Brisley couldn't find any reasonable excuse for me not to go, as their home was only three doors away from ours, so reluctantly, she agreed. To her way of thinking, as the family lived on the same street, she knew exactly where I was. As usual I was given strict instructions about how I was to conduct myself, and to be home no later than eleven. I knew she was not pleased about my going, but I was so excited, I didn't care.

Seeing him up close and personal for the first time, my initial impression of him had been correct; *he was a handsome boy.* It came as quite a shock when I realized I was actually his date for the evening. Believe it or not, this was *my* very first date. There had been a few boys in the past who had shown an interest, only to be quickly rebuffed by *the woman* and they went rapidly on their way.

I remember the evening so well. If I close my eyes I can see him talking and laughing with his friends, holding my hand and introducing me as his new girlfriend. I think I was in some sort of daze. I could not believe that this handsome fellow had singled me out. It was a wonderful evening, beautiful young people laughing, dancing, eating, drinking and above all *happy*. There was a small part of me sending out warning signals, but I was too deliriously carefree in those few hours to think about them. Toward the end of the evening, some of Paul's friends said they were going on to a pub in the City that had a discotheque behind the main building. I remember him saying, "Let me get my girl something warm to wear, and we'll follow you there." I knew I shouldn't have gone, but it was harmless, it was his birthday and I so wanted to go. It was the first time (and come to think of it) the last time I'd ever been on a motorbike. He loaned me one of his mother's jackets, and off we went. I put my arms around his waist and snuggled into his back. He was wearing a heavy knitted sweater which smelled of Old Spice. I was consumed with the sheer overwhelming feeling of pure joy. It was a truly memorable evening in more ways than one. We danced and laughed and during the evening I felt I had the world on a string. I didn't realize at the time that Chris Brisley had seen me leaving with Paul on his motorbike. We returned a little after midnight, and he dropped me off at my front door, saying that he would call me the next day. He gave me my first kiss, telling me I was drop dead gorgeous. It was such an innocent evening. The strongest drink was a glass of sherry, with young people enjoying being together and listening to the music.

As I opened the front door, *she* was in the hall waiting for my return; she must have been standing there for hours. She started screaming and hitting out at me the minute I entered the house. She had worked herself up to a complete frenzy during the time I was away. Obviously it had reached an all-time high when she saw me riding away on the back of Paul's motorbike. Again she dragged me up to my bedroom by my hair, her favorite thing to do, punching me so hard that I had the wind knocked out of me. The beating seemed to go on forever. Such a wonderful evening, completely devastated by one woman's hate and jealousy. It was then she punched me in my face catching my jaw with her clenched fist. I went down and stayed there. All the time she was screaming at me, my only thought was hoping that Paul hadn't heard what was happening, and how completely embarrassing it would be if he had. But I knew he had, and I also knew it was the end to any future of ever seeing him again. That night I curled myself up into a ball and lay there, wishing I had the courage to get up and leave, but even if I had, where would I go?

The next morning there was no sign of Chris Brisley. I stayed in my room and kept out of her way. Needless to say it was a day without food, but I didn't care; I wanted to shut myself away from the world and *the woman.* My bedroom window was open and looked out onto the back of the houses. I could hear people talking and laughing, and I knew one of them was Paul, my wonderful new boyfriend who I would never see again. My jaw was bruised and excruciatingly painful, and for a week I could hardly open my mouth. Paul's mother never spoke to Chris Brisley again, and her son never did call me for another date. I guess he was too sensible to become embroiled with such a crazy woman and her daughter. Whenever I saw his motorbike at his home, I usually steered clear and hoped that I would never see him again. It was all too embarrassing, and, yes, quite heartbreaking. I was so glad when they eventually moved away.

To this day I still have a slightly lopsided mouth. Thank goodness for lipstick and lip liner. I don't think anyone has ever noticed, but certainly my jaw is forever knocked sideways by her brutality.

Luckily, apart from my jaw, most of the bruising was to my body, so, with the careful application of make-up I felt somewhat ready for the up and coming Monday morning and my new job. I decided not to say anything to *the woman* until I either got thrown out on my ear, or managed to con my way into this new world.

Mr Michael greeted me at the salon entrance and immediately wanted to know what the hell I'd done to my face. I thought the bicycle story was becoming a little too worn out by now, so I told him I'd slipped on some wet grass and had fallen on to a stone wall. I don't think for one moment he believed me, but at the time, he was much too interested in getting the salon ready for action. Still, the first day went fairly well, mainly because I didn't have to do anything. I had my hair washed and styled by a young man called Brian, who asked me where my preferences lay. I was completely dumbstruck by this question, for it was quite obvious he was gay. As I grappled with my answer, he smiled and assured me he was talking about my hairdressing skills. It was then I took the bull by the horns and told him I knew nothing about the job, but desperately needed the money. We then went into a conspiratorial huddle, and, suddenly, I had found a friend. For him, I think this was the most exciting thing that had ever happened in his young life. I will never know how he managed it, but it was decided that I should work with him for a few weeks so I could learn Bernard's way of operating with the clients. Brian had been sent over from Bernard's Bristol salon to ensure the smooth running of this new salon. For the first week I was absolutely glued to his side, watching him cut with scissors and razor, handing rollers and hair clips as he set and styled each client. Oh my God, it didn't take me too long to realize how I hated this job, but I knew I simply had to stick it out; the alternative didn't bear thinking about. It didn't take Brian or me too long to learn that I had very strong fingers, and I was soon helping him with perms. The styling then was quite different from today. Most women had perms, and then their hair would be set into various curly or wavy styles. By the second week I was quite efficient in the art of the permanent wave, as it was then called. It was at that time Brian suggested to Mr Michael that I should do all the perming for the salon, as he quite rightly realized that it would take me much longer to learn how to cut hair and style hair. Unlike today, where hairstylists have their own clients, at Bernard of Mayfair, it was not encouraged. When free, each stylist would take any client as they came in for their appointment. It was a crazy way of doing things, and so, if the client liked a certain stylist, they would make excuses until their particular girl was free.

So now, thanks to Brian, it seemed I had a job I could do. The client's hair would be cut, and I would then perm. And after I'd finished, the women would be turned over to someone else to get set into whatever style they wanted.

After the fifth week at Bernard's I told *the woman* that I had found a job in a new hairdressing salon in Bath. The first words out of her mouth were, "How much are they paying you?" There were no questions as to how I got the job and what on earth did I do there – did I wash towels, or sweep floors? No, just how much money was I getting. At least for the moment, she seemed satisfied with my salary, but hoped it would be raised soon, so that she could then take a part time job and not have to work so hard. In all the time I worked there, she never once asked me what I actually *did*. That's how interested she was in me.

I got on really well with my new-found job, and, no matter how coarse or strong the clients' hair, I could always wind it up on to those small rollers and keep the women happy. So now, apart from my weekly salary, which went straight to *the woman* unopened, I was now doing very well with tips.

Brian, who had become a good friend to me, and knew a little of my circumstances, told me that I should get a post office savings book, and start saving my tips. It didn't take Chris Brisley too long to realize that I must *get* tips, and so her hand would be out each evening for the tip money. I would dutifully hand over approximately half, and keep the rest. I did as Brian suggested, and got my savings book. Definitely a *déjà vu* moment as I thought of Ken Brisley and my weekly pocket money all those years ago. However, this was to be my escape money – if indeed I ever had the courage to escape.

Around this time, Chris Brisley lost her job as a nurse. Again, I don't know what happened at the private nursing home, but she came home one night and said that she would not be going back. Her next words were, "You'll have to get a pay rise or find a better paying job." I sat looking at her, wondering how much more of my life she would suck out of me.

The next day I talked to Brian at length. I knew that, even if I gave up *all* my tips, it certainly would not be enough to keep her happy, or, indeed, to pay the bills. It was Brian who suggested I should go and see Bernard himself and explain the situation. He could only say no. Bernard rarely came to the Bath salon. Maybe he would come a couple of times a month, and, as he'd only just visited, I knew that it would be too long to wait until he came again. It was decided between Brian and me that I should go to Bristol and beard the lion in his den, so to speak. The thought of having to ask this man if he would give me a rise in order to continue working for him made me squirm with embarrassment. But I knew that if I didn't get a rise I wouldn't be able to stay at the salon. Although I hated hairdressing, I *really* loved the fact that I was out in the world, and spending my working life with normal people. Most of the staff were young, and although we worked hard, we also had a lot of fun, and I guess that, to a certain extent, I lived vicariously through them. Only Brian knew I did not have a happy home life. He certainly didn't know how bad it was, but he knew enough to cluck over me like a mother hen.

The bus journey to Bristol was simply awful. I kept going over what I would say. I tried all sorts of different scenarios, but in the end I decided to tell it like it was. The Bristol salon was much bigger, and was simply swarming with staff and clients. I hadn't had time to put any makeup on, so I sat there looking pale and washed out, feeling very drab in my school uniform coat – yes, I was still wearing it. I had to wear clothes until they either got too small for me, or were literally falling apart. I sat in the reception area feeling like a condemned prisoner waiting to be executed. Eventually, I was shown into Bernard's office. It was the first time I had ever spoken to him, for when he came to Bath all the staff would be working like slaves hoping he would not stay too long, or find anything untoward like dusty corners or worse still unclean equipment.

He was a large, rather impressive man, sporting a goatee beard, and was immaculately dressed. Needless to say I was completely overwhelmed and quite tongue-tied while I tried desperately to act normal. Eventually I got my story out, even telling him that I was not actually a fully qualified hairdresser. Why on earth I told him, I'll never know, but for some reason it truly amused him, especially the fact I'd got one over on Mr Michael. I also told him how Brian had helped me from my very first day and because of him I was now in charge of the perming salon. He picked up the phone and ordered coffee and sandwiches, then asked, "How much money would you have to earn to allow you to stay in my salon?" I shook my head. There was no way I could sit there and give him a figure for my untrained skills. We sat looking at each other. Then he said. "Does your father or mother not work at all?"

I suddenly leaned forward and literally banged on his desk. "My parents are dead, and she's divorced, and not my mother."

He sat back and looked at me, not quite believing my sudden violent outburst, and I must say neither did I. Of course, then I knew I'd lost all hope of any help from my boss and squeaked out an abject apology.

It's strange, but throughout my life, when I have thought all was lost, a rainbow would break through the clouds and envelope me with beautiful colours. This day was no exception.

Suddenly he said, "I will give you a rise on one condition." He looked very stern, then carried on. "You are to tell no one. I don't want my staff stampeding to this office begging for a rise. Your circumstances are very different, and I think you need my help."

The relief was overwhelming. I wanted to get up and hug him but luckily restrained myself assuring him I would not let him down. I then nibbled on ham and lettuce sandwiches, washed down by very strong coffee. His parting words to me were, "You have an extraordinary face, and a little make-up would not go amiss. I shall also expect you to learn the art of hairstyling post haste, for, at the moment, you will be earning more than my top stylist here."

I left very quickly before he could change his mind. Another hero who probably would never know how much he helped me.

I arrived back at the Bath salon just after lunch, and thanks to Brian, no one had missed me. I told him about my successful meeting with Bernard and swore him into secrecy. He was a true loyal friend, and my first introduction into the gay world. It was an easy friendship with no sexual strings attached, just a young man looking out for a very bruised teenager.

The next few weeks were fairly quiet. *The woman* was happy that I was making more money, and, for the moment, she could put her feet up and take life a little easier. Her words, not mine. With her spending idle time at home, the house did not stay very tidy for long. I think housework was a forbidden activity as far as she was concerned. So, I found that I was doing a full day's work at the salon, and then coming home to clean, cook, and wash up, before I could even think of going to bed. Luckily, I was young, and, I guess, very resilient or completely stupid! But even then, I could not function in a dirty environment. So my life literally revolved around the salon and the house. I felt completely stifled, and again, envious, listening to my workmates making plans to catch the latest film or go to the local Chinese or Italian restaurant for dinner. Again, it was Brian who came up with a great idea. I would tell the woman that to make a little more money, I was going to do some hairdressing in the evenings. It would mean giving up some of my precious tips, but at least I could occasionally go out in the evening and start to feel like the young girl I was. When I told her, she thought it was a great idea. I think the only time we ever really got on was when I was making money for her.

By now, all the staff at the salon knew her, at least by sight. She often loomed like a black cloud outside the salon, waiting for me to finish work, but Brian was the only one who knew a little of this woman's personality, and what he saw he didn't like.

I was now cutting and setting hair, as well as perming. I would work like a thing possessed, garnering as many clients as I could throughout the day. Chris Brisley still expected me to hand over my tips each evening, and I still wanted to save as much as I could, so my cinema and restaurant trips were kept to one special evening every two weeks. It was heaven, and, needless to say, I was the life and soul of the party. Very innocent, just a group of young people spending time together and having fun. I always so enjoyed those stolen moments until after it was all over and I would stand outside the front door of my home with my stomach churning and my heart beating so fast I thought it would burst. Was this the night she'd find out what I was doing? Was she waiting on the other side of the door ready to pounce on me and drag me upstairs to kick hell out of me for daring to lie to her? I can tell you it took a lot of guts to put that key into the door, and each time I stood there, I vowed that this would be the last time I would play truant; my nerves couldn't take it. Most nights, she was already in bed, and would call out the minute she heard the door shut. I would climb the stairs, hand over the money to the outstretched hand, and then, thankfully, go to bed. The fact was she never did find out about my wicked evenings, though there was one *very* near miss.

There were two cinemas in Bath. One was called The Beau Nash, after a famous gentleman who had resided in the City many years ago; the other cinema was called The Odeon. When I started this adventure, I hadn't taken into account that *the woman* was an avid film fan. I have known her to go to an afternoon matinee, then cross the road to the second cinema and watch whatever film was showing there. One evening, a group of girls, along with the faithful Brian, who seemed to be permanently without a partner at the time, decided to have a Chinese meal, then go and see the latest film at The Beau Nash. We were quite a noisy crowd as we entered looking for our seats. A few people turned and glanced our way, hoping we would all settle down quickly, as the film was about to start. I found my seat, as Brian literally fell upon me clasping me in a firm embrace, much to my complete astonishment, let alone the group. We all knew he was gay and I started to giggle, because I thought he was playing the fool. But what he whispered in my ear sent shock waves through my whole body. *The woman* was sitting three rows in front of me, and giving our group one of her most piercing stares. It seemed forever before she turned back to the screen and, with a quick wave to the others, Brian and I beat a hasty retreat out of the cinema. He took me home and made sure I was okay, and had got over the shock, before he left. If she had seen me it would most certainly have been the end of my scant hours of freedom. It was a long time before I had the courage to spend another evening playing hooky with my workmates.

Wendy at Age 4

Wendy's 5th Birthday at
the Photographers

Wendy at Blackpool Age 14

Wendy Modeling Age 20

Wendy with her Yorkshire
Terrier, Deda

Actor and Friend Robert Wagner Visits
Wendy and Raymond in Virginia

Wendy and Actor, Robert
Wagner Arriving at LHR

Raymond on White Charger

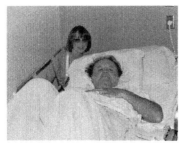

Wendy and Actor, Rod Steiger
After his Heart Surgery

Wendy and Sir Bruce
Fosyth, UK Entertainer

Wendy with John Phillip Law
on the Set of The Golden
Voyage of Sinbad

Wendy with Actor, Rock
Hudson on the set of The
Martian Chronicles

Wendy and Actor, George
Segal

Wendy and Actor,
Patrick Macnee

Wendy at Cocktail Party with
Actor, Cary Grant

Wendy and Husband,
Raymond

Wendy and Judith Dress
for Dance

Wendy with Actor, Joseph Cotton.
Raymond's Best Man at their Wedding

Wendy and Actor Tom Selleck
on Set of Magnum Pi in Hawaii

Wendy with Actor, Sir.
Roger Moore

JUDITH

Around this time, a girl named Judith Chamberlain came into my life. The first time I saw her, she was at Bernard's in the salon setting someone's hair. Her hairdressing skills were being tested by Mr Michael, and she passed with flying colors. To me, she was stunningly beautiful with her dark hair swept up into a highlighted blonde chignon, and I have never seen such beautiful eyes on anyone else. They were very blue, and framed with a double row of lashes that cast a shadow across her face when she blinked. She was a couple of years older than me, and seemed so carefree and full of life.

Judith's parents lived in Devon, at a place called Newton Abbot, so she was staying in Bath at the home of her then boyfriend, who was in the navy and away most of the time. I think she only saw her parents on the odd weekends, and that all seemed pretty mature and urbane to me. One lunchtime I do remember being introduced to her father, who was visiting her at the time. They seemed to have a really good relationship, and I envied her that. I could only imagine what it must be like living away from home and being completely free to make one's own decisions.

As for me, I was still wearing flat shoes, plain clothes and no make-up, unless I was very daring and had the time to put some on when I arrived at work in the morning. Judith always looked perfectly groomed, always wore high heels, and sported the latest fashion.

We were instantly drawn to each other. I had a zany sense of humour, and took great pleasure in making her laugh. In fact, when we were together, we were always laughing and looking back; I guess we were probably quite annoying. Eventually, Mr Michael separated us, with Judith working in the downstairs salon, and me upstairs. Quite a wretched event. Still, we often managed to sneak our coffee break together, but our working days weren't quite so much fun any more.

The inevitable day arrived when she asked me to go and see a film with her one evening. At the time *the woman* was becoming even more controlling. She would often stand outside the salon, waiting for me to leave. My precious evenings out with my friends were now a thing of the past, so I had to tell Judith that, in the unforeseeable future, any evening activities were out. It was then that I reluctantly told her about my life with Chris Brisley. I always found it very difficult and excruciatingly embarrassing to tell anyone what my home life was like, and how controlled I was. I felt somehow it was my fault, and now, looking back on those wasted years, I guess that in a way it was. I should have tried to overcome my paralyzing fear and stood up to her, but oh, those cold black eyes! Even to this day, if I think about her I can still see them.

Apart from Mabel Redwood, Brian, and now Judith, no one else knew what kind of life I was leading. I was always too ashamed to ever let anyone into my world.

HIGH HEELS AND RUSSELL AND BROMLEY

It was nearing Christmas again, and because I had worked extra hard, and as Bernard had given me a rise in salary, Chris Brisley was quite pleased with me. She told me that she didn't have time to buy Christmas or birthday presents for me, *not that she ever had,* but this year I could buy myself a present. This was unheard of, and I was truly excited. As I was going to be nineteen in a matter of weeks, I felt that the time had come to buy my first pair of high heels. There was a wonderful shoe shop at the bottom of Milsom Street called Russell and Bromley. Every time I passed by I would stop and breathe all over the window looking at those beautiful shoes, and I promised myself one day I would buy a pair. My grandmother had sent me some money for both Christmas and my birthday, and, for the very first time, I was allowed to actually spend it. Would wonders never cease?

On Saturday afternoon, I simply flew down Milsom Street and did my usual breathing bit. There was such an array of beautiful shoes that I was heady with excitement, but I saw the shoes that were to be mine. Venturing into that hallowed place for the first time was an experience I will never forget. A sales girl glided over to me asking if she could help. I had truly found my nirvana. "I want those beautiful pair of high heels," I blurted out, feeling all eyes on me as I awkwardly pointed to the pair I'd seen in the window. After measuring my feet she disappeared into the back of the shop, while I tried to look as though I shopped there all the time. The box and the girl arrived back and as she set those high heels before me, for a few seconds, I sat and stared at those incredible shoes. The shop assistant must have thought me quite silly *but* to me this was a pivotal moment in my life. It was the start of a love affair between me and shoes that is still as strong today as ever.

They were of the softest, fawn-coloured leather, with a two-and a-half-inch heel, and they fitted perfectly, though walking in them was another matter. As I teetered across the store to look at them in a full length mirror I felt like a princess. I was an elegant girl for the very first time in my life. The price was beyond belief, as I had never owned anything so expensive before. Thank goodness I also had some of my savings in cash, as grandmother's present nowhere near paid for them, and I most certainly was not going to leave without them. I wanted to wear them out of the shop but knew I would never make it to the top of Milsom street if I did. No, I would keep them for very best. I would wear them each night in my room before I went to bed, that way I would get used to them, and, yes, I would feel beautiful.

As usual Chris Brisley was in a black mood when I arrived home but for a few blissful moments I was impervious to it or her, I was on cloud nine. She pointed to the Russell and Bromley bag asking me what I was carrying, I told her it was my present. I was commanded to open the bag and as I did a slight drizzle of apprehension ran through me. The drizzle soon turned into a thunderstorm as *the woman* stared at my lovely shoes.

"*Have you completely lost your mind?*" she screamed, as I clung to my present.

"You told me I could buy something."

"But not shoes, for God's sake, and certainly not these shoes. You don't have the legs for them, you will never have the legs for them, and you would look idiotic in them; besides, you are much too plain." She grabbed one of them and tried to get her foot into it, but thankfully her feet were too big. I stood there in abject misery looking at my beautiful shoes being stretched and contaminated by her.

"You will never learn. You will always have to be taught a lesson." Her lips turned into a hard line, and right there in front of me, she literally tore the heel off the shoe, then threw it on the floor. I was stunned not quite believing what had happened. I cradled the other now useless shoe, like a baby, in my arms as I felt huge sobs rumble up through my body. How could anyone be so cruel, and how could I be so stupid as to believe she would let me keep them.

I kept the one shoe for a long time. I hid it under my bed, and sometimes I would take it out and look at it. It was beautiful and one day I swore I would wear such a pair and Chris Brisley wouldn't be around to stop me.

The next day her mood was no better but she took great delight in taunting me and showing me the broken shoe, assuring me that I would never be sophisticated enough for the finer things in life, and my ugly feet would forever be ugly. As she taunted me, she was boiling a kettle of water for tea, and suddenly she lifted the kettle and poured some of the scalding water over my feet. I screamed out with pain as the water burnt my skin. Those evil eyes stared down at the now reddening area. "Well now, if possible, your feet are even uglier." The burns quickly blistered and for the next couple of weeks I could hardly bear to put my feet on the ground, and certainly couldn't wear a shoe. Work was out of the question and they were told by Chris Brisley I had a bad bout of influenza.

The red marks are still there to this day, and it took many years before I could look at them and not see her face, laughing at me and reminding me how ugly I was.

Russell and Bromley is still at the bottom of Milsom Street, and when ever I go back to Bath with my darling husband, Raymond, we *always* visit.

It was just after my birthday that I made a life-changing decision. For many years, my dead parents had kept me sane, whatever sane was. But I now knew it was time for them to leave. They had been with me for so long, and had cushioned me through some of my most traumatic times, but they couldn't stay with me. They were in my head, locked away where only I could run to them. They had seen me through a horrific childhood, and I am still absolutely convinced if I had not had them I probably wouldn't have made it through; but I knew they would have to go. So one memorable night, I sat in my bedroom until well into the early hours, and then I knelt by my bed and prayed. Apart from praying in the convent, I had never done this. I had prayed many times, but not actually kneeling by my bed. I fervently prayed my parents would understand why I was doing this. I told them that I had to move on, and however painful it was, I had to live in the real world if there was ever going to be a chance for me. It was an emotional and gut-wrenching experience, and I could almost feel them leaving me. I desperately wanted to pull them back, keep them close to me but somehow I knew that this was the right time, no matter how difficult it was, and although they, especially my mother, are forever in my thoughts, from that moment on I stopped building my life around them. I was now completely on my own.

***

A couple of months later, *the woman* was asked to look after an elderly man who was quite sick but still living in his own home. To my delight Chris Brisley moved into his house, and stayed there for a few precious weeks. Although the house was within walking distance from our home, I hardly saw her. She would still pop up every now and again, to make sure I was toeing the line, and her hand would always be out waiting for any money I'd accrued from tips.

During those few short weeks, Judith and I became very close. We had the same sense of humor and would talk for hours about nothing important, just girl talk, which I hadn't experienced before. For the first time I felt and behaved like a normal teenager. Without the cloud of Chris Brisley hovering over me, I began to venture out again. We would spend busy and hectic days in the salon, but after work would reward ourselves, by either going to the pictures or to a new coffee bar called *The Salamander*. Cappuccino coffee had become the rage, and small coffee bars were opening up all over England. Judith and I would go there, order our coffee, and sit at one of the tables, feeling very sophisticated. We lived in a totally different world then. We didn't smoke or drink. We weren't particularly interested in the boys who hung around the bar, and besides, Judith was sort of engaged; but for those short precious times we were young girls wanting to be *young girls.* Judith never really talked about her navy boyfriend, and I got the impression he was far more interested in her than she him. That was fine by me. I wanted her all to myself. She always made me feel that life was worth living.

On the occasions when Judith met Chris Brisley she saw what kind of woman I was living with. I know that even Judith was afraid of her. On one particular Saturday, I was a little late leaving the salon, and, as I was walking toward the bus stop, *the woman* suddenly appeared out of the blue and flew at me, like the crazy woman she was. Watching Judith and me laughing must have made her see red. She almost shoved Judith into the road and demanded to know what I'd being doing. I tried to explain that we had had to work late, but in no way did it pacify her. She thought Judith and I had been up to something, and whatever we said made it worse. It was the first time *the woman* had lived away from the house, and her fear of losing control of me must have been a constant battle. Apparently the old man had his daughter staying with him for a couple of days so Chris Brisley had decided to come home for a long weekend. As I said goodbye to Judith I saw the look on her face and knew she was worried about me. She was right to worry. It must have taken all *the woman's* will power not to batter me right there on the street. We sat on the bus in total silence and I could feel the dread creep up inside of me until it reached my chest and I thought I would choke with fear. I was a child again and, as always, all the bravado I felt while she was away from me evaporated like a puff of smoke when she was near. A short walk up the road to the house and I knew what lay ahead. She literally punched me in my stomach as I turned from closing the door. I went down like a sack of potatoes and lay there trying to get my breath while she kicked me in the chest and then ordered me to make her lunch, clear it away and go to my room. There was nothing to eat for me, but, as usual under those circumstances, my appetite had long since dissipated. I would do my chores and run up those stairs like a frightened animal as fast as my legs could carry me. Why, oh why, couldn't I stand up for myself? But I knew I couldn't. Just seeing her sapped all the energy out of my body. With my bedroom door firmly closed, I could undress and yet again inspect my now very bruised body in privacy.

I would often lie in bed at night and wonder what life would be like if she were gone. If she were to disappear then I would be free, but free from what? I simply had no idea what freedom truly meant. I imagined going back to University, and having a home of my own. I would spend hours decorating it and choosing furniture but then, more often than not, no matter how late, she would call for me to do some late chore or run an errand, and I would get out of bed, dress and the spell would be broken. I would *never* get away from her. There's a saying: 'Sticks and stones will break your bones but words will never hurt you.' Well it wasn't true, not for me anyway. The things she taunted me with, especially about my mother, were so brutal that I knew beyond a shadow of a doubt that I was ugly. I was skinny and awkward. I did not have one redeeming feature, and I sometimes wondered if she was right in what she said, especially how very disappointed my mother would have been to have had such a plain and stupid child. The more she told me, the more I morphed into a pathetic creature. I would agonize for hours through many a night, wondering why God had made me so ugly and unwanted. I would get up the next day, and try not to look at myself in the bedroom or bathroom mirrors; if I did it was so depressing, for I always looked the same. This lasted for many years to come, and, to a certain extent, still lives with me today.

On Monday morning, I arrived at the salon feeling completely worn out and still very sore; but with no bruising on show, no one knew what sort of weekend I'd had. Only Judith suspected that it had been a rough couple of days, but even she didn't know the extent of the physical abuse.

That morning, Chris Brisley gave the old man whom she had been looking after a week's notice, saying that she had problems at home, and would not be able to continue nursing him. His spaniel had just had a litter, so he gave her a puppy as a present. God knows why she accepted it but when she brought this tiny bundle home I was determined never to love it like I had Paddy. I didn't want to get my heart broken again. However the little Cocker Spaniel was named Julie, and, after two or three weeks of being completely ignored by *the woman*, became my sole responsibility.

There were times when I would arrive home and Chris Brisley would be all sweetness and light. On those days the name Wen would be on her lips, very cringe-making. It usually meant she wanted something, or maybe she'd had a particularly nice day. On one occasion she seemed happier than I'd seen her in a long time. My God! She'd met a man, *and* apparently he liked her. I did wonder what sort of cretin he was, for by now, she was certainly not the most attractive of the female form. I was soon to find out. His name was Frank. He was in the Royal Air Force and stationed at Colerne. There was a large base there and still is to this day. Colerne is a small village about eight miles away from Bath, and most of the soldiers based there came into Bath for their entertainment. Chris Brisley liked to go to the York hotel which was situated at the top of Broad Street. Though she smoked like a chimney, she didn't drink a lot, but loved the small bar which was in the hotel and to the left of the main entrance. That was where she first met Frank. I met him when she invited him to dinner. I was ready to dislike him on sight, but found him fun and most charming. God knows what he saw in her. I found out that he was stationed at Colerne for around eighteen months, and would then be going back to his regiment in the north of England. So, whatever the relationship, I gathered it would not be of a permanent kind. I could never imagine that anyone wanted to sleep with this woman, but I guess they did, for while the relationship lasted she was a different woman. I also found out that Frank was married, so my hope of their getting together on a permanent basis was dashed pretty quickly.

FIANCÊS AND ROBERT

It was at this time that we went into our RAF mode, for want of a better phrase. Chris Brisley started to spend a lot of time at the Colerne barracks, where they would have weekend dances and lots of other entertainment. After a couple of visits to our home, Frank asked me to join them one Saturday evening. I expected her to say no, but for once, she readily agreed.

Frank had a car, so we were driven to the dance in style. I don't think I've ever seen so many young men gathered together under one roof. It was noisy and fun, and for once, Chris Brisley was behaving like a normal human being. She was so taken up with Frank that she hardly noticed I was there. Very soon I was inundated with dance requests, and started to enjoy myself immensely. Halfway through the evening, a young man asked me to dance. His name was Robert. He was a very tall, good-looking man and for the rest of the evening I only danced with him. I seemed to float in his arms. It was all very romantic and slightly surreal. Here I was, having a normal wonderful evening with *the woman* dancing past me every so often and not taking the slightest interest in what I was doing. I wanted the evening to go on forever.

I began to think that the only way I could ever leave her was to get married, though I wasn't sure if I would be exchanging one controlled life for another. In the past, whenever I thought of marriage, which wasn't very often, in my mind I would always see a faceless dark shadowy figure whirling around in front of me. The vision always frightened me, and from quite an early age, I vowed I would never marry. There would never be another person in my life who would dominate me. Still, here was a very presentable man, obviously interested in me. I looked at him then across the room at *the woman*. I thought *my God, anything and anyone had to be better than existing with her*. Then I told myself I was being stupid; even if

I wanted to get married she would never agree to it. Poor Robert, he was completely unaware what he was getting into. As the evening progressed, I found out he was twenty-four, heading for a promotion and definitely thinking of staying in the RAF. It was obvious, even to me, that he was determined to get on in life. I decided he would be perfect. Love certainly didn't come into the equation.

It turned out to be an amazing few months. Chris Brisley was hardly around, spending all her time with Frank, and I spent as much time as I could with Robert. It was the very first time in my young adult life that, although with a few strings still attached, I had a fairly normal existence. It wasn't too long before Robert told me he loved me. Was I in love with him? *Sadly, no.* I wanted desperately to be in love, but I wasn't ready to love anyone. I didn't know what love was. He was a wonderful person who was opening a door for me, and he had no idea what was on the other side.

In a few weeks Robert proposed and although only a few steamy kisses had been exchanged, I was still very much a virgin, telling him I was determined to wait until I got married. I was happy that at least the intimacy hurdle had been passed. He readily agreed with me, then promptly set the wheels in motion for a very early wedding date. I was completely swept along with it, even though I knew I'd got myself into a ridiculous situation; but I truly didn't know how to get out of it. One Saturday we went into Bath and chose a very pretty garnet engagement ring, so now the only thing left for me to do was to tell Chris Brisley, who was still completely immersed in her social life with Frank. It was decided that we would take her out to dinner one evening and then break the news. Robert came to the salon to pick me up from work and when the manager saw him, his first words were, "Wow, what a good looking fellow, how on earth did you manage to get him?" In that second, all my new found self-worth totally disintegrated, and the evening loomed over me like a black cloud. I knew everything was completely out of control, but could do nothing to stop it.

We went to the York hotel for dinner, and I sat through the meal with my stomach tied in knots, wondering what her reactions would be. Robert, on the other hand, was in high spirits. I envied him his uncomplicated life, and instead of feeling excited, I felt sorry for the mess I was in and even more sorry for Robert, for he truly didn't know what he was letting himself in for. He wined and dined us in style, complimenting her and hung onto her every word and in true Chris Brisley style she was in her element exuding charm. After dinner we were shown into the hotel sitting room for coffee. *Then he dropped the bomb.* He went down on one knee, bringing the ring from his jacket pocket and asked me to marry him. I almost hyperventilated on the spot. Why, oh why, had he done it in this way? Why hadn't he first asked her if we could get engaged? My eyes immediately flew to her face. Her coal black eyes were riveted to the ring. She said nothing, but I could feel the anger seething up from inside her. At first I thought she was going to hit me but instead in a very tight hushed voice she turned her gaze on me and said. "What the hell have you been up to, you little whore?"

For a second, Robert was completely dumbfounded then he stood towering over her. I could see he was shocked. I had never told him about the real Chris Brisley, and I know that if I had, he wouldn't have believed me. How could he, when every time he met this woman, she had been happy and gregarious. I wanted those precious weeks to go on forever, and, in my stupidity, I thought Frank had brought out something good in her. How wrong was I? Suddenly she saw that while she was having a fling I was slipping away from her. The two went at each other like a couple of wild cats while I sat back in a complete trance. I knew my little break from reality was over. Robert couldn't help me. No one could. I was underage, so without her consent, I was toast, and burned toast at that. I was transfixed to the tableau in front of me. How could I do this to Robert? How could I have even thought it would all work out? And how could I say I loved him when I didn't? Liking someone a lot does not turn into love, no matter how much I wanted it to. I realized I had done him a grave injustice. I also realized I'd thrown myself back into the ring and was now once again about to be torn into pieces. Robert gave me the ring, saying he would wait until I was twenty-one. She laughed at him, saying it would be the longest three years in his life. In the end I asked him to leave the hotel. I walked with him to the entrance and gently told him he was better out of it. I know he was completely stunned by Chris Brisleys' verbal abuse. He wanted me to leave with him immediately, and to hell with the consequences, but of course I couldn't do it; I knew she would find me and drag me back. I told Robert there were too many pitfalls and if he stayed around the result could be catastrophic. That may have seemed a cowardly thing to do but I was doing it for him; he certainly didn't deserve to be swallowed up in all this crap. What a lucky escape he had! I never saw Robert again, but a couple of years later I heard that he had got married, and at the Abbey in Bath, no less.

I couldn't leave the house for over a week after Chris Brisley had dealt with me. The beating and the screaming was so loud, the elderly woman who lived next door came to find out what was going on. I crept to the top of the stairs to listen as my reputation was being annihilated and hear the neighbor commiserate with her. It was even suggested that I be taken to a doctor to see if I was pregnant as that could be the only reason any man would want to marry me. He was a really special person, and when I think of him now, I hope he has had, and is still having, a wonderful life.

DAVID

Eventually Frank went back to his unit in the north of England, and Chris Brisley became more psychopathic than usual. Now she turned her full attention back to me with a vengeance. Everything I did was wrong. Every look I gave her was considered insolent. I was back to being the brunt of all her hate and loathing. No malicious word or deed was spared on me.

She still went to the bar at the York hotel, and also to Colerne at the weekends. Everyone who knew her liked her immensely. She could turn the charm on for all she met at the drop of a hat. I was often absolutely amazed at how quickly she would become a completely different individual, especially as, a few minutes before, she'd been bashing hell out of me. Her other dark persona was strictly for me. During this period I kept a low profile and stayed out of her way as much as possible. The only time I ever saw her smile at me was when I dutifully brought my tips home and handed them over to her. I was still saving around a third of them, and was accruing quite a tidy sum. Nothing earth-shattering, but if I ever left her, at least I would have some money to get started with. *If I ever left her.*

One Saturday evening, she told me *we* were going across to Colerne. There was a birthday party for one of the officers, and we both had been invited. I stood staring at her with my mouth open for it was unusual to say the least that any sort of invitation would ever be forwarded to me through her, especially after my abhorrent behaviour with Robert. I wasn't sure if I was happy about having to spend an evening with her radiating charm from every pore as I found it quite sickening. Still, any invitation coming from her was not in any way an invitation that could be accepted or turned down according to my mood; it was absolutely mandatory.

The evening turned out to be fun. Chris Brisley had latched on to a Sergeant Schofield. Apparently she'd met him a couple of weeks before, and I could see that she felt it was the start of something good, especially as he was a widower. It turned out that he was looking for a housekeeper, and thought she would fit nicely. So did I. I thought it a wonderful idea. Maybe she would disappear for a few weeks, *or maybe even longer*.

During the evening I met David. He had just arrived at the base, and as I was one of the few unattached girls there, he latched onto me like a drowning man. He was average in height, with average looks, and a fairly average view of life; still, he was easy to talk to. No fireworks exploding, no immediate, dramatic, earth-shattering attraction, just a nice person to spend an evening with.

As I was now nineteen, I began to realize that there was something else going on in Chris Brisleys' head. As well as being a complete bitch, I think she was a sexually twisted woman. She actually liked men to find me attractive, then, if they came too close, she would stamp on them as she would a bug and then, as usual, give me hell for even looking their way. During the next couple of months, while she made plans to move into Sergeant Schofield's home – needless to say, I had to move with her – she was encouraging David to take me out, but, as always, it would be a controlled outing. If it was to the pictures I had to be home at a certain time. If he invited me to a dance at his base then she would have to be there. If he was asked to dinner it was *by her,* then she would sit and watch us, like a cat playing with a mouse before it pounced. I didn't like him enough to put up with her shenanigans; also, he was too nice to be drawn into her web. So the next time David brought me home from a date I told him it would be best if we didn't see each other again. He then absolutely floored me by telling me that he had asked Chris Brisley if he could marry me. I was completely dumbfounded, for she'd said nothing to me, and I knew she would never let it happen. She was playing with him, watching him and dangling him like a carrot in front of me. To make matters worse, he produced a ring from his jacket pocket and asked me if I would make him the happiest man in the world. It was a warm summer evening, and we were standing outside the Perfect View home as I tried to explain that, although I liked him a lot, I wasn't ready to marry anyone yet; I was too young and, sadly, super as he was, I wasn't in love with him. His face changed from astonishment to complete disbelief. God knows what *she* had told him, but in the next instant, he threw the ring over the embankment and walked away, leaving me standing there not knowing quite what to do next.

When *the woman* asked me how my evening went, looking at her watch to make sure I was back no later than her given time, I told her David had left and I wasn't seeing him again. She seemed quite satisfied with my answer. I think she was getting bored with my little romance, as she put it. That was until I told her he had produced a lovely diamond ring asking me to marry him and when I declined he had thrown the engagement ring over the embankment. She went completely berserk. How could I be so stupid to let him do that. What on earth was she thinking? Did she imagine David would give me the ring as a consolation prize for not agreeing to marry him? She spent the next day over the side of the embankment looking for the ring. I am extremely pleased to say that she never found it.

I met David again a few years later when I was living in Devon. Someone in Bath had given him my address, and he called to say he wanted to meet me again. We went out to dinner at one of the seaside restaurants in Brixham. He was completely amazed at the transformation in me. He was a sweet, charming man, and I am so glad we laid ghosts from the past to rest. For a couple of years, we kept in touch, and then he wrote to say that he was getting married. It was a closure I was happy with.

SERGEANT SCHOFIELD

William Schofield was near retirement, and when his wife died, he bought a house in Chippenham, just outside Colerne. He had two sons. At twenty-two, Leonard, was the eldest son, and already in the RAF, stationed at Colerne. Richard, a year younger, was still away at University. Their father, Bill, as he liked to be called, wanted his own place, where he could put down some much needed roots and have a home for his boys until they got married. He and his wife had lived with the constant moving every few years, and now he was ready to settle down. The house at Perfect View, unbeknown to the old boy who owned it at the time, was rented out by Chris Brisley on a short term let to a very strange man who smelled of dead fish, probably because he worked at the local fish market in Bath. Cases were packed, and we duly moved to Chippenham to live with Bill Schofield and family.

Needless to say, our stay at the Schofield residence turned out to be a fairly short stay, I think five months at the most. It was a strange time, almost like a black comedy, for at first Chris Brisley was on her best behaviour, most certainly viewing the house as her future home, and Sergeant Schofield as a good possibility of being her future husband. Bill Schofield, on the other hand, was looking for nothing more than a housekeeper, someone who would clean his home and cook his meals. Since I was the only one who ever dusted or vacuumed a carpet in her lifetime, she was completely screwed. Now that I was into a much longer journey to get to work each day and home at night, she could only rely on me at the weekends. It was a ridiculous scenario, where I would come home at midday on a Saturday, sprint around the house like some demented creature trying to get it cleaned while Bill was either out at the barracks, or with his buddies. It didn't take too long before he began to realize it was me doing most of the housework, washing, ironing and even the odd meal here and there, while she would privately and constantly bemoan the fact to me that I was a lazy incompetent idiot who didn't know how to do anything properly. I would work as hard as I could because I wanted to stay. Whilst there, I wasn't getting the almost daily beating or tongue lashing which she usually meted out, and if Bill queried anything, she would lie to him, saying either that she had hurt her foot in some way, or was not feeling too well. He'd smile and let it go, but I could see it wasn't going to last. Her mask was slipping and he would often catch the tail end of her verbal abuse to me if he arrived home too early or too quietly. I think the only thing he enjoyed about our stay was Julie, our little spaniel. She would often trail after him, and there was a time before we left when I thought he was going to ask her if he could keep the dog, but nothing was ever said.

One Sunday, Leonard asked me to go for a bike ride with him. It was a warm sunny afternoon and I readily agreed. He borrowed a neighbour's bicycle for me and off we went. It was wonderful. The English countryside is so beautiful, especially in the south. I was loving every minute of it, until I fell off the wretched bicycle. Leonard was by my side in a second, fearing I might be hurt but I was fine, the only thing hurting was my pride and the bike. I felt really silly sitting at the side of the road alongside a bicycle looking as though it had seen better times. We had quite a long walk home and the neighbour was none too happy to see the state of her bicycle. Still, during that walk, Leonard asked me out to a dance the next weekend.

Over the next few months, Leonard and I got to know each other and spent many happy weekends roaming the countryside. He was a really nice person to be with, but for me there were no heart-stopping moments, which was sad for both of us, because even though I so desperately wanted a new life I was, thank God, over the thought that marriage would be the answer to my prayers. One Sunday afternoon, Leonard told me that he wanted us to get married, so that was the end of our friendship; and also, around the same time, it was the end of the working relationship with Chris Brisley and Leonard's father. He told her quite bluntly that he wanted a housekeeper, and she wasn't even close to being that. Angry words were exchanged, and we packed our suitcases and headed back to Perfect View in Bath, with the fish-smelling tenant staying on until his lease agreement was up.

As soon as I could, I headed up to see Mabel Redwood and told her the whole sad story. Although my freedom was again curtailed, at least I didn't spend hours on buses getting to and from the salon.

HARRY LAPHAM

It didn't take Chris Brisley long to get back into the swing of Saturday evenings spent at the RAF club in Colerne, though this time I was never invited.

It was during one of those Saturdays that she met a man called Harry Lapham, who was around the same age as her and had never been married. He was a really nice man who was rather timid and quite shy. Whenever I think about Harry, I feel so sorry for him, for he never stood a chance. Here was a man who had made the air force his life. He was paid well, so for her, had good prospects. Apparently, some years earlier, he'd bought a cottage somewhere near Colerne ready for his retirement. I remember one afternoon having tea with Mabel and telling her that as far as Harry was concerned, Chris Brisley was in for the kill. It was one of my happiest moments when she arrived home one evening and announced that she was getting married. Poor, poor Harry, but oh, how I wanted them to get married, and as quickly as possible.

The wedding was duly arranged. What a glorious day! Mabel and I, along with a few other people trooped off to the registry office and I almost hyperventilated as they made their vows and then left for a week's honeymoon in Weymouth. A door had been opened for me.

Sadly, it didn't take Harry long before he realized he'd made a terrible mistake. His wife was not the charismatic woman he'd thought her to be. A leopard doesn't change its spots, and very soon she had him on a tight leash, hand open for his pay and any savings he had in the bank. Whenever I saw him, he looked like a frightened rabbit caught in the headlights and not knowing quite which way to turn. The only time he stood up to her was when he absolutely vetoed her moving into his cottage which he adamantly said was for his retirement and not before.

About three months after the wedding, Harry announced he was being posted to Aden (as it was called then) for two years. I knew immediately he had put in for the posting. It didn't even cross his mind that she would want to go with him. I guess she figured she had me well under control, but knew that with Harry, two years would be too long to be away from her, and her meal ticket might never return. They argued a lot about Aden, from the searing heat to the vastly different way of life and the fact she'd never travelled abroad before, but he didn't stand a chance.

So, four weeks later, I was taking the now Chris Lapham to the train station in Bath, and almost walking on air. As I helped her on to the train, I couldn't believe it was real. I almost had to pinch myself to make sure this wasn't a dream. Even as she was boarding, she was verbally giving me a long list of chores to do while she was away. The last command she gave was to make sure I fed the dog! As if this was anything new. If I hadn't fed the poor animal, it would have starved to death years ago. Chris Lapham was going out of my life, and somehow I knew that she would never fully be a part of it again.

Before she left, she'd asked my grandmother to come and stay with me. Her excuse was that I would simply have no idea how to look after myself, and she was worried about me. Of course she was worried. There she was, in between a rock and a hard place. Both Harry and I were integral parts of her life, and she didn't want to lose either one. My grandmother stayed for a couple of months, and then realized I was quite capable of looking after myself; besides I think she missed her home. It was during this time that, with Mabel Redwood's help, she truly realized what a terrible mistake she'd made all those years before.

Judith now became a regular overnight visitor, and we had the opportunity to become really close friends. We were a happy trio, and I'm quite sure it made my grandmother feel young again, with two girls filling the home with fun, and an awful lot of laughter.

GRANDMOTHER'S BIRTHDAY

It was my grandmother's eighty-fifth birthday, so Judith and I decided to give her a party. Both uncles were invited. Uncle Bob worked at St. Martins Hospital, and as the party was on a Friday, he said that he couldn't get time off. Uncle Cyril said he would be delighted to come. Judith and I asked some of the staff at the salon if they would attend, so it was an evening of two older people and a lot of very young people. My grandmother was in her element.

I hadn't seen Uncle Cyril since I was that very young child standing before him on the day of Aunt Maude's funeral, and really had very little memory of him, so when this *really* handsome man came through the door, I was so shocked I nearly dropped the birthday cake. I was now twenty, so I guess he must have been in his early fifties. All the girls gravitated to him, which I could see he loved. I stood by, quietly looking on, feeling my heart rate soar madly. I started to flirt with him; after all I was a grown woman and the fact that he was my mother's brother meant nothing to me. I hadn't seen him in years.

The evening was a great success and I could see that my grandmother was thoroughly enjoying herself until she noticed Cyril was paying a little too much attention to me. Suddenly, I heard her say, in a very loud voice, "*Cyril*, remember she is your niece!" She wagged her finger at him, and he gave her a shrug. Turning to me he kissed my nose saying. "It's so easy to forget." He then spent the rest of the evening flirting with Judith, while I drank everything I could get my hands on.

By the time the evening was over I was starting to feel like death. The only alcohol Judith and I usually had was a ghastly drink called Babycham. It was the in thing of the day, and tasted rather like apple cider, with hardly any alcohol at all. I don't think either of us liked it very much, but it made us feel extremely adult, especially as it was always poured into Champagne glasses. The only thing I remember about the end of the evening was the humiliating fact that Judith had to pull me up the stairs with Cyril pushing at the rear while I held a bowl in front of me in case I was sick. What a way to end my grandmother's birthday, and how embarrassing that this attractive man should see me in such a state.

Needless to say, I was too ill to go to work the next day but as it was a Saturday, and a half day at the salon it wasn't too bad and in any case I didn't give a damn. I was too concerned about the lunch, for I had foolishly invited Cyril to join us before he went back to London. All I wanted to do was lie in bed and die quietly. I managed to get up and get dressed without being sick again, while ignoring my grandmother who tutted every time she saw me. I was intent on getting through this lunch as quickly as possible.

Judith, bless her, came home with a cheap bottle of wine and some nice cod fillets, while I cooked potatoes and peas. All was going quite well, until we started to lay the table. The stainless steel fish cutlery had definitely seen better days so I decided to give them a quick clean with some Ajax cleaning powder while Judith prepared the Cod. A little while later, my Uncle arrived for lunch with flowers *for the sick child* as he put it, and I went off him completely. All was going well in the kitchen, except I couldn't find the Ajax powder I'd put out on a plate ready to clean the knives. I then noticed that Judith was busy frying two pieces of the fish, and realized she had battered them with the cleaner mistaking it for flour. I'm afraid to say that we both became quite hysterical at this, wondering who we were going to give the fish to. I didn't feel like eating, so luckily Grandmother and Judith had the untainted ones. We gave Cyril the Ajaxed Cod, and both took great delight in watching him devour it. He never said a word about the lunch, just kept asking what the hell was the matter with us for we spent the whole meal trying unsuccessfully to behave like young ladies but dissolved into fits of uncontrollable giggles every time Cyril took a bite, I guess we were hoping to get some sort of reaction from him, but he either thought we were lousy cooks, or his taste buds had been severely anaesthetized by the cheap white wine. It was a few years later before I saw Uncle Cyril again but under not such happy circumstances.

ENGLISH TRIFLE

The calamity with the Ajaxed Cod certainly didn't put me off cooking. Watching Mrs Briggs in the BLESMA kitchen all those years ago had always made me feel happy. I enjoyed the warm atmosphere of the kitchen with her bustling around, opening ovens, putting saucepans on the hob and getting all hot and bothered if all the food didn't cook on time, and to her satisfaction. Mind you, she always cooked for at least thirty to thirty-five patients each day, so I thought of her as some kind of miracle worker. Now with my grandmother staying with me for the summer, and the memory of Mrs Briggs telling me that cooking was common sense, I felt I had a responsibility to look after grandmother as best I could, though on looking back, I think she rather wistfully hoped I would always bring food in. She didn't cook. In fact, I don't think I ever saw her in the kitchen, as far back as I can remember.

My first real adventure into desserts was to make an English trifle and those who know how easy this dessert is to make will be surprised that, when finished, mine bore no real resemblance to a trifle at all. I bought fresh raspberries, a raspberry jelly, custard powder and a *very* large round jam sponge. My grandmother was excited, because not only was trifle one of her favorite desserts, she was sure that it was something I could easily manage. I put the raspberries in a cut glass bowl, then the *whole* sponge cake on top, and lastly the jelly. This would go into the fridge until set. I then made the custard, which I thought should be made fairly thick, so that when the whipped cream was spread over my creation, the custard would be firm enough not to sag in the middle. I must say when finished and decorated I thought the trifle looked like it should and I was more than pleased by the oohs and aahs from both Judith and grandmother as I carried it to the table with some pride.

As it was a Sunday, we had roast Lamb for lunch, with all the trimmings. I could hardly wait to sample my first dessert, *but* the problem was how one could get a serving spoon into a trifle that was a bit like digging into very heavy clay. It was like a *really* over cooked fruit cake; not only did it weigh a ton, it tasted horrible. I couldn't understand it, what a disaster. My long suffering grandmother smiled rather sadly and said, "Better luck next time."

I don't know why Judith and I didn't bin it straight away, but we decided it shouldn't be wasted so we gave a portion to Julie the dog. We stood over her as she gave it a sniff and then, with a disdainful look at us, left the kitchen. Undaunted, we then took it out to the garden for the birds. I think it was our 'waste not, want not' era. Sadly, even the birds turned their beaks up at it. So the next day the now infamous trifle was scraped up off the grass and brought back to an outside drain and I tried to poke it through the grid while Judith ran the kitchen water to wash it away. It still wouldn't budge, so in the end, we had to lift the drain cover off, to get as much of the now disgusting mess into some aluminium foil and put it in the bin. We both ended up sitting at the dining table, screaming with laughter. I think my poor grandmother thought we were both having a fit.

RICE PUDDING

I've always had a sweet tooth, so while never having a problem with savory dishes, such as Sunday roasts, I longed to finish a meal with a really nice dessert. *The woman* was a terrible cook, but the one thing she could make was a great rice pudding. Having got over the disastrous trifle episode, I thought I would once more try my hand at making a dessert. In those far-off days, very few people had cookery books, and I was no exception; and I never really thought of getting one. Anyway, I decided that if *the woman* could make a rice pudding so could I.

I had already bought the pudding rice, and stood for ages in the kitchen agonizing over how much rice I should put in the dish. I started off with a few dessert spoons of rice, but it looked so pathetic that in the end I put the whole packet in, with probably an equal amount of sugar. I poured a pint of milk into the dish, stirred it vigorously and then into the oven. I knew it would take about an hour to cook, but even so, I hovered over the oven like a worried parent waiting for her child to do something wonderful.

When at last I took the pudding out of the oven I knew I had failed yet again. The whole pudding was so heavy that I could hardly pick it up and it had literally come away in a solid mass from the sides of the dish. I turned it upside down and it made a loud thud as it hit the plate. I felt hysteria rise up in my throat as I thought of my poor long suffering grandmother sitting in the dining room, no doubt hoping against hope that I had at last made a dessert to be proud of.

I carried it into the dining room on a now cracked plate and solemnly showed her the results of my culinary labors. She looked at it and then solemnly said, "If you make a few more of those, you will be able to build a house." I returned it to the kitchen without saying a word.

It was not until some time later, when I bought a Robert Carrier cookbook, with a wonderful recipe for French rice pudding, that I had the courage to try again. I am proud to say my rice puddings have never failed since, but I often think of my grandmother and the expression on her face as she stared yet again at one of my culinary disasters.

***

During my grandmother's stay, and while I was tidying her room, I found two unframed photos of my mother, tucked away in a drawer. One was taken on her twenty-first birthday, and the other on her wedding day. I knew the framed ones were at her home, so I asked her if I could have them; then at least I would have something. To my astonishment, she refused; even when I said there were duplicates at her home, she still refused me. I was stunned. When she was away from the room, I would take them out of the drawer, look at them, then carefully put them back again. Eventually I could no longer take it, and one morning, I took them out of the drawer, and never put them back. I still have them today, and my darling husband had them framed for me. Was it a bad thing to do? I don't know. The only thing I do know is that, at the time, I desperately needed something, anything to hold on to. I was still floundering in a world where any family I did have didn't really have me.

About a week later, my grandmother became seriously ill. I had never seen her in the middle of an asthma attack and it was one of the most frightening experiences I have ever witnessed. I thought she was going to die. I called Uncle Bob, and she was rushed to hospital. He came to see me later that evening and told me the attacks were now more frequent, and as frightening as they were, she always pulled through. He also said that when she was better, she should go home. She was far happier in her own surroundings. I'm not sure whether those were his thoughts, or whether my grandmother had conveyed them to him.

Judith and I settled into the house at Perfect View, and I couldn't believe life could be such fun. Although her boyfriend was mostly away in the navy, I think he was pushing her to get engaged. We never talked much about him, and I always felt the day would come when she would bid him farewell. Anyway, while he was away, she met a boy called Michael, though for some reason he had been nicknamed *Sos*! We never did find out why. He had a friend called Tony, and after a couple of weeks we four became an item. It was the first time I really had fun dating. Both Judith and I liked them, but not in a romantic way. Still we saw a lot of them, until Judith told me she couldn't take Sos any more. The foursome was duly disbanded and we settled for the Salamander coffee house, pictures at the weekend and various strange meals during the week.

THE COAL SHED

Judith and I were avid film goers. First, we would go to the Salamander for coffee, then off to see the latest movie and usually ended up at the local Chinese restaurant. On this particular evening we went to see a film called 'Psycho' with Anthony Perkins and Janet Leigh. It scared the living daylights out of us. When the rocking chair turned, revealing the hideous decaying face of Bates's mother, I literally jumped on to Judith's lap. Even a good slap-up meal after the film didn't help to get the rocking chair sequence out of our minds. We caught the bus home, with each of us vowing we'd never go to see that sort of film again.

When we arrived back at Perfect View, the house felt cold and damp, so I decided to light the fire, as neither of us were early to bed people. Ah, to be young again!

The coal shed was outside, so I gallantly volunteered to fill the coal bucket, while Judith made a hot chocolate drink. It was dark outside, with a fine drizzle starting and as there was no light in the coal shed, I must have taken longer than usual for Judith was worried and came to see if I needed help. As I was coming out of the shed, I saw a dark shadow looming over me and I imagined it was Anthony Perkins's dead mother. I was so scared that I turned and fell full length back into the coal shed. Judith thought it was the funniest sight she'd seen in a long while, because by the time she managed to get me out of the shed, I was covered from head to foot in black coal dust. From then on, I made a silent vow always to make sure that the coal bucket was filled during daylight hours.

Yes, life was good, and by now, I had quite a healthy savings account, which I had transferred from my post office savings into a bank account.

One weekend, while Judith was away with her boyfriend, who was home on leave, Mr Crouther, the landlord of Perfect View, a strange old boy who looked and smelled as if bathing was a forbidden luxury, came to tell me he needed to sell the house. I remember sitting staring at him, not knowing quite what to say. When I asked why, he said that he'd got himself into a spot of bother with the bookies and needed money. Well, for me, there was a simple solution. *I would buy the house!* I couldn't think what else to do. Trying to find somewhere else to live seemed insurmountable. I told him I would pay a lump sum upfront, and then pay the mortgage off each month at the same price as the rent. At first I thought he would decline. We sat looking at each other for what seemed like an eternity. He stood, walked around the room for a few minutes then came back to me and shoved a very grimy hand out saying it was a deal. After he left, my euphoria lasted all of a couple of hours, for though I had a few thousand saved it was nowhere near enough for the down payment that would satisfy Mr Crouther. My next task was to go to the bank as soon as possible and ask them for an overdraft. My thoughts then honed in on Chris Lapham, wondering what she would make of it. Somehow, I didn't think she would be happy at all. Still, she would be away for at least another eighteen months, and if all went belly up, I knew that Harry had a cottage somewhere in the country, so at least they would not be without a home.

My meeting with the bank manager on the following Monday was during my lunch break, and by the time I got to the bank I was almost certain the overdraft would be refused. I had set out all my expenses plus my weekly salary and kept my fingers crossed. At that time, unmarried females of my age did not get mortgages or overdrafts. It was always feared they would get married, leave work, and have babies. But this bank manager smiled as I gabbled on, telling him that this was a good business venture. Though he shook his head once or twice, to my great relief he eventually said I could have the bank mortgage. I flew back to the salon as if on wings, not truly comprehending just what I had achieved. *So I now owned a house*!

I didn't have a phone in the house, but whenever necessary, I would ask my neighbour if I could use hers. On a warm Sunday morning, she knocked on my door, telling me that Mrs Lapham was on the phone. I nearly had a heart attack on the spot. Whatever the reason for the call, I knew it wouldn't be good. Sure enough, as soon as I picked up the receiver, without even saying hello, she told me curtly she would be home within the week. When I weakly asked about Harry, her reply was that he would be staying for the full two years. She gave no reason for her return, and I didn't ask. I had some serious thinking to do. Judith and I stayed awake long into the night when I told her that *the woman* would be returning home.

As we sat drinking hot chocolate into the early hours, Judith said. "Okay, so now you have no option, you'll have to leave."

"If I leave her, I can't stay in Bath. She'd probably kill me within the week. Besides I now have literally no savings."

"I'll talk to my parents and ask them if you can stay with them until you get sorted out. My boyfriend and I have split up at last, and I am ready to leave Bath."

It all seemed too good to be true, and for me, Devon seemed an oasis from a very stormy sea. During that week, Judith made me pack a couple of suitcases so that if things got really nasty, I could make a hasty exit. As it turned out I was *very* glad of those suitcases. We hauled them into a taxi and put them in the staff room at the salon. Judith's parents readily agreed to my staying with them, and by the time this was all set up Chris Lapham had returned.

The last day at Perfect View will be seared into my very soul forever. For many years after I left her, I would wake up in the night, drenched in sweat from the same terrifying nightmare. I would struggle to reach reality, for in my dreams I was still in *her* clutches and those black empty eyes would bore into me while she told me I could never leave her. Well, leave her I did.

It was a week since she had returned from Aden. A whole seven days with questions firing at me from all directions. I think that deep inside her, she was so very afraid she had at last lost control of me, for, unknown to me, she and Harry had separated. Still, for that week, nothing had changed. We both slipped back into our roles, and it was as if she had never left. I fought so hard to walk out but those months away from her were rapidly fading, and the resolutions I'd made with Judith were being slowly stripped away. I was the terrified child again.

It was on the Wednesday that *the woman* saw Mr Crouther in town, and he told her about me buying the house. She was waiting for my return at lunchtime, and as I walked through the door, she literally screamed at me, asking me who the hell I thought I was. "You're a mere nothing. You always were and always will be. How dare you think you can do things behind my back? You think you're so clever buying a house." Her hand went out as she asked for the papers. I readily gave them to her, signing the mortgage over to her. It wasn't that I gave into her, I knew that if I left her, I didn't want to be saddled with a mortgage on a house I now didn't want. It was a huge relief, for even though I now had no money, I felt that the last problem had been removed, and I could now leave without any loose ends, still hoping and praying I would have the guts to do just that. We stood in the living room, eyeing each other, me wondering what was coming next for I could see she was getting ready for yet another battle.

I was unaware that, during the few months living on my own, with Judith staying for most of the time, the next door neighbour had taken a keen interest in what we did. The neighbour was a typical spinster, a dour old woman in her seventies, who hardly ever smiled, and thought the world was going to hell in a handbasket. Apparently, she'd seen the suitcases leaving the house and felt it her duty to tell Chris Lapham that, while she was away, we girls had had a few parties where young men entered the house; though she couldn't be sure if they'd ever stayed overnight, there was a lot of music and noise going on. When *the woman* told me about this, I remember thinking this was quite a Dickensian scene, with the wicked witch holding all the cards again, *as usual*.

Her eyes became mere slits, as all this information was spewed out with such venom that one would have thought at the very least Judith and I had set up a brothel. Her first question was, "Why were you taking suitcases out of this house?" Her second question was,

"How many men have you and your friend had to stay while I was away?" I stood before her completely dumbfounded by these questions, wondering how on earth she could know. Then it dawned on me. It must have been the neighbour. The most ridiculous thing was that the only person I had shared a bed with was Judith. I was far too terrified to let anything happen, and besides, as far as sex was concerned, I was still an innocent. I thought that kissing someone you liked was absolutely wonderful. I had no wish or desire to go any further. Also, the world was not so sex-oriented as it is today. I think nowadays most young people seem to have sex on the first date. From a very young age, I vowed that if I ever managed to get away from the Brisleys I would *never* be owned by anyone ever again. Sex meant just that, being owned by someone. So, on that fateful day, I was standing at one end of the living room with the window behind me staring across at her. She made everything in life seem so dirty. I don't think I ever hated her as much as I did then. Here she was once again back in my life and here I was *still* taking crap from her. My mind went completely blank.

"Are you thinking of leaving me?" she suddenly asked, literally smirking at me. "You'll never leave me, but if you do, you'll end up in the gutter, which is exactly where you belong. Your mother must be turning in her grave. I've thanked God every day she is dead and will never know what kind of person you are." *The woman* took a couple of steps closer and almost whispered, "Are you leaving? Just say yes or no." She kept repeating those words as she moved closer and closer toward me. Her large body casting a dark shadow over mine.

It seemed forever that I stood staring back at this terrible creature. In my head I kept saying *just say yes, for God's sake say yes* and let it all happen.

Then it did happen. I've heard that, when someone is under incredible stress, the mind can do strange things. Well, I guess my mind did just that. As I whispered *"Yes,"* I literally floated across the room, and stood outside my body. I was actually standing looking at a young girl who was the image of me. It was the word *yes* that changed my life forever. Somehow I knew it was me, yet this girl was so strong as she stood for the *very first and last* time before this woman who had completely annihilated the first part of her young life. I was not afraid, I was calm, and I knew this was the turning point in my life. I didn't know what lay ahead; I didn't know how far her rage would take her. I knew my life would begin or end with this altercation.

From then on, all hell broke loose. She started to scream at me, telling me Harry, her new husband, didn't like married life and had asked for a divorce and there was no way in hell I was going to slink away as well. Poor Harry, it didn't take him too long to realize what a horrendous mistake he'd made, but I was so relieved for him that he had got out before she ruined his life as well.

As *the woman* ranted on, the girl started to talk. I know this will sound strange but it really was as if I was watching another person. I was in awe at how she stood up to this woman.

"If you leave me you'll be even less than you are now, which isn't much." she screamed. "You will never get away from me. I will hunt you down like a dog."

The girl told her that if she was to end up in the gutter, it would be a damn sight better place than living another minute with her. She then told the woman how she'd completely destroyed her life so far, but this was the end. She wasn't going to ruin any more of it. She also said how much she hated the woman, she hated her for all the years she'd battled with this overwhelming and destructive emotion that had crept into her heart and sat there like a stone for as far back as she could remember. No child should grow up with those terrible feelings No one should ever hate another human being as much as she did. Maybe, one day, in a far-off place, she would leave the hate behind her, but oh not yet, *definitely not yet*.

The girl then disappeared as quickly as she had materialized and I was suddenly standing there all alone. For what seemed like an eternity we stood staring at each other. Then the most overwhelming thing happened. *I wasn't afraid anymore.*

With that, *the woman* launched herself at me, grabbing my arm in a vice-like grip and propelling me out of the room and up to my bedroom, literally throwing me across to the other side of the room. But in those precious moments I had changed. I didn't know what she would do to me, I only knew at last she had no terrifying hold over me. I stood watching as she opened the wardrobe, grabbing my clothes and tearing them to shreds. "If you walk out of this house, you walk out with the clothes you stand in." She was quite maniacal, and, as usual, completely out of control. She opened the dressing table drawers, throwing the contents on the floor, stamping on anything looking worthwhile, and then smashed the now empty drawer over my head. She was between me and the door, but I knew somehow I must get to the door before she killed me.

"If you're thinking of leaving me, you're even more stupid than I thought you were. Do you think your so-called friend is going to worry what happens to you?"

I wanted to scream back at her that Judith was the only person in the world who cared what happened to me.

I moved toward the door, but she was faster than me and blocked the exit. She shoved me back into the bedroom, snarling "You'll never leave me. You don't know what it's like out there. No one will want you, you're just an ugly awkward human being who has no purpose in life." She punched my face and I saw stars, she punched me again and I felt my nose start to bleed, I saw her fist coming at me for a third time but this time she hit me in the stomach. I had never *ever* touched her in any aggressive way, but I was now hell-bent on leaving this house alive, and I knew without a doubt that she wasn't going to let me go. I propelled my body into her with all my might. She was so surprised that she lost her footing, and fell against the wall with me on top of her. She kicked and punched at every and any part of me within her reach, then, with all my might, I elbowed her and ran past her. I knew by the look on her face that it was time to leave. I simply flew down those stairs with her careering madly after me. I ran out of the house and down the road like a thing possessed. My only thought was to get as far away from her as possible. I ran without stopping all the way to the salon to tell Judith

I had left the woman.

When I arrived at the salon I looked as if I had been hit by a truck but I didn't care. Susan, one of the older hairdressers, took one look at me, and, without asking any questions immediately drove me to her flat to get me cleaned up. I wanted to leave Bath as soon as possible, but I actually stayed until the end of the week so I would get paid! For it would be all the money I had in the world. It was incredible, but the manager seemed completely oblivious to the comings and goings concerning me. For the rest of week I still looked a mess, but nothing was ever said. Susan brought me to work each morning and took me home each evening; she was like a human shield, saying that if Mrs Lapham came anywhere near me, she would bat her over the head and somehow I believed she would. Judith, who had already given in her notice, made plans for us to travel to Newton Abbot on the Friday evening. I never saw Susan again, but I will always be thankful to her for taking care of me during those last days in Bath.

I don't think I have ever experienced before or since the feeling of absolute and utter elation. It bubbled out of me even while I was still living so close to her. I was away from Chris Lapham forever. So now, at twenty-one, at long last, I was free. I was free.

FREEDOM IS JUST A WORD

Of course the euphoria didn't last; how could it? I was not equipped in any way to take charge of my own life or make my own decisions. *She was still there in my mind*, still controlling my thoughts. I would see her around every street corner, would wake up sweating at night knowing that she was in the room waiting to kick hell out of me and drag me back, never to have the courage to leave her again.

My last week in Bath was horrendous, and I knew I had to start growing up fast. As each day drew to a close I was always amazed that *she* didn't come into the salon. Maybe she was frightened by the new me, and thought I would create a scene there. Little did she know that I didn't think my other me would come to my rescue again. I was so terrified of how I would react if I came into contact with her before I left Bath, because I didn't think I'd be strong enough for a second round.

Each day seemed to go on forever, and, as skinny as I was, I think I lost a considerable amount of weight. I remember how worried Susan was when I couldn't eat, and when I did, it didn't stay down for long. *Oh God, I had to get away from Bath and her.* Brian was the one person I found it difficult to say goodbye to. We held on to each other, while he literally sobbed on my shoulder. He was a wonderful friend to me, and, in his way, most certainly helped me to move on with my life.

At last, Friday evening came, and Judith and I were sitting on the train, heading for Newton Abbot and the new life ahead of me. Judith's father was at the station to meet us. I'd met him on a couple of occasions, when he'd come to visit Judith in Bath; she'd obviously told her parents of my circumstances, for he was very sweet, telling me that he and his wife were looking forward to my staying with them until I got settled.

I was only two years younger than Judith, but the childlike

creature who arrived at her parents' home must have been a strange sight. Judith wore her curly hair long, and as usual, it was swept up in a sophisticated chignon. Mine was short and wavy and not exactly flattering. She was always beautifully made up, whereas I still had to learn the art. My two suitcases were duly unpacked with great care. Judith and I had bought the clothes while Chris Lapham was in Aden. They were feminine and pretty, so perfect that I found it very hard to even put them on. I thought everyone would look at me and wonder why someone so plain would be wearing such beautiful clothes. Actually, they were quite ordinary, but I had chosen them; so, to me, I was now a woman of the world, and they were lovely. I carefully hung them up, not wanting to get a single crease in them; and to this day I still have a phobia about that.

Later, as I sat in the front room looking across at Elsie and Raymond Chamberlain, I felt completely and utterly tongue-tied. Here were two strangers who had invited me into their home and I couldn't even string a single sentence together; but I silently thanked God for Judith's friendship and their generosity, for without them, God only knows what would have happened to me.

After the weekend, Judith went back to Bath to work her notice out, and to collect any remaining things from her boyfriend's parents' home. I was now truly alone, living with two people who didn't know me, and often must have wondered what the hell Judith was thinking about, making friends with such a strange and introverted girl. But they never saw us when we were out together. Only then did the real me shine through. We always had a lot of fun. It was then that I would let my hair down and learn to be me. I could make Judith laugh, and I revelled in that. In fact, I realized that I was actually very witty, and people enjoyed being in my company. It was like being back at school, and being the class clown, but I always had to be with someone I knew, like Judith. I couldn't be witty or amusing if I was with people I didn't know. It was then that those demons would come out, and I would become silent and awkward.

When I was alone with the Chamberlains, I was polite to the point of absurdity. I would only speak when spoken to. I was very afraid that, any day, they would ask me to leave, for although I wanted to stay in this state of limbo, realistically, I knew it was impossible. I never went out, for although Judith was sure that Chris Lapham didn't know where I was, *I knew she would find out.* I had nightmares almost every night that she was standing over me with a hatchet, telling me I was never going to get away from her. Realistically, I always knew she would come looking for me; it was just a matter of time. I imagined I could see her face wherever I looked; sometimes I thought I would go out of my mind. A knock on the front door would make my heart race so much that I would feel faint. The Chamberlains became worried about me, and asked if I wanted to see a doctor, for although I had not told them anything about my life, or the fear of her finding me, Judith had obviously filled them in on a few things. I know they had no idea of what had happened to me as a child, and through my teenage years. I was much too embarrassed to talk about it, for I always felt somehow it was my own fault; it certainly was my own fault that I'd stayed for so long.

A couple of weeks later, Raymond Chamberlain sat me down in the sitting room, and asked me what was I going to do with my life. I was never quite sure if he was telling me to move on, but I do remember feeling quite sick with anxiety because, although I kept pushing it to the back of my mind, I knew the time had come for me to find a job, and somewhere to live. Back then my biggest problem was still going out alone and being paralyzed by the fact I *was* alone. I still had the terrible overwhelming phobia that everyone was looking at me, snickering at how ridiculous I was. I could still hear her telling me *what a stupid person I was and how I was just a monosyllabic idiot.* So I wanted to be by myself, somewhere safe where I didn't have to make decisions and see people. But I knew this was a fantasy, a place where I had lived most of my life. Now it was time to face reality, do the things I had always dreamed of doing. *Easier said than done.*

Raymond Chamberlain was really very kind to me, and I began to see him as the father I always wanted. He took time to find addresses of salons looking for stylists and told me to go to see them, and to get the best salary I could. And so, dressed in my new clothes, I dutifully took the bus into Torquay and did the rounds. By the end of the first day I had no less than three job offers. I felt completely elated. I chose the salon where I felt they wouldn't expect too much of me. It was also agreed that I should stay on with the Chamberlains until I settled into my new job before taking the next step. Now, at least, I could pay for my keep, which made me feel better, and I'm sure, made them happy. In the weeks that followed I began to feel less anxious, though it was a slow and often painful procedure. I would go to work and then almost run home, to hide myself away until the next day, and the same routine would start all over again.

Judith arrived home, and confided in me she didn't want to live too near her parents. She was used to the freedom she had had while living in Bath, so she started looking for jobs further afield. Eventually she found a job in Salcombe, and although we saw each other at various weekends, it was the beginning of a gradual separation between us. We were still very close friends, but Judith didn't need me as much as I needed her. It was a painful and learning time for me, for I had to let this friend go and find her way in life while I continued on a path of my own.

The first time I was asked out by some of the girls who worked in the salon, without even thinking I immediately apologized, saying I couldn't go, because I had things to do that evening; then I realized I could, there was nothing and no one to stop me. I called Raymond Chamberlain to say that I would be home late, and duly went to the pictures. Halfway through the film I felt so ill that I had to leave; my stomach was in knots, and I felt sure I was going to throw up. *She was still there in my head!* And it didn't matter how hard I tried telling myself that she wasn't waiting outside the cinema; a voice inside my head told me she probably was. I slunk out, and ran all the way to the bus stop, not daring to look right or left until I was safe inside the Chamberlain home. I was a complete mess. The very thought of her would give me heart palpitations, real heart palpitations, and try as I might to move on, I was still governed by her, even in her absence. Even when she was away in Aden with Harry, there were many times when I would be out during an evening, and suddenly I could literally feel her presence and imagine myself arriving home, with her waiting for me on the other side of the door. Now here I was, a grown woman, leading a life without her, yet she was still there. Would I ever be normal? Would the time ever come when I wouldn't think about her? And would the time ever come, if I saw her again, when I would not crumble under her terrifying stare, that had governed my life for so many years? I couldn't move on, but I wanted to move on more than anyone will ever know.

The next step was to find a flat, for I began to suspect Mrs Chamberlain was getting bored with me living in her home. I completely understood, for it must have been like asking someone to stay for the weekend and then finding that they had moved in for good. I was again lucky, for one of my clients happened to mention that she had a flat in her home, and was looking for someone to rent it. That evening, she took me to see it, and I paid for the first month's rent on the spot. The flat was in Paignton, a few miles from where I worked in Torquay. It was a nice flat. I had my own front door, a bed sitting room, with a small kitchen and bathroom. It was situated in a very pretty area, with a short walk to the beach. It took me another three weeks to pluck up the courage to actually move in. The Chamberlains had to almost throw me out of their home before I made the move.

So here I was, living in a flat in Devon, earning a living, and mistress of my own life. Sometimes it felt so good, and at other times I was scared senseless. I had always dreamed of a life without her but now I wanted so much more. I had never set out to be a hairdresser, and if I was truthful, I wasn't very good at it, maybe because I never had the basic training and maybe it was because I never wanted to be a hairdresser! Still, I was most certainly in the right area to get away with what scant skills I had. Devon is mainly a holiday resort, so, luckily for me, most of my clients were vacationers just wanting their hair styled while they were on holiday. If it wasn't up to their usual standard, they accepted it, knowing that they probably wouldn't be seeing me again.

I always thought that at some point Judith and I would share a flat, but it never happened; she got a job in a yachting village called Salcombe, where she eventually met her first husband. I missed her a lot but I guess it was all part of growing up. We had our own lives to lead, and although we would always be very close friends, we wouldn't be sharing a flat. It was absolutely gut-wrenching for me.

At the weekends, I would still take the bus back to Newton Abbott and stay with the Chamberlains. Sometimes Judith would be there, but if she wasn't, I was quite content to sit with them and watch television. I still couldn't face going out anywhere alone. If Judith came home, we would go into Torquay on a Saturday evening. There was a well known discotheque in one of the big hotels there. We would go and drink our usual Babycham, then dance the night away, mostly with each other.

A couple of years later I remember venturing out alone to attend a party. The minute I arrived I knew I had made a bad mistake. As usual, I stood in the corner of the room watching the interaction between the party-goers, wishing the floor would open and swallow me. I felt self-conscious and overdressed. I prayed no one would come over to speak to me, and also prayed they might, for I felt exceedingly conspicuous standing there, all alone. Eventually, a rather tall, willowy girl walked toward me, and smiling she said, "Oh my God, I do wish I could stand alone and look so sophisticated and sure of myself. How do you do it?" I was so taken by surprise, I wanted to laugh out loud and tell her that the only thing I was doing was planning an escape. Instead I gave her what I hoped was an enigmatic smile and said, "When you've been to one party, you've been to them all." For the rest of the evening she was my constant companion, pointing out various people of interest whom I knew I would never see again. Still, when I eventually arrived back at my flat, I felt the first flicker of exhilaration. The girl thought *I* was sophisticated. Maybe other people thought the same about me. But those times were far away, and I still had a long road ahead before I could consider myself a woman of the world.

CHARLIE'S AUNT

I loved the small flat in Paignton, and had now stopped rushing back to the Chamberlains every weekend; and although I was still very introverted, I was quite content to come home each evening, cook dinner and watch television. At first I didn't know that the two elderly women who owned the bungalow were lesbians, and when I did, it taught me to always accept people for who they were and who they chose, for it was obvious they were very happy together. Some years previously, they had adopted a girl named Judy. She was about three years younger than me, and was away at college, studying to be a teacher. When I eventually met her, we became instant friends, and whenever she came home for holidays or the odd weekend, we would spend hours together, talking and wondering what our future lives would be like. Even then, Judy looked like a school teacher. She was a little plump and rather plain, except that, when she smiled, her face lit up. I was still stick-thin, so she nicknamed me Wispykins and I, in turn, nicknamed her Mugwump! I still have some poetry books she gave me.

Many evenings, when she was at home, she would curl up on my bed, and we would recite poetry, or listen to music. For me, it was a wonderful time. I worked hard, paid my rent on time, and that was all I wanted.

One of the girls at work belonged to an amateur dramatic group, and asked me if I'd like to join. The thought of doing something quite so daring overwhelmed me, and it was completely out of the question, so I declined. But eventually I thought "Why not? Nothing ventured, nothing gained!" That attitude stood me in good stead during the next few years. The group had just started reading for a play called *Charlie's Aunt*, and I was asked to play the part of Amy Spettigue. It was great fun, and I really looked forward to those rehearsal evenings, though I almost lost the part, because, at the start, we only had the use of a small room at the town hall, as the local theatre was fully booked up until two weeks before the play was due to open. We would all sit in a circle and each read our lines. I felt so self-conscious, and stumbled over the words in a low flat tone. The director was mortified, and was, I know, frantically looking for someone else to take my place. It was only when we eventually got to use the stage that I blossomed into a budding actress.

Opening night had a full house, along with Judith and the Chamberlains, my two landladies and friends from work. I was so busy peeking through the side curtain to view the audience that I missed my cue and almost fell headlong onto the stage. Still, I did very well after that, and thoroughly enjoyed the whole experience. However, it did not spark any lasting urge to become a thespian. The opportunity to join the exciting world of the film business came my way later. Satisfied that I had done something different, I gladly went back to my small flat and what I thought was a safe life.

ROBERT SAVARY

I was still working in Torquay when I met a handsome French man called Robert Savary at one of the local coffee bars. He was thirty years old, and taking time out to see the world before settling down. He told me that he had another few weeks in Torquay before he flew off to Greece. We had a couple of dinner dates at one of the local hotels, where they combined an evening of dinner and dancing, which was all very romantic. At nearly twenty-two, I decided it was high time I became a woman and who better than Robert? I could enjoy the whole experience with no strings attached. On our second date, it became obvious his thoughts were running parallel with mine.

Eventually the whole night was planned rather like a military operation, right down to the rather skimpy baby doll pyjamas I bought for the occasion! So one Saturday evening Robert booked us into a small B&B in Brixham. He picked me up at my flat, with me clutching my small vanity case and we drove to Brixham in complete silence. The owner, a rather large woman, showed us into the bedroom saying that dinner would be served in an hour. As she left she gave me a motherly look as if to say *here's another lamb to the slaughter.* It was a pretty room with a large double bed overlooking a small cove. In the corner of the room there was a hand basin with a dressing table to one side. The room is seared into my memory. Passionate kisses were exchanged, and I began to relax, feeling the excitement of events to come.

I'm not sure whether the landlady said anything to the other guests, but I certainly felt very conspicuous as Robert and I sat down for dinner. It seemed that, every time we spoke, the dining room fell silent, as if all were eager to glean any spicy details of our romantic evening. There was no doubt Robert was a very handsome man, so much so that people often stopped to give him an appreciative once over. I felt very smug as the women eyed him with open envy. Dinner ended rather too rapidly for me, and I was beginning to feel decidedly nervous. It's all very well thinking of losing one's virginity but doing the deed was another matter altogether. Robert had no idea that I lacked experience and was thoroughly looking forward to ravishing me, *as he put it.*

We arrived back in the bedroom, and I, along with my vanity case, disappeared into the bathroom. I showered, powdered and perfumed myself and donned my very pretty jammies, stood behind the door for another ten minutes, then bravely walked out into the bedroom ready for the event to come only to be confronted by Robert who was stark naked and washing his feet in the hand basin. To say that I was riveted to the spot is a complete understatement. Any romantic thoughts I had flew straight out of the window, for I can assure you there is nothing less attractive than the sight of a naked man in such a ridiculous posture. Robert was completely oblivious of the effect the scene had on me, and went on performing his ablutions with great gusto. I spent the rest of the night being chased around the room by a very frustrated man, until I managed to lock myself in the bathroom. The morning came at last, and when I timidly ventured out into the bedroom, Robert had left and I was met by a very worried landlady who wanted to know if I was all right. When I assured her that I was, she kindly brought me breakfast, before getting her husband to drive me home. So there I was, still very much a virgin, and wondering whether I would stay that way for the rest of my life!

CHRIS LAPHAM FINDS ME

She was still there, filling my waking hours with indecisions and controlling my nightly dreams. There were times when I thought this woman would always have total control over me forever. In my head, I questioned everything, always unsure, always the child in an adult world. I had lost my childhood, but still couldn't get to grips with this new world that was opening up for me. There was a wall in front of me, and try as I might, I couldn't climb over it, for I knew if I did, as sure as hell, she would be waiting on the other side.

The inevitable day came when I returned to my flat from work, to be greeted by Judy, who was home from college, asking me if I would join them in the garden. I could see by her face that this was not a social invitation. Suddenly, I felt my legs go to jelly, and *I knew* something catastrophic was about to happen.

Along with Judy, the two older women were sitting by a pretty pond, and beside them was a garden table laid out for tea. It should have been comforting but it wasn't. I made it to a chair without collapsing and then said. "She's been here, hasn't she?" All three nodded in unison.

I had never really told them about Chris Lapham or my life, except maybe snippets here and there when Judy and I were together, talking about various happenings in our past. But I could see by their faces that the meeting with her had left an indelible impression on them, and not for the better.

So now this place and my little flat was no longer a sanctuary. She had been here, and had contaminated it. I literally sat and, once again, felt the energy seep away from my body. It was like I had some awful disease eating away at my very soul. I was now in my twenties, and still this woman could unravel me in seconds. The thought of looking into those dead black eyes again made me literally want to throw up with dread. Judy poured tea, not quite knowing how to handle the situation. I must have looked terrible, for both women stood and moved to my side. One took my hand while the other asked me if I wanted a brandy. Suddenly I felt so very tired, my whole body seemed to fall apart and I was thankful I was sitting for there was no coordination in any movement. A terrible lethargy washed over me like a black cloud, a feeling I had not experienced since leaving her. It was a weariness invading every part of my being, making those few precious liberating months a mockery. I would *never* be free of her. I think in those moments my brain ceased to function properly. One part kept saying, *she can't hurt you any more*; yet the other part said *oh yes she can, just you wait.* The sad truth was that I wasn't yet ready to tackle this woman for a second round, and even though I knew I would never go back to her, I also knew she was determined never to leave me either physically or mentally.

We all sat in complete silence, they drinking tea and me staring into the small pond and absently thinking how pretty it was, with all the colourful summer flowers around it. It was the first time I had ever seen a dragonfly up close. It was quite large and a beautiful iridescent blue in color. I watched it swoop and dive over the water, and then fly away. I wanted to be that dragonfly. I wanted to fly away to a far-off place where she could never find me.

I knew it was time to move on. I gave my notice to the salon and told the women that I would be leaving the flat as soon as possible. I knew they understood, and I also knew they were sorry to see me go, but not half as sorry as I was.

I moved back and stayed with the Chamberlains until I found another job, and somewhere else to live. The Globe hotel was one of the biggest hotels, and was situated in the High Street in Newton Abbot. There was a small hairdressing salon to the left of the entrance, and the hotel manager was looking for someone to rent the salon. At the interview, I was told that I could rent the salon on a monthly basis, but I would be my own boss. After twelve months, if I wanted to lease the salon he and I would discuss it. It was exciting, and although I was still stuck with a job I hated, I felt I was moving up the ladder, and would even have two other hairdressers working for me. Now came the time when I would have to be far more careful with my clients, for unlike Torquay, Newton Abbot was not really a holiday town. Most women who would now frequent my salon were women who lived in the area. I decided to, at least, take a course on razor cutting which was all the rage at the time, having tried it once and almost having cut my finger off! Hair-tinting and bleaching was another matter altogether, I was simply hopeless at it. My poor clients never really got the same hair colour twice; still, they kept coming back.

I then found a really super unfurnished flat in an old house just a twenty minute walk away from the hotel, so, once again, I had a place to call my own. During this settling-in time I tried not to think of *Mrs Lapham* and whether she would try to find me again; but I was back with all my old hang-ups, imagining I was seeing her around every corner. There were times when my nerves were so shot to pieces that I could hardly function, only wanting to finish work then run home to my flat, lock the door and hide myself away from her and the world.

It was during this time that I met Anthony. He worked for a company called Cable and Wireless, and traveled around the world. His mother, a wealthy widow, became a client, and would come to the salon for her weekly hair appointments. After a couple of months she decided I was just right for her son. He was working away in some exotic place, but she assured me that as soon as he returned, she would set up a meeting as she thought it was high time that, at thirty, he got married. I must confess I didn't really take too much notice, for a lot of mothers thought I would be just right for their precious sons.

Well, Anthony arrived home, and I was duly invited to dinner to meet him. He was the sort of man you would pass in the street and never really notice, but he was pleasant and very easy to be with. Apparently, he started out in life studying to be a concert pianist but, as he put it, after years of hard work he never quite reached the very high standard necessary to attain his dream. I often listened to him playing, and thought he was extremely talented. Anyway, for a few months we spent a lot of time together. He was very sophisticated, taking me to concerts and some highly intellectual plays, which were extremely boring, but I was having fun, and spending time with an older man made me feel safe and very grown up.

I had started taking cooking seriously, and decided to ask Anthony to dinner to show off my skills. I agonized for simply ages deciding on the menu and I also bought a record of Beethoven's Piano Concerto No. 3 in C Minor, which I thought I would nonchalantly play while we were having coffee. The meal was a great success, the coffee poured. We both sat in silence listening to the music, while I kept thinking how impressed he would be by my choice. When the record finished, and whilst pouring a second coffee, I asked him casually if he enjoyed the piece to which he answered that it was extremely interesting, as he'd never heard it played at high speed before. How embarrassing was that?

The day came when Anthony asked me to marry him. He was off to India for a two year stay and wanted us to be married straight away so we could go together. I couldn't imagine why this worldly man would find me attractive enough to want to marry me, and, being very enthralled by this, I immediately said yes. What another terrible mistake! The second Anthony's mother heard, the news the wheels were set in motion. For the next few weeks my feet hardly touched the ground. After the first excitement wore off, I knew *yet again* that I couldn't go through with it. I wasn't in love with Anthony, though I kept telling myself I was and this would be a good marriage. I would be so far away from *the woman* that she would never find me. I spent many sleepless nights agonizing over the mess I'd got myself into and feeling very sorry for my now fiancé. Anthony's mother was like a mother hen on steroids! I have never known anyone move so fast in preparing for a wedding. It was to be held at the local church, and the reception was to be in the gardens of the family home, with the tent already erected. The material was chosen for the bridesmaids, Judith being one of them. Wedding-dress books were sent to me by the dozen. The engagement ring was bought, and wedding presents were already arriving. It was a whirlwind of activity, with me looking on while being tossed here, there and everywhere. Anthony's mother was a force to be reckoned with. She was in her element, and nothing and no one was going to stop her. One of her main concerns was that I was still working, and she wanted me to finish as soon as possible, but there I stood my ground, and somehow managed to stop her from storming into the hotel telling the manager I would be leaving.

A couple of weeks before the wedding a friend of mine invited Anthony and me to dinner. Along with her family we sat at the table with me listening to them babbling on about how exciting this wedding was, and suddenly I couldn't take any more. I stood, rushed from the room and out of the house, leaving Anthony and my friends wondering what on earth was going on. I ran to the nearest phone box and called the Chamberlain's, begging them to come and pick me up. Later that evening I called Anthony to apologize for my terrible behaviour. The next day he came to the flat, and I quietly told him I couldn't marry him. I told him that, if I did, it would be the cruellest thing I could ever do to him; he deserved someone who truly loved him. Over the next few days, all hell broke loose, with his mother pounding on my door demanding what was going on. She was determined that the wedding should go ahead, even telling me to go away with Anthony for a long weekend. That will tell you how desperate she was. In those days, one wasn't encouraged by parents to have a naughty weekend together. I handed the ring back to her, telling her how sorry I was, but I would not change my mind. Just before Anthony left for India; I saw him standing across the road from the salon, it made me feel so sad, and I almost went out to him, almost said I'd made a mistake, but I didn't; instead, I watched him until he eventually walked away. He was a truly nice person and I hope he met someone who made him a very happy man. Somehow, I'm sure he did.

One weekend, while visiting the Chamberlains, Judith's father gave me a letter addressed to me, and sent to their address. It was from Ken Brisley, telling me he'd met someone at a BLESMA convention who knew where I was now living. Would I ever be able to hide from my past? He'd remarried and wanted to see me again. My first thought was there was absolutely no way, then I realized I wanted *him to see me*. I wanted him to know that, no matter how painful and as yet incomplete, my journey had moved on, and I was slowly picking up the pieces of my life. I was no longer the skinny child he could knock off chairs if I didn't achieve his very high standards, no longer the child who would listen to his verbal abuse, fuelled by her hatred of me.

So the day came when he and Alice, his new wife, drove from Blackpool to spend a holiday in Devon. The Chamberlains laid on a lunch, and I sat with nerves as tight as a drum waiting for their arrival. Ken really hadn't changed very much, and even then, I had to steel myself to make eye contact with him. It was like looking down into a muddy pond and seeing his reflection come slowly to the surface. But Alice was absolutely wonderful. She was a little plump Yorkshire woman who was sweet, loving and gentle, all rolled into one person. She most certainly brought the best out in Ken, and whenever I saw them together I had to pinch myself and come to terms with this new man. Until they died, a few years later, which was just hours apart from each other, I kept in touch. I think mainly I wanted him to know that I had survived.

Life became lonely once again, just work and home, so I decided to buy a dog. I was watching a hilarious show on television called "Green Acres" with Eddie Albert and Eva Gabor. In the show, Eva Gabor had a small Yorkshire Terrier, who was the cutest thing on four legs. It took me some time to find a reputable kennel that bred Yorkies, but eventually I found one in Brixham, and there she was: a tiny little puppy, just waiting for me. That evening, I took her home and I have been in love with Yorkshire Terriers ever since. I named her Pickles, and from then on she went everywhere with me.

So there I was, with a small business, a nice flat and a dog. The scene was set for me to become the quintessential spinster! The next project was to buy a car, but first I had to pass my driving test. I was recommended to an instructor, a Mr Bowes-Lyon, who happened to be a cousin to the Queen Mother. I felt that, with his Royal lineage, he would be the right choice and signed up for six lessons. It was with great excitement that I sat behind the wheel for the first time. I, listening intently to his instructions, started the engine and off we went. It all seemed so easy until I saw a couple of my clients. I waved like mad, honking the horn at the same time, determined that they should see me driving, then completely lost control, and drove straight up on to the sidewalk, almost killing them on the spot. From then on, each time I went for a lesson it seemed to be total chaos. I couldn't get the hang of the gears, and my poor instructor would cover his ears, screaming at me while I ground away at them. Driving down a hill was also another hazard, as I felt completely out of control; I would put the gears into low and crawl at around twenty miles an hour, with simply miles of traffic piling up behind me. By the third lesson, those sharp descents always a challenge, my instructor would find routes that were flat and straight. When I arrived for my fifth lesson, I had a new instructor and was told that, sadly, Mr Bowes-Lyon had a nervous breakdown and would not be instructing me any more. I was firmly convinced that I contributed to his sad state – if not wholly, then certainly a big part of it. Still undaunted, I carried on and after the second attempt I passed my driving exam.

There was a garage a few miles outside of Newton Abbot that sold mostly small cars, and I had seen a white Morris Thousand for sale on their courtyard. That weekend, I visited the Chamberlains, and told Raymond Chamberlain I wanted the car more than anything and had worked out that I had enough money to put half down, and the rest on hire purchase. He sat me down and told me never to buy anything I couldn't buy outright. I should save the rest of the money, so that, when I did buy my car, it would be totally mine. I was simply heartsick; I so wanted that little white car. Anyway, we went to see it, and I told the garage owner I wanted it, and would probably be able to buy it in a couple of months. His answer was, "If it's still here, then it's yours." For the next two months, I saved every penny. With the money firmly in my hand, Raymond Chamberlain drove me to the garage, and my car was still there. It was bought and paid for, and all mine. I drove it home feeling like royalty, wondering if Mr Bowes-Lyon had got over his breakdown yet! I have never forgotten the advice Judith's father gave to me all those years ago, and have never bought anything I could not afford to buy outright.

I now had my work, a car and my flat with just my little Yorkshire Terrier for company and, at the time, it was all I required. I wanted to disappear from the outside world and *her*. I still looked for her around every corner, imagining that she would turn up, either at work or at the flat. I would hear her voice still telling me I was a useless human being, with those cold flat tones sending iced water through my veins. She'd found me once, and who was to say she wouldn't find me again? I would lay awake for hours, wondering how I would react; and although I felt she would never pull me back into her life, I also knew that the very sight of her would have a devastating effect on me. She'd ruled my life so completely from four years of age until I was twenty-one. That's a very long time to have such a huge chunk out of one's life, and not an indoctrination that could be sloughed off like an outer layer of unwanted skin. Believe me, I so wanted my mind free of her, as if she never existed. I often wondered whether, if I saw her lying in the middle of the road, I would rush over to help, or just step over her. My answer to that question still haunts me to this day.

UNCLE CYRIL

I kept in touch with my grandmother, and was happy to learn that she was now living with my great aunt Maude, whom I'd never met, but from my grandmother's letters she sounded happy and content.

It was a sad day when I received a phone call from Uncle Cyril saying my grandmother had passed away. So there it was, the one and only person I'd ever craved love from throughout my childhood and young adult life had gone. On looking back, I often wonder if I'd ever really known her, this rather mysterious woman who'd played such a big part in my yearning to belong to someone, yet never fulfilling the emptiness still surrounding me to this day whenever I think of her.

I went to the funeral, and tried not to show how devastated I felt. The ceremony was short, with Cyril saying a few words, as one does at funerals; then it was back to his home for the wake. It was there that he made the mistake of starting to talk about *the woman* and what a dreadful person she was. I stood almost to attention, listening to him babbling on about how she came into my life. He then made the most terrible mistake of saying, "I said at the time you should never have gone to her." I can honestly say I almost decked him I was so incensed. I told him what I thought of him, then quietly walked out of his life, sadly realizing I'd never even been in his life. I drove through the night back to Devon, knowing it would be the last time I would ever see Cyril again.

It was very easy to slip into a daily routine; I would work hard at the salon, drive home with Pickles, take her for an evening walk, then shut myself away where no one could get at me. I felt safe when the door was locked and the curtains drawn. It was my world, my place furnished to my taste, and I thought of nothing beyond that. To this day, I am a solitary person, happiest when I am in my home with my husband. He's the only person I truly need. Our home is called

Fox Haven, and yes, for us it is and always will be our haven.

While I was living in Devon, I met David Emerson. On our first meeting he told me that if he were an artist he would paint my portrait; thinking he was being facetious, I told him that if he *was* an artist I would let him. It turned out that indeed he was an artist, and a very good one. He painted two pictures of me; one I still have, and the other he sold to Sammy Davis, Jr.

David also introduced me to a man who was looking for models, for a line of clothes named Susan Small. The clothing line was particularly styled for women sized two and under. I most certainly fitted into that bracket, for I was still as thin as a bean pole! My first trip down the runway was at the town hall in Plymouth and caused quite a stir, as I was so nervous I fell off the raised stage at the end and almost landed on a rather large gentleman's lap, but I loved modelling, and I also loved the money! On a chance meeting at one of the shows I was introduced to an agent looking for models, especially photographic models, to work for Chanel. I was given a date and an address in Exeter for the interview, and was so excited I couldn't sleep for a week. On the day, I wore my most tailored suit, plus the highest heels, and sat in the waiting room with six other hopefuls, all striking various poses as they waited for their turn. I got the job, and modeled for Chanel and various other couturiers for the next eight years. At the time, it was a hectic period in my life and I was away from the salon for a few days each week. The two girls who worked for me were exceptionally good, and with the salon doing so well, the girls asked me if I would hire an apprentice. I could now leave the hairdressing side to the professionals, and get on with the work I loved. Later, when I moved to London I still worked for Chanel.

I had now rented the salon for over a year when the hotel manager asked me to go and see him during my lunch break. I thought all dire thoughts, and was absolutely convinced he wanted to get rid of the salon. Indeed, it turned out it was exactly what he wanted to do, except the great part of the meeting was that he asked me if I wanted to buy the lease. There would be a thirty-year lease on the property, but I would have to buy the furnishings. As I left the meeting my head buzzed with excitement. I drove to the Chamberlain home and talked with Raymond; under these circumstances, he thought a bank loan was permissible. During the next week I took all the salon records along to my friendly local bank manager, and in under an hour, I came away with the loan I needed and the realization that I was going places. For the next nine months, I worked every hour possible, modelling for different shows and doing a lot of photographic work. In a very short period, I had paid off the bank loan and had hired another fully qualified stylist. Chris Lapham was steadily moving to the back of my mind and life.

A few months later, a client of mine invited me to a party to mark the completion of her new home, which, at the time, was reputed to be the most modern home in Devon. It was all glass, and, apart from the kitchen, was completely open-plan. Once again, I had the dilemma of whether I should go or not. Still, what had I got to lose? If I didn't like it I could leave. So, putting on my best party dress, I set forth in my little Morris Thousand on a very dark night in the pouring rain. The minute I arrived, the hostess rushed me over to meet a tall thin man she'd picked out for me. I hated him on sight, as I stood listening to him extolling the virtues of women staying barefoot and firmly in the kitchen, and although I'd only just arrived, I knew it was time for me to leave. I also knew I couldn't go through the front door as I would be seen by all. Weaving my way through the crowd, I eventually found the kitchen, relieved to see that it had a back door. I opened the door, and saw that, by now, the rain had turn into a deluge, so I would have make a quick dash to the car. I took two steps and disappeared over a complete mud bank of unfinished landscaping. I fell and slid all the way down, rolling over a couple of times while I tried desperately to stop the fall. At last I reached the bottom, and, as I stood, I realized that there was simply no way out to the front drive. I would either have to stay there until the party had ended, or claw my way back up the mud bank to reach the back door. I eventually made it back to the kitchen, and was literally covered from head to foot in thick mud, my hair plastered firmly to my head with the wet mud running in rivulets down my face. *What to do?* I knew I couldn't stay outside the house for the rest of the evening, I just wanted to get home so I opened the door and, with as much panache as I could muster, I sailed through the house, passing the astonished guests, not looking at anyone as I made it to the front door, dripping mud along the way while everyone stood staring at me in stunned silence. Needless to say, I was never invited again.

ANDREW DONALLY

One Monday morning, when Pickles and I arrived at the salon, there were a lot of people coming and going from the hotel. I soon found out that a film company had moved into the hotel for at least two months, as they were making a film on the moors. It all sounded very exciting. A couple of weeks later, with all the staff finished for the day, when I was about to close, a man walked into the salon, asking me if I cut men's hair, as he was in need of a trim. He had extremely curly hair, so although I'd never ventured into that area of hairdressing I thought it would be pretty easy. As I snipped away, I found out that he was one of the producers of the film, which was called *The White Colt*. Later on it would be re-titled *Run Wild, Run Free* for America. They were afraid that the English title might be confused with a gun rather than a horse. The producer's name was Andrew Donally, and he was to change my life for the next fourteen years.

The film starred John Mills, Sylvia Syms and a young boy called Mark Lester, who had just finished starring in the remake of *Oliver Twist*. The director, producers and stars were staying at the hotel, while most of the crew and the lesser cast were staying in smaller hotels or bed and breakfast establishments around the area. The film was about an autistic boy who lived with his parents on the moors, and fell in love with a wild horse. It showed how he tamed the colt, and, to a certain extent, tamed himself.

It had Newton Abbot abuzz with excitement, for I think it was the first time a film company had stayed there. In the first couple of days, I saw Andrew Donally glancing through the salon door each time he passed into the hotel. One week later to the day he came back, and asked me if I would cut his hair again. At the time I thought he must have a phobia about short hair, and told him it didn't look any different from the last time I cut it. He then laughed, and said he was plucking up courage to ask me out to dinner, and the haircut was the first step. He was a sweet man, rather like a teddy bear, and sixteen years my senior. I instantly became very interested in the film world.

He took me in his chauffeur-driven car to a small restaurant in the country outside Newton Abbot and I quizzed him on what went into making a film. I truly think I was hooked from the very first evening. The next afternoon, he came into the salon and said he had a business proposition to make. The film was being shot on the Moors, and, as Sylvia Syms didn't need to look too groomed, they hadn't brought a hairdresser with them. Would I be interested in doing any hairdressing needed? For instance, the boy who was doubling Mark Lester when riding the colt needed to have his hair bleached to match Mark's very blonde hair. And although Sylvia Syms did not need to look coiffured, there would be times when she required something done to her hair. I jumped at the chance. I had three qualified hairdressers and an apprentice working in the salon, so I knew it was in very good hands. I was absolutely sick with excitement.

On the first day I had to be at the hotel by five a.m., along with the other crew members, to get the bus that would take us to the location. It was another world, full of bustle, lights, cameras and people rushing here and there, all looking as though they were getting nowhere fast, but all knowing exactly what they had to do. I think it was the first time in my life I knew what *I* wanted to do. I had absolutely no idea how I was going to achieve this major change in my life, but I had no doubt I would.

My first hurdle was to bleach the hair of the little boy who would be doubling Mark Lester. As I said before I had never been really good at any sort of colouring and always strictly kept away from bleaching. But what could go wrong? The poor boy came to the salon one evening, and I bleached his hair until clumps of it fell out, poor little fellow. Luckily he had enough left so that no one really noticed what a state his hair was in, and as they did all the filming on him at the beginning of filming, he didn't have to go through the ordeal again; but he most certainly had a very sore head for quite some time. While on the location, I had to set Sylvia Syms's hair a couple of times, which was fine, for her role was that of a rather harassed country wife. I also had to cut John Mills's hair, which wasn't so good; in fact it was a complete nightmare, and, at the time, I was so very glad there were no mirrors in the makeshift hairdressing caravan. I do know that his wife, Mary Haley Bell, was quite aghast when she saw what I had done to her famous husband. That, coupled with the fact that, early on, I thought she was the mother of Mark Lester's stand-in, kind of froze me out of their inner circle.

Still, I was in my element, but knew I had to set my sights on something other than hairdressing if I wanted to make it in the film industry. I became friends with Andrew Donally's secretary who told me that she was leaving at the end of the film and I decided that would really be a good job for me.

One afternoon, while I was sitting in one of the caravans, Andrew came in. I hadn't seen too much of him in the past couple of weeks and was still rather in awe of him, for he was the producer, and all roads led to him. He sat beside me, then suddenly smiled.

"How long have you been hairdressing?"

I was so surprised by this question and for a moment didn't quite know how to answer. "I own a hairdressing salon," came my defiant reply.

"I know, and owning it very well, but I don't think you were born to be a hairdresser."

I laughed. "Are you firing me?"

"No. I think you'll do, as long as you don't have to bleach any hair again."

I knew this was the man and this was the time when I should tell him I wanted to join the film industry. He sat listening to me as I told him about my journey into the hairdressing world and how I wanted out. I could see it amused him.

"Okay, so you want to work in the industry. What can you do?"

I thought for at least two seconds. "I hear your secretary is leaving."

"Yes, so she is."

"Well, I think that's the job for me."

At this Andrew laughed out loud. "Are you as good at that as you are at hairdressing?"

"Infinitely better."

"You can type and do shorthand?"

"Typing isn't a problem," I answered with fingers crossed. "I don't do shorthand, but I can write very fast." I almost laughed out loud at my audacity, *but* I knew he was hooked; besides, I also knew that he was in love with me, and love and judgement don't always go together.

"All I can say is, you'd better be typing by the time we start our next film and you will also have to move to London." With that, he left the caravan, and I nearly had a heart attack on the spot.

From then on I spent almost every day on location. It was the very first time I realized there was a life that didn't consist of just work and home. There were exciting and colourful people leading extraordinary lives, and here I was, about to join that wonderful industry of make-believe.

All too soon, filming came to an end and the production team moved back to Shepperton studios, which was situated about an hour from London. I bought an old typewriter, and got to work learning how to use it, with lukewarm success. I was still pretty sure I could wing it; I mean, how much typing could there be? Most of the work was done either on location or on set, and I thought it would be the odd letter or two. How wrong could a girl be?

The next few weeks were a whirlwind of activity, getting things sorted out in Newton Abbot and ready for the imminent move to London. I was lucky with the salon, for I knew someone who had asked me on numerous occasions if I was interested in selling the business. I gave my landlord one month's notice and made arrangements to put my furniture in store until I found somewhere to live in London. It was during this time that Andrew told me he'd found a flat in St. John's Wood, and would I move in with him? My furniture was promptly moved into the smallest room, looking rather silly and nondescript, in a very large beautiful flat. It had previously been an Arab Embassy and was in desperate need of a complete overhaul so, for a few weeks, we were to stay with Ed Harper and his partner Joanne Stewart at their rather small rented flat near Primrose Hill. Ed had been the production manager, and Joanne the wardrobe mistress on the film in Devon, and I got to know them quite well; I really liked them, and was looking forward to seeing them again.

I left Devon on Christmas Eve. I caught the evening train to London and sat by myself in a first-class compartment with Pickles. I remember telling her that we were on a really big adventure, but if I had the courage to admit it to myself, I was a little scared of what that adventure entailed. I was moving to London to work and live with a man I hardly knew and hadn't even slept with. What was I thinking? The train pulled into Exeter station, and a fascinating couple got on and entered the carriage in a flurry. The man looked to be in his eighties, and the woman quite a bit younger. She was extremely beautiful, and looked like a character out of the film *Dr Zhivago*. She wore a coat down to her ankles, with a dark fur collar and a Cossack hat. She smiled at me, and I thought she was one of the most exotic women I had ever seen. I was transfixed by their conversation, and it became obvious that they were connected in some way to the entertainment industry, for they had been to see a play in Exeter, and were extolling the performance of some young boy whom the elderly man was interested in managing. As I listened to their conversation, I wanted to tell them soon I too would be in the entertainment business but they were so wrapped up in their conversation, and I satisfied myself with the knowledge that we were all three leading an exciting life. When we reached London they quickly left the train and disappeared into the crowd. I silently thanked them for making the journey go that much quicker, and for keeping the butterflies in my stomach at bay for a few hours, for I didn't truly know what the future had in store for me.

Over the next fourteen years, I worked on some incredible films. *Run Wild, Run Free* (1969), *Cromwell* (1970), *Nicholas and*

Alexandra (1971), *The Golden Voyage of Sinbad* (1973), *Summer Wishes, Winter Dreams* (1973), *The Internecine Project* (1974), *Conduct Unbecoming* (1975), *Sinbad in the Eye of the Tiger* (1977), *Dominique* (1979), *The Martian Chronicles* (1980), *Story of D. H. Lawrence* (1981), *The Zany Adventures of Robin Hood* (1983).

Paddington station was packed with travellers, all excited about the Christmas holiday, and, as I waited on the platform, I suddenly panicked. *What if Andrew didn't come to meet me?* I would be stranded in a city, with absolutely nowhere to go. But there he was, bounding through the crowd, arms outstretched, while I stood letting the feeling of pure relief wash over me.

After depositing my suitcases at the flat, we dined out at a smart Italian restaurant with Ed and Joanne. Then back to their flat for champagne, as the clock struck twelve and we all madly opened presents bought for each other, though Andrew and I decided we would open our personal presents when we were alone. It was so strange, for it was the first time we'd spent a night together and here I was about to embark on a new life with this man.

We sat up in bed each holding a small Christmas wrapped gift and arguing about who would open theirs first. Andrew insisted it should be me. I tore off the wrapping, and opened the box only to shut it quickly. "You have given me the wrong present. This is your present." Andrew assured me that it was his present, pointing to the wrapping. "I took great care choosing the Christmas paper." I opened the box again, and looked at a beautiful and rather uniquely designed St. Christopher on a gold chain. I stared at it, while a now very agitated Andrew kept asking me if I liked it. Without saying a word I passed my present to him and gestured for him to open it. It was simply unbelievable that we'd given each other a St. Christopher, but not just any medallion, *the two were exactly the same.* Life can have some strange twists and turns, every so often. Our relationship started on that Christmas Eve, which was not earth-shattering but was gentle and easy.

New Year came and went, with me trying to fit in working full time on the pre-production of *Cromwell*, a film which had locations in Spain, with the rest of the filming to be done at Shepperton studios in England, plus sorting out workmen, who were now updating the kitchen and decorating the St. John's Wood flat.

For the first few weeks, I hardly saw Ed and Joanne, but as things started to gear up for the move to Spain, I spent more time with them. Being young, and still completely naive, I was utterly taken in by this couple. They were charm personified.

One day, while Andrew was working late at the studios and the three of us were sitting around talking about nothing in particular, Joanne suddenly asked me if I realized that Andrew was an alcoholic; I was absolutely astounded. As I hardly drank, I didn't know anything about alcoholism. I sat looking at her, not sure how to answer.

"You'll have to watch him," she said, seeming quite happy about this mind-blowing information.

I thought about it for a minute. Yes, Andrew always had a drink when he came home, well, maybe two or three; but I thought that's what people in the industry did, and at the time, it seemed rather sophisticated, though after our conversation I started to watch Andrew's intake with more awareness. To my very limited knowledge of how an alcoholic should behave, Andrew certainly didn't fall into that category. He didn't slur his words or totter around, he wasn't abusive, nor did he behave badly. He just went to sleep very early in the evening, sometimes even falling asleep at the dinner table, but I put this down to long hours at the studio. I was fairly certain Joanne had made a mistake. Still the nagging doubt had been planted in my head, and from then on, never quite left.

One morning, while we were having breakfast, Joanne and Ed told me they'd been looking at properties to buy. I listened to their tale of woe about not having enough money to put down on a small house they'd fallen in love with. I felt indebted to them for letting Andrew and me stay with them, so I offered to lend them the money I'd received from the sale of my business, and immediately handed over a check. They thanked me profusely promising to repay me at so much a month. They also asked me not to tell Andrew as they thought he wouldn't approve. The weeks went by, with no mention of repayment from either of them. So I now had two dilemmas: one, how would I approach this delicate subject to Ed, and two, I now had no money at all, and as Andrew hadn't discussed how much I would be earning on the film, and as yet, no contract had been signed, I was too embarrassed to have to tell him I was flat broke. While we were still staying with Ed and Joanne, I eventually plucked up courage, and asked Ed how long it would be before they started repaying me as promised. He literally laughed in my face, and more or less told me I could whistle for it. It was a salutary lesson that people sometimes have a thin veneer of niceness, but, underneath, there can be a very rotten core. That evening I told Andrew we had to move into the flat straight away, no matter what unfinished state it was in. The next couple of days were a nightmare. Andrew was oblivious of the underlying tension, as he was now working very long hours at the studio, and I wanted to get away from Ed Harper as soon as possible. We eventually moved into the flat, and on our first evening there I told Andrew about my stupidity, and the resounding slap in the face I'd received from our so-called friends. Poor Andrew, he felt so bad for me, and sorry we had not discussed finances before. I told him that I didn't want to be kept by him but would need to have some help until we had sorted out my salary, for I was convinced I would never see my money again.

Andrew took me to his solicitor who, after hearing my tale of woe or stupidity, told me that it would be difficult to retrieve the money, as there was nothing in writing and they could say it was either a gift or repayment of a debt. Undaunted, Andrew decided to ask Gerry Crampton and Terry Plumber, who were a couple of stuntmen, to come for drinks at the now almost finished flat. When he told them the story of how Ed Harper had refused to pay back a loan of ten thousand of pounds, Terry Plumber wanted to know *if he should rub him out, or just teach him a lesson.* I nearly choked on my Vodka and tonic, saying weakly that I thought the latter was preferable, and within two weeks I received a cheque for the full amount. Needless to say, Ed Harper never worked for Andrew again.

A week later, Andrew confessed that, just after he met me, he'd moved out of his home, which apparently came as a shock to his family and left me almost speechless. I knew he had three children, but until that very day I never knew he was still married. For me his confession was bad enough but I now wondered if I was the cause of the breakup, even though Andrew vehemently denied it. I was living on shifting sands again, not really knowing if I could trust Andrew, for I still hardly knew him. How could I be so stupid, for I had automatically thought he was divorced? I told him I would still work for him but should move out of the flat; but he assured me he and his wife had been living separate lives long before he met me, and she'd agreed to a divorce as long as the children were taken care of. I realized that where men were concerned I was still very much a child, with a lot to learn.

It was around this time that I met Sandra Dorne and Patrick Holt. They were both actors and lived in Maida Vale, just ten minutes away from St. John's Wood. I first met them at a dinner party that film producer Irvin Allen was hosting. Patrick had worked with Andrew on a film called *The Long Ships*. I struck up a friendship with Sandra, which at times was both volatile and eye opening. Not many people will remember an English actress called Diana Dors. She was a big busted blonde who was the epitome of what most English men dreamed about. Well, Sandra could have been her twin, and, seeing that Diana had already made her mark on the silver screen, it was bad news for Sandra Dorne. Any acting roles for a blonde curvy woman always went to Diana Dors. All the time I knew Sandra, she hardly ever worked.

A couple of months after I had moved to London and settled into life with Andrew, I accepted an invitation from Sandra to have lunch in the city. She picked me up at the flat and drove into London. As we were driving down Oxford Street, a young man in a snazzy sports car cut in front of her, giving the finger as he did. Well, that was my introduction to four-letter words, in fact *every* four letter word Sandra could think of came out of her mouth. I was completely speechless, as was the young man when she eventually flew past him, still very loudly hurling verbal abuse. Boy, my convent education never prepared me for this volatile woman!

I was still somewhat in shock as she led me up to the restaurant of Fortnum and Mason, and later, while we sat waiting for our dessert, she asked me a question.

"Are you in love with Andrew? Or are you in love with the film industry? I think if you're honest it would be the industry. It has that effect on people, and although he's nice, he's not really your sort."

Her question took me completely by surprise, as I was still coming to terms with his revelations concerning a wife. Still, I thought her extremely rude, and I sat staring at her unable to answer. The first words out of my mouth should have been *of course I love Andrew,* but in all honesty I couldn't answer. It was a question I had never asked myself and I certainly didn't want to think about it then. As crazy as Sandra Dorne was, *and she was crazy*, where some things were concerned she was one shrewd cookie.

At last I answered. "If he's not my sort as you say, what *is* my sort?" She smiled and said, "Oh, you'll know when he comes along."

That evening as I sat in the flat with Andrew I kept thinking of what she had said. I looked across at him. I knew he was in love with me, but it was not an earthy passionate love one always imagined would happen. It was a gentle love. He always called me his baby doll and from the start of our relationship he treated me like a precious child, someone he could take out of the box and say *look who I have. Bet you never thought this would happen to me.* He certainly got a kick out of showing me off, and because I was much younger than him, I was often mistaken for his daughter. I can honestly say that I loved him very much, but what did being *in love mean*? Let's face it, my journey into that world had always left me uncommitted both emotionally and physically. I still wasn't ready to completely belong to anyone, and often wondered if I ever would. So when Andrew came into my life, I'm sure he took the place of the father I never had, it just felt right. For me, it was a sad evening; I couldn't tell him how I felt. How could I, when I didn't even know myself? I did know that Sandra Dorne was right about one thing. I was in love with the industry, and for the next fourteen years it was the glue that held Andrew and me together.

I absolutely loved working at Shepperton Studios. There were always lots of well known actors floating in and out of the office to see Andrew, all hoping for a part in *Cromwell*. Richard Harris and Alec Guinness had already been cast to play Cromwell and King Charles I. It was a big budget film produced by Irvin Allen, with Andrew as associate producer. I loved every minute of it, and worked hard to be the perfect secretary. We were almost through pre-production, and getting ready to leave for Spain, and Andrew seemed pleased with my progress. He simply had no idea how much paper and Tippex I was going through in order to hand him the perfect letter folio for signing at the end of each day. Still, I knew I was getting better when I only had to re-type a letter twice, instead of maybe three or more times. It was hard work, and I hadn't even got to the real work yet; that would come when we eventually settled on location in Spain. Then there would be masses of contracts for both actors and crew to be typed. I spent many a day on location, wondering whether I had bitten off more of than I could chew. One wrong word, and it was out with the Tippex, and hoping my boss would not notice.

On the last day at Shepperton, we celebrated at the bar with various actors and stuntmen, all looking forward to seeing everyone again in Spain. Andrew and I spent the weekend packing for the upcoming months on location. On Saturday afternoon, Gerry Crampton and Terry Plumber suddenly arrived at the flat. Gerry had heard through some friends that Ed Harper was so mad that he'd had to pay back the money he was going to trash the flat while we were away. So here was Ed Harper rearing his ugly head again. Looking back on that evening now always makes me laugh. As far as I was concerned, stuntmen were just stuntmen. It took me some time to learn that a lot of them had quite a nefarious start to their adult lives, but only a few minutes to learn that Terry Plumber was definitely one of the nefarious breed. I guess that transitioning into the film business kept most of them out of trouble and out of prison. Having said that they were a most wonderful and colourful bunch of men. And, later, I was to learn that director Ray Austin had brought both men into the industry.

Andrew made drinks for us, and again we all sat around as if we were going to have a congenial chat about life in general. Suddenly, Terry said, "I should have had this prick rubbed out the first time and that would have settled matters. I think we should get this sorted before we go to Spain." I laughed weakly, hoping it was again a joke but I could tell by the look on Terry's face he was deadly serious. Gerry seemed quite happy with this proposition but Andrew shook his head. "Just let him know that if *anything* happens to the flat while we're away, we'll know who to blame. A couple of weeks later, Gerry and Terry joined us in Spain. Apparently Terry had again scared the hell out of Ed by warning him he must hope nothing happened to our home because if it did he'd be straight over to sort him out once and for all, saying that, even if he wasn't responsible, he'd still get the blame. We never heard from Ed Harper again. Later I heard that he and Joanne went to live in South Africa.

CROMWELL AND SPAIN

We arrived at the airport in Spain, to be met by a Spanish location manager who looked as though he was about to have a seizure on the spot. Apparently, the hotel we were going to stay in, along with Alec Guinness, Richard Harris, other actors and some of the crew was nowhere near finished. And to make matter worse, Alec Guinness had already arrived at the hotel. When Andrew saw the location a couple of months before, the hotel was already built, but with still a lot of interior work yet to do. At the time, the Spanish construction company had assured Andrew that it would be ready by the promised date. The hotel was in a small village, very near to Sierra de Urbasa, where we were to shoot some of the major army scenes. We drove in near panic to find out how much needed to be done. Andrew rushed into the hotel, while I went into the hotel garden and tried to reassure Mr Guinness, who was sitting on what appeared to be an exceedingly uncomfortable wooden bench, looking small and very forlorn with all his suitcases at his feet. In my most professional manner, I assured him everything would be quickly sorted out. I soon realized my assurances were a wee bit premature to say the least. Apparently most of the bathrooms had yet to be finished. The windows were at the hotel but not actually fixed, and the dining room and entrance floor was not due to be laid until sometime the following week. All hell broke out, ending up with Andrew having a screaming match with the owner, while Mr Guinness was still sitting patiently in the garden with nowhere to go. Though the hotel was nowhere near finished, I found out that the wine cellar was well stocked, with various assorted Spanish wines. I grabbed a couple of bottles, a bottle opener and glasses and an hour later Alec and I – we had now moved on to first names – were both sitting together on that wooden bench getting plastered on warm Spanish wine and agreeing that if we had another bottle we wouldn't really care where we slept.

I don't know how they did it, but by early that evening Andrew, along with anyone he could find, managed to get everyone booked in at other various hotels in the area.

From then on, Alec Guinness and I formed a warm friendship, and whenever he had a glass of wine and if I was anywhere near him he would raise his glass and say "Here's to unfinished hotels, an English Rose and Vino Tinto de la Casa."

My baptism into film locations was well and truly set. We were to shoot all the battle scenes on Sierra de Urbasa, which is a mountain range topped with a beautiful plateau. We had literally hundreds of extras dressed in their battle gear. Many of the horses were trained by some of the top Spanish riders. A lot of very eager English actors, playing smaller roles, said that they could ride, but they either fell off or clung to the poor horse as soon as the command to gallop was given. If an actor wanted a job, he said he could do everything and anything. One actor galloped straight through the huge meal tent, causing complete havoc then disappeared out the other side and over the hill. Various stunt riders raced after him and brought him and the horse back to safety.

The Sierra de Urbasa location had been specifically picked for its lush green and uninhabited area. Also, as a bonus, our location manager was told it hardly ever rained in that area. Well, the minute we started shooting it started raining. Not a light drizzle but endless hours of torrential cold rain soaking every person and animal within minutes. I remember that, on the third day, a rather large Robert Morley, who played Edward Montagu, 2nd Earl of Manchester, was sitting on his horse rehearsing a scene, and as we watched, we could see the poor animal slowly sinking up to its fetlocks in the mud. Later, as the horse was being winched up out of the mire, Robert, still playing Edward Montagu, solemnly and loudly declared "I want you all to know I bear this horse no ill will." It was the only bright spot in an otherwise very wet and cold day.

Still, nothing could, or ever did, dampen my love for the film industry. We would get up at the crack of dawn and drive in a convoy to the location which was already a hive of activity. Huge temporary buildings had been erected to house thousands of costumes, along with hairdressers and makeup artists. There were stables for the horses, rows of honey wagons, motor homes and the now famous meals tent with a kitchen/caravan at one side of it, where all the meals were prepared. All actors, crew, stuntmen, extras and stand-ins had to be fed and fed well. Logistically, it must have been a complete nightmare for the caterers to come up with really good food for such a vast number of people. But each day the food, which was plentiful, was fantastic, starting with breakfast, then lunch, and various snacks and beverages throughout the day. The caterers were then rarely mentioned on film credits, but they did an incredible job, and often in truly impossible situations. I'm glad to say that they now get the credit they deserve.

As the shooting continued so did the rain. We were told it was a record amount of rain, and at that time of the year it was virtually unheard of. Because of the atrocious weather, script pages were often rewritten within hours, and the daily call sheet soon boasted every colour of the rainbow. Different colours from the original script signified changes in the daily call sheet. Actors were seen sitting, walking, riding or standing, all riveted to their lines and the various changes, all bemoaning the fact they'd already learned theirs for that day and couldn't remember the new ones in such a short amount of time. It was a mad fantasy world where we were all cut off from reality, and I never wanted it to end. By the end of the Spanish location, I was fairly adept at typing, and was happy to see Andrew becoming more relaxed as he read through my various work at the finish of each day.

Through Andrew, Patrick Holt came over to Spain to play Captain Lundsford. It was one of the very few times Sandra would leave her dogs to accompany him. Though Sandra hadn't worked for years, she still played the actress to the hilt, in fact I think she was a much better actress off the screen than on. Once she and Patrick were installed in their hotel, she became quite a liability, demanding cars to take her shopping or pick her up at the hotel any time she wanted to come to the location. In the end, Andrew put his foot down reminding her that she was not working on the film, and was therefore not entitled to transportation. Thus the beginning of a love/hate feud between the two. Andrew really didn't care, but at times I found it quite difficult to have a harmonious relationship with her and to keep peace between them. Andrew really liked Patrick a lot, so, at the end of the day, we would often dine with them in the hotel, or sometimes go out to one of the local restaurants if the filming had finished at a reasonable time. The meal would always start off with happy banter until Sandra would drink a little too much Spanish wine, or Patrick would decide to pick her up on her grammar; he was a stickler for *proper English* as he called it. He would then tell her she was talking rubbish. Whatever the reason, more often than not they would end up in a fierce argument while Andrew and I sat watching the spectacle, both vowing never to have dinner with them again. It was a difficult situation to be in, as I always reminded myself that she was the one person who had taken me under her wing and made me feel welcomed when I first moved to London. Still, if any friendship is stretched too far, like an elastic band, it will surely snap.

Eventually, shooting in Spain came to an end, and we all returned to England. The rest of *Cromwell* was to be filmed at Shepperton studios, and while we were away on location the sets at the studio were finished with lavish interiors and massive exterior buildings. Walking through some of the exterior sets was rather like being back in London during the 1600s, with the scaffolding up and the platform ready for the execution of King Charles the First looming in the background.

They were halcyon days, with incredibly early mornings and very late nights. Each morning, a car would arrive at St. John's Wood for Andrew and me and sitting, or rather lying, in the back was the director Ken Hughes, who lived close by. I always sat with him while Andrew, who revelled in early mornings, sat up front going through copious notes, and impatient for the day to start. Not so for Ken and me. Ken always looked as though he had slept in his clothes, with his bleached hair standing on end and the ever-present cigarette in his mouth. He was a wonderful, funny and highly talented man but, in those early morning hours, he looked as though he'd seen better days. Whereas I wanted to curl up in a little ball wondering what the hell I was doing up at this ungodly hour. At that young age I was a night bird, with Andrew always fading fast at around seven p.m.

As the months went by, I began to realize that Joanne Stewart was right; Andrew really did have a drinking problem, and I had no idea how to cope with it. Each morning he would be up at the crack of dawn, full of energy, which would last throughout most of the day, only to be slightly dulled by the afternoon after a too often liquid lunch at the studio restaurant. By early evening he would often fall asleep at the dinner table or soon after. Andrew was *never* a nasty drunk, he was a sleepy drunk. Which became very scary when he stopped working for Irvin Allen, and had to start driving to and from the studios himself. I spent hours pleading with him not to drink and drive, and if I wasn't working at the studio with him I would be waiting for him to come home, praying he would walk to the front door without that drinker's gait, but always disappointed. It began to consume my whole life, and I told him that he would have to stop drinking or we couldn't stay together. I know he certainly tried, but I knew nothing about alcoholism, and soon realized I was fighting a losing battle. When he was home at the weekends, although I felt cruel, I wouldn't let him drink, and as improbable as that was, he was fine. On Saturday, we would often go out for dinner, and on Sunday we would have the traditional English lunch, then take Pickles out for a country walk. On those days, Andrew didn't drink anything stronger than a cup of tea. No slurring words or falling asleep at the table; in fact, I began to live for the weekends, knowing that once he got to the studio during the week there would be nothing I could do to stop him. Living with Andrew became a rollercoaster of emotions. Here I was, beginning to branch out into this new world, and once again I was trapped in a relationship, with me becoming Andrew's watchdog. I hated always having to decline invitations for various dinner parties because I knew he would never get through the evening without falling asleep, and I would see the looks of pity on people's faces as I either tried to prop him up or make excuses and leave early. It didn't take long for the invitations to stop.

Why did I stay with him? Well, it certainly wasn't because I was afraid to leave him. I think it was because he was such a nice man and I knew he truly loved me. He wanted nothing else than to be with me. I was his baby doll, and as long as I was there sitting beside him, that was enough for him, and maybe, at the time, it was enough for me. Also I was still transitioning from being a very immature person who, sadly, still needed a prop, no matter how flawed the prop was. We were really two lost souls trying to get a grip on life, and not quite sure how to go about it.

Then there were quite a few occasions over the years when Sandra Dorne had too much to drink, and those four letter words would come fast and furious. I would either drag her out of some restaurant or drive her home only to hear her little girl voice on the phone the next morning calling me with abject apologies and the sincere assurances that she would never behave badly again. Needless to say, it didn't last. Sadly, in the end, the elastic broke and I could not take any more of her wild erratic behaviour. A while later, I bought a house in Horsell, Surrey to be nearer to Shepperton Studios, and thus Sandra moved somewhat gently out of my life.

Around this time I met a rather strange man named Brian Johnson. He spent a lot of his time studying Yoga and would often sit on the floor doing very strange contortions with his limbs. During one of our many conversations on the subject I told him I was a chronic insomniac and he said he thought practicing Yoga would help. I started going to classes and after awhile I could train my mind to stop thinking about my past and let my body relax and would get at least four to five hours sleep each night. When our Yoga teacher left the area, I took over her evening classes while I was still living in London. I loved teaching, though it was mainly the Yoga exercises but once I moved away from London life got so hectic I stopped practicing and soon slipped back into endless nights lying awake waiting for the morning to come.

BIRTHDAYS AND HOLIDAYS

Birthdays come and birthdays go. I'm sure everyone who celebrates a birthday either a few days before Christmas or a few days afterwards has, at some time, suffered the same fate as I did. Most years, if I was lucky enough to receive a present for Christmas, I was told that it was also for my birthday.

From when I was a very small child, I always suffered that fate, for my birthday is on the 5th of January. Even my grandmother fell into the trap, and would either forget all together, or send a present for both dates. The Brisleys never recognized the 5th of January and hardly celebrated Christmas, so I was starved of any of the usual childhood excitement and the wonderment of holidays and other milestones in my life. In the scheme of things, it shouldn't be considered too important but to a small child who was starved of any form of love or acknowledgment as she was travelling through life, it was quite devastating.

As I grew into adulthood, I became almost obsessive about these events that take place each year. First of all, Christmas was an important religious date for me. My Catholic education was still very much a part of my inner self, though I never did get back into the routine of regular Sunday church visits. The other side of me was absolutely enthralled by the glitz and the excitement of packing presents, decorating trees, going to various parties and cooking all the holiday fare like mince pies, Christmas cake, sausage rolls and, of course, Christmas pudding. It was *my* time. A time when I could have all the excitement I never had as a child. I would not hold back. Each year I would try to outdo the last by a bigger tree with more beautiful ornaments and more lights. I wanted to wow my friends, but most of all, I wanted to fill the black hole that had been my childhood.

Andrew was such a sweet man, but surprise gifts were not his forte. My yearly enthusiasm and excitement around Christmas probably scared the hell out of him, and on looking back, I think he was slightly embarrassed by the amount of presents I bought him. Bless him, he too would give me my Christmas present, and then solemnly tell me that it was for my birthday as well. So, here I was, a grown woman, still desperate for presents to open on these special occasions. I most certainly didn't hanker for wildly expensive jewellery, fabulous furs, or exotic holidays. I just wanted to open a fancy wrapped present; the money it cost, or lack of it, was not important to me. It was the mystery surrounding the whole ritual and magic of a present. Yes, it was the child in me, who still exists to this day. The excitement of a wrapped present is great, and the disappointment of nothing, even greater. What a messed-up person to be hung up on something so insignificant in this world of far more important things! But there it is: good, bad or indifferent, that's me.

AL PARKER

A couple of years into our relationship, Andrew had a meeting with an agent called Al Parker, who was then in his late eighties. He was quite a famous character in the film business, and was either revered or feared by most in the industry. He had actually discovered the silent movie heartthrob Rudolph Valentino.

We were invited to his flat in Mayfair to have tea with him and his wife Maggie Parker, also to meet an actor called James Mason. At the time, Al Parker was agent and manager to Mr Mason, and both Andrew and Al wanted him to read a script of an upcoming film. Since I had long been a fan of the actor, I was really excited about meeting him.

As we were getting dressed, I suddenly said. "Oh my God, I know who these people are. They're the couple who were on the train on Christmas Eve, when I first came to London." Andrew smiled benignly, replying that it wasn't very likely. I don't know how, but I just knew.

Sure enough, as soon as we were ushered into the flat by their housekeeper, there they were: Al Parker, seated in a chair, looking very old, fierce and imposing, with Maggie Parker looking small, dainty and still incredibly beautiful. It was an afternoon I will never forget: to be sitting in the same room with James Mason and also, at last, to put names to the faces who had so fascinated me on that Christmas Eve train journey! Throughout my life, I have often had strange experiences and happenings that cannot be explained. They just happened.

I saw Maggie Parker many times after our first meeting, but the evening of my first dinner party at the flat in St John's Wood was memorable to say the least.

Andrew wanted to invite Maggie and Al, along with some other friends in the industry, to dinner. I readily agreed. Invitations were sent out and Maggie's answer was that, as much as she would love to come, Al didn't go out at night, as at his age, he was early to bed, and would never stay out late. I duly promised that the dinner would be served at a respectable hour and thus secured their delight in coming. I hyperventilated throughout the day, making myself sick with worry, and sure the dinner would be a resounding failure.

Everyone arrived on time, and all were given cocktails and canapes. Al was enjoying holding the fort with the select guests, and all was going well. I began to congratulate myself as I went into the kitchen to start the last part of the cooking, only to see the leg of lamb, that was supposed to be almost cooked, still sitting on top of the cooker looking cold and forlorn. I had a complete meltdown but had the good sense to immediately turn off the vegetables and wondered what on earth I was going to do. Having signalled Andrew for help, *who by this time was well and truly happy* and no help at all, I poured my guests more cocktails trying to keep everyone happy for the next couple of hours, as I feverishly served extra canapes and managed to keep out of eye contact with Maggie, as Al became the life and soul of the evening with each new cocktail. Eventually, we all sat down to dine at ten p.m. with everyone completely smashed, and with no comprehension of what they were eating. It was well after one a.m. in the morning as I poured Al and Maggie along with my other guests out of the flat, all saying they had never enjoyed such a great dinner party. It was one hell of a baptism into the art of entertaining with an eclectic, and may I say, a rather eccentric group of people.

Now, on looking back, I realize it was a strange time in my life but one I wouldn't have missed, for in those years I grew up learning what it was like to have to make decisions; for although Andrew was strong in his field at work, he was a man who, in his private life, would forever let the world go by, and us along with it. He couldn't face the fact that we were not compatible in any way at all, and whenever I tried to bring the subject up there would be tears, and such sadness that it was yet again swept under the carpet and we limped along trying to make the best of a very bad relationship. I think the trouble was that, although I was not in love with Andrew, I truly *loved* him. He was the very first person in my life who really cared for me, and, until the day he died, I know he always felt that way. How can anyone hurt a person with so much feeling? There were many times when I would tell him we had to part. I even said I would still work for him, but our personal relationship was getting us nowhere at all. The real problem was that, with Andrew, as long as I was with him, and, in his life, everything was fine, I just had to be there. For a number of years we had a relationship based on a deep friendship. To the outside world, we were a couple. I think a lot of people even thought we were married, and although there were many times when Andrew asked me to marry him, I think we both knew that would never happen. In a way, I was again living a home life of isolation but this time it was of my own making. My working life was full of people, with the hustle that went along with the film business. It was still exciting and with *Cromwell* now behind us, we were ready to move on to the next film *Nicholas and Alexandra*, which would be made entirely on location. Maybe it was an excuse but there really was no time to sort out our personal problems.

NICHOLAS AND ALEXANDRA

In 1971, Andrew and I moved to Madrid in Spain for the year-long production of the film Nicholas and Alexandra. We took an apartment near the film studio, which housed all the interior sets for the film which was situated outside the city. I think it was the last big film to be made at the studio before it was torn down.

Andrew was the associate producer, with Sam Spiegel producing the film. Sam had made many big and memorable films such as *Suddenly Last Summer, Lawrence of Arabia, Bridge over the River Kwai,* and many more. He spoke seven languages fluently, was a highly talented man, and a terrible womanizer. At seventy, he could still chase a young girl around his desk. This he did frequently, whenever I went to his office, it seemed to be one of his favorite things to do, and I always told him he was a little too old to catch me. Although I was still working for Andrew, I also worked for the publicity department, which was a little slow-going, as the film was to take over a year of filming before its release date; so publicity was really not a priority. It was interesting though, and let me see another side to filmmaking. Another one of my jobs was to meet the actors at Barajas airport, take them to their various hotels, and see that they were settled in. With a whole year of filming, many actors streamed in and out of the airport each and every day. A lot of actors would come and go frequently, as it was cheaper to send them home until they were needed again than to pay their daily *per diem* and hotels.

It took Sam and Andrew quite a long time to find a Rasputin. In life, he was regarded as a religious healer who eventually crossed paths with the Russian royal family. It was certainly not a healthy relationship, but apparently Alexandra was completely fascinated by him. And Sam wanted someone who looked dark and mysterious to play the part.

After searching for the right actor, Sam found Tom Baker, who he thought would be wonderful in the role. Tom was hired and due to arrive a week later. I was sent off to Barajas airport to meet him. I remember asking Sam how I would know what the actor looked like, as there were no photographs of him and I was going to the airport during rush hour. Sam laughed and told me all the male Spaniards were midgets, and, as Tom Baker was well over six feet, it would be easy to find him. Off I went and stood waiting amidst the commuters and holiday people all converging into the airport arrival area at an alarming pace. Sam was indeed correct, most of the Spanish men were quite short in stature. At last I saw a man head and shoulders over the rest of the crowd, and, rushing over to him I went into my long speech of welcoming the actor to Madrid, etcetera. After I'd finished, and got no reaction from this rather handsome man, I realized Sam was wrong; not all Spaniards are short, and this poor man, who obviously didn't speak any English, hadn't a clue what I was talking about. As he hurriedly made his escape, I heard a soft deep voice behind me thanking me for meeting him; he had thoroughly enjoyed watching me make a complete ass of myself with some poor unsuspecting man, who surely thought I was there to accost him.

So there Tom Baker stood, towering before me. Although certainly not handsome, he had a striking face, topped with a mass of unruly curly hair. He also looked as though he'd slept in his clothes for a week. But it was the voice: it was like dark chocolate melting on the tongue, filling one's senses with an addiction of needing so much more. I was completely enthralled by him and from then on we became firm friends. Over the next few months, I would spend a lot of time at Barajas airport ferrying Tom to and from England, and we would sit in the passenger terminal talking about everything and nothing. In fact, one time he almost missed the flight back to England, and had to be rushed on to the plane amid a lot of angry and impatient passengers. Tom eventually went on to play *Doctor Who*, and it was one of his most famous roles in television history.

Another one of my many airport tasks was to meet the continual arrivals of Sam's many girlfriends, who came in quick succession, with not one of them over twenty-five; and I never met the same girl twice. On other occasions, I would also go to the cargo side of the airport to pick up the large containers of Beluga caviar that Sam was partial to, and would take to his yacht for his naughty weekends. On several occasions Andrew and I were invited to his yacht, along with the girlfriend of the moment and various actors who Sam thought would add to the enjoyment of the weekend. It was a fun experience with everyone tucking into the copious amounts of caviar and Dom Perignon.

The day I met Curt Jürgens at the airport was indeed not easily forgotten. I'd seen this German actor in a number of films, and in reality, he lived up to his screen image. He was a very imposing man, simply dripping with charm from every pore. I stood before him, and by now, like a well-trained parrot, reeled off my usual welcome speech before escorting him to his hotel. The accommodation varied according to an actor's ranking, though all were looked after extremely well. However, Curt being considered the upper echelon had a large suite in one of the bigger hotels. I noticed that Sam had ordered champagne, and an exotic bowl of fruit along with two champagne flutes. Mr Jürgens took this as a sign that, along with the champagne, I was to be the designated girl for the evening. Sam had no compunction about whether or not a girl was either married or involved with anyone else; all women under a certain age were simply fair game. As soon as the hotel porter shut the door, Curt was at my side, arms circling my body and telling me this would be a memorable evening for both of us. It took me quite a while to convince him that I was not part of Sam Spiegel's welcoming party. At first, he couldn't believe I had turned down an opportunity to spend an exotic – his words not mine – evening with him, and he felt sure I would later regret it. After a few more minutes of trying to extricate myself from him I made a mad dash to the door, arriving back at the studio looking as though I'd been dragged through a hedge backwards. I must say that whenever I saw him at the studio, he was the perfect gentleman, always bowing low and kissing my hand, it was only on the last day as he bid farewell to cast and crew that he turned to me, and loudly said, "There will come a time when you'll regret that you didn't spend the night with me, for I would have taken you to heights which you will probably never know." Then, turning on his heel, he marched out of the studio. I, along with the actors and crew, stood there absolutely speechless at his audacity. Obviously I was in the minority where being bedded by Curt Jürgens was concerned.

One of my most favorite actors was Jack Hawkins, who was much loved by everyone who knew him. Sadly, some years earlier, he had had throat cancer, and had lost his beautiful voice. It was wonderful that he was still in such great demand, and there were two actors, Charles Grey and Robert Rietti, who would dub his voice whenever he worked. He once told me, in his now raspy whisper, that I was one of the few people didn't treat him like a deaf mute or as slightly retarded, for people would either shout at him or painfully articulate while wildly throwing their arms around as if it would help him understand them. I very quickly got used to his way of speaking, and absolutely adored spending time with him.

Lord Laurence Olivier was also working on the film, though sadly he was not in good health at the time. He was another one of those great actors who were mesmerizing. There was an aura around him, making him seem a little unreal to us mere mortals.

On my thirty-first birthday, Sam Spiegel threw a birthday party for me. It was held in a private dining room at a well-known restaurant called the Thirty-One Club, which, for that occasion, was very aptly named. Kirk Douglas, a close friend of Sam's, was also there. I sat with Laurence Olivier on one side of me and Sam on the other, as Sam yet again asked me to be in the film with no strings attached, while his very gay butler, who went everywhere with him, kept making strange faces at me as he stood behind him. It was such a hilarious scene that I got the giggles, and Sam, who thought or hoped I'd had too much to drink, kept stroking my leg under the table and trying his best to move his hand up as high as possible, with me rapping his knuckles with a dinner fork. It was a memorable, fun evening, and after dinner, I danced the night away with some of the greats: Lord Laurence, Kirk Douglas, Michael Jayston, Curt Jürgens and the lovely, Maurice Denham.

DON JAIME DE MORRO Y ARAGON

Jaime was the son of the Spanish royal family, and elder brother of Queen Fabiola of Belgium. His mother was Blanca de Aragon who lived in absolute splendour in Madrid. Andrew and I were invited to dinner quite a few times during that year, and I was captivated by the grandeur of her home. A white-gloved butler stood behind each chair at the very opulent table, and it was there that I first met her charming and very bohemian son, Jaime. He really was the black sheep of the family, but what a charming black sheep! Jaime, along with many other ventures, had dabbled as an actor in the film business, and wanted desperately to work on Nicholas and Alexandra. It was obvious that his mother loved him dearly, but frustration plainly showed on her face as she spoke of his wayward life. She wanted him to be in Sam Spiegel's film, for, as she put it, it would be a step up for her son. As there really weren't any acting parts for Jaime, I'm convinced that Sam made up a role for him. He would be playing *Minister reporting to Grand Duke Nicholas.* It pleased his mother, and, from then on, Jaime practically lived at the studio, and in my office, where he would bring me succulent treats each morning and sneak me out of the studio when the coast was clear for hilarious rides through Madrid in his open top car. It was clear that he was a firm favorite with the Spanish people, for wherever we went, hordes of onlookers would wave and scream at him. I simply loved every minute of it, and I adored Jaime. No, I wasn't attracted to him in any way; but oh, what fun we had! We were like two small children playing truant from school.

Most of the actors were fun people to work with. However, there were a few who were very aloof, and some extremely unpleasant. Luckily, they were few and far between, but at times they made life very difficult, especially as they would often run to me with their grievances, hoping that those grievances would be either passed on to Andrew or Sam, which never happened. We were like one huge family living in a make-believe unit where the outside world couldn't reach us. England, with its normal everyday trials and tribulations, ceased to exist. I think that's why I always loved film locations, for again it was a part of me where I could shut myself away from reality and where *she* could not reach me. I never really told Andrew about my childhood; sweet as he was, he wasn't the sort of person who would understand, and by this time we were slipping more and more into a working relationship, and most definitely, it was the glue holding us together. When you are working flat out with unbelievably long hours, personal lives went out the window; at least ours did.

It's incredible how quickly those months flew by, but *Nicholas and Alexandra* came to an end, and I was once again packing for the homeward journey. We had been through all four seasons in Madrid. And it had been a magical experience with colourful individuals, wonderful costumes, glittering ball scenes and magnificent sets. About a year later, Andrew and I went for a holiday to Alicante, to stay with Eddie Fowlie, who had been the prop Master on the film. He had a small hotel near one of the coastal bays, and as we walked into the entrance hall, it was like walking onto the set of *Nicholas and Alexandra*! Eddie had literally brought most of those lavish sets from Madrid and had installed them in the hotel; even Andrew had to laugh at Eddie's sheer audaciousness, for we were both very sure that not one item had been bought.

CONDUCT UNBECOMING

In October of 1975, we started production of the film called *Conduct Unbecoming*. It was a film about the British Army in India, with locations in Pakistan, and then back to Shepperton studios for the interiors of the filming.

We flew out to Pakistan with the main cast, plus some English crew, and landed in Rawalpindi Benazir Bhutto International Airport. (As it's called now!) We stepped off the plane and walked to the arrivals terminal. The first thing to hit us was the sticky heat, with a pungent aroma I have yet to define! The area was literally teeming with people of all denominations either coming or going, but most of the human mass were beggars, taxi drivers and small children, all rushing at us, trying to grab our suitcases, begging for money or pleading with us to take their transport. We literally had to fight our way out of the airport to our waiting cars. It was incredibly overpowering, and rather frightening. As we drove through the streets to the hotel, it was like watching a film unfold, for the scene before us was surreal: cows and oxen crossing the road in front of us, with some walking exceedingly slowly ahead of the car. Again, people rushing at us and banging on the windows, all wanting money, and all dressed in what can only be described as rags. As we passed the Lai Nullah river which runs through Rawalpindi, I saw many women squatting by the river washing their clothes with what I thought were piles of dirty clothes near to them waiting to be washed, until the clothes suddenly moved, and I realized that they were people who, in all probability, lived right there. The streets were noisy, dusty and, again, crowded with a human mass, all trying to move with the flow. For me, it was an unbelievable sight, which was even more noticeable when we reached the hotel and were received with an air of grandeur so disproportional from the real world just beyond the hotel entrance. Andrew and I were shown into our suite, which could have matched any upper-class London hotel. It was as if we had stepped into an alien world and out of reality.

Each day, while shooting some of the army scenes, we would break for lunch, which was located in a huge tent that travelled with us whereever we went. We would dine as if we were royalty, with lobster and other various succulent delicacies washed down with wine. God knows how anyone managed to work after that. Michael Anderson, the director, was very concerned about getting food poisoning, and would only eat eggs *at every meal*! Quite a lot of the crew did go down with stomach bugs, but Michael sailed through the whole location without a twinge. When we arrived back in England, he said he never wanted to see another egg again.

Rawalpindi was incredibly hot, dusty and noisy, but I wouldn't have missed it for the world, although it did give me pause for thought. During our stay, we were all treated like royalty, with invitations to cocktail parties each evening after the days filming. A shining black Mercedes would meet us at the hotel, and we would be driven to the Governor's mansion, once again along those wide bumpy dusty streets, at a snail's pace, so the driver wouldn't kill, or be killed by, any of the animals who seemed to loom up in our direction at any given time. There was much honking of horns and screaming from drivers, which made little or no difference to the speed of our journey. We would then at last arrive at a gated entrance, guarded by what can only be described as characters straight from the film *Porgy and Bess*. As we drove through the magnificent gardens, the gates would slowly close behind the car, leaving those moving ragged heaps piled up outside, and us entering into a universe of such opulence. It was simply mind-blowing to think that there could be such a divide of wealth and poverty. Each evening, we were invited to a different party, and we met the same English people, all with similar gated entrances to their homes. Most of the cocktail crowd either worked for the government or had high-powered international jobs in that part of the world. It was fun for us during our short stay, but must have been mind-numbingly boring for those who lived there.

The location manager, who had traveled to Rawalpindi a few weeks before us, put together what can only be described as a rag-tag Pakistan location team, with drivers who would take us to the various locations in the area. On one occasion, the location team had to find a train where we could film without the hordes of camp followers descending on us every day and driving everyone completely crazy. Well they certainly found a train, albeit a broken down one that had been abandoned well away from any sort of civilization. It was in fact miles beyond the boundaries of the city, and it would take us about two hours to get to this barren location. We were up at some unearthly hour, and started the journey, with Andrew and me in the lead car, followed by around ten other cars, all carrying the artists and crew needed for this shoot. We left Rawalpindi and made our way through the rugged hills toward our destination. The transport left a lot to be desired, and I was thankful that we all arrived at the location without any breakdowns. I was impressed by the train, for although it had been abandoned years before, and was old, it had been spruced up and was certainly what was wanted for the film. After a very hot and gruelling day of filming, we all thankfully piled back into our cars for the long journey back to the hotel.

About ten minutes later, our driver suddenly stopped the car, with all of the cars behind us stopping in a cloud of dust, rather like bumper cars almost crashing into each other. Our driver, who incidentally, seemed to be the only one who could speak some sort of limited English, gathered all the other drivers, and started a screaming match with them, with Andrew getting ready to blow a fuse. Eventually, our driver sat back in the car, turning to us, and very calmly, said that we should put any money and jewelry we had in our shoes, as the cloud of dust gathering in the distance behind us was a group of outcasts, who roamed those waste lands looking for people to rob and kill. As far as I know, none of our crowd had any jewelry or money on them, and Andrew screamed at him to get going and to drive like hell. It was an hysterical journey, as we watched the dust cloud turning into shapes of men on horseback getting closer to our cars by the minute. I had visions of our being front page news in such papers as the *Daily Mail*, regaling its readers with the tale of an English film crew killed by Pakistan marauders on the outskirts of Rawalpindi. I have never been so glad as when the journey came to an end. Needless to say, we *all* got completely inebriated that evening and thanked God we'd got the footage we needed from the location.

On another occasion, Mike, one of the wardrobe assistants, and I, had the day off, so we decided to go into the bazaar to see what everyday life was really like. We had a map of the city, so off we set. Mike was well over six foot tall, with a mass of white blonde hair. As we entered the bazaar, it was rather like turning on a switch, suddenly people of all ages converged on us like a black cloud, all wanting to touch us, pulling at our clothes and gesturing madly at Mike's hair. We began to run through the warren of tiny alleyways, twisting and turning, with all looking exactly the same. Eventually, the deeper we went, the more the crowd of followers increased in size. The noise was simply deafening; all were vying for our attention. Out of breath, and exhausted, we stopped, looked around us and realized that we were completely lost. Everywhere appeared exactly the same. Small shops were haphazardly put together on either side of a dirt track. Most of the shops consisted of tin sidings with some sort of roof, all open at the front. We passed one that was completely on fire and I wondered whether we should say something, as no one especially our crowd, seemed either notice or care. There was an old man sitting cross legged on the ground in front of the burning structure smoking a pipe, completely oblivious to the world while his shop went up in flames. I thought the whole area would go up in smoke in a matter of seconds. For the next hour we tried desperately to find our way back to the main road; we played crazy charades to our followers, throwing our arms up and pointing at nothing hoping they would understand our predicament, we even asked a couple of the shopkeepers who were also sitting outside their shops, smoking some strong smelling stuff that definitely wasn't tobacco, but no one understood us. I began to panic and wondered if we'd ever find our way out of this rabbit warren. Suddenly I saw a brightly-coloured building with a strange, thatch-like roof and remembered we'd seen it before. We did an about-turn, and eventually reached the opening leading to the main road. Our crowd of followers seemed to melt away as quickly as they had appeared, and we stood laughing hysterically, thanking God we were both okay. We were hot, dirty and both wanting to throw our clothes away as soon as we reached the hotel. When we happily arrived back and told the concierge of our adventure he ran around the entrance hall like a demented idiot, telling us that many people had disappeared in the bazaars, never to be seen again. I guess we had a lucky escape!

That very night, I was rudely awakened by a deep rumbling coming from somewhere underneath my room. At first I thought it must be an approaching storm, only to realize it was an earthquake, as the room started to shake with ornaments, and pictures falling to the floor. The alarm was raised, and we all rushed out of the hotel in our sleepwear. Luckily, it was a small quake, but it most certainly rattled a few nerves. I found out later that Pakistan has a lot of earthquakes, and is one of the most seismically active countries in the world. A couple of years later, that area had a really large quake, with many buildings destroyed.

FIRST VISIT TO CALIFORNIA

While we were still living in London, in the mid-seventies, Andrew and I set up our own production company called Wendrew. He was still working as a producer for Irvin Allen, while I started learning how one set up an independent film company that was not under one of the major banners, such as Columbia, Metro-Goldwyn-Mayer, or Warner Brothers. It was around this time that the huge Hollywood-type films like *Cleopatra, Lawrence of Arabia, Cromwell* and *Nicholas and Alexandra* were fading, with the smaller, independent companies now coming to the fore. It meant that one literally touted a script to anyone who had money and was interested in investing in the film industry. It always helped to have at least one named actor to go along with the project. Certainly someone who would, hopefully, entice the public to go and see the film. Andrew had an option on an interesting script title, *Down Every Dark Alley*, which we both felt would make a good mid-budget film. There was a lot of interest in our script, which was exciting, but much too early to get over-confident about. There are always many scripts floating around studios with agents and hopeful actors, so one had to be in the right place at the right time to get any project off the ground. Very early on we were lucky to find a star-struck English businessman who was willing to invest half the money in the film. It sounded easy and very exciting. We just had to find the other half. If the subject was good, it was somewhat easy to get some of the money up-front. The stinger was getting the other half, and much more important was getting a distribution agreement; without that, the project was dead in the water. Andrew had some contacts in America, and, as he was still working on the post production of *Nicholas*, he asked me to fly out to California for a couple of meetings he'd set up. To say that I had mixed emotions at this request was an understatement. I was elated at the thought of going to California, and completely terrified at the prospect of meeting these money moguls who I imagined worked in offices one only sees on the silver screen. How wrong can a girl be?

I arrived in Los Angeles on a Saturday, and was met by a chauffeured limousine and driven to the Beverly Hills hotel – such luxury! – and I thought it could only get better. I was still very unsure of myself when out of my own environment, and suffered from acute anxiety, but I had Sunday to go over my pitch, as Andrew had put it, and I was determined not to let any opulent surroundings put me off my stride.

At nine a.m. on Monday morning, armed with a large manilla concertina file holding the script, budget, schedule and anything else I thought important, I gave the taxi driver the address and sat going through my notes for about the hundredth time. I suddenly felt very calm and self-assured. I was dressed in a business suit, also wearing what I thought was a very fashionable pair of unnecessary glasses, and heels so high I could hardly walk in them. Still, I looked the part, and who wouldn't be impressed when they met me?

The taxi eventually stopped at a rather seedy-looking building in an equally seedy part of Los Angeles, and when I queried the address, the driver assured me it was correct. As I tottered into the lobby I was met by an elderly doorman who gave me directions and floor number. He gallantly lurched forward to hold the lift door for me while I followed, feeling quite certain that if my meeting took too long this poor man would have surely bitten the dust by the time I returned to the lobby.

The office was on the top floor, and I had visions of this being the penthouse suite, but as I stood outside an exceedingly shabby door I removed the glasses, wishing that I could do the same with my shoes. The so called money man fitted the building to a tee. His name was Hank Sterner. He was short, fat and along with the room, looked as though neither had been cleaned for quite a few months. The penthouse vision went straight out of a rather grimy window. Still, I have to say he was friendly, asking if I wanted coffee or anything stronger, and the meeting started off well with him extolling the virtues of the script, though he wasn't too wild about

James Coburn, who had agreed to play the lead. After going through what we had in the way of pre-production money, schedule, and the promise of half the money upfront he proceeded to then pick holes in the script saying that, if he came into the project, he would like some changes made; but he kept assuring me the story was good. It just needed a little rewrite here and there; again he asked me if I'd like a cocktail. Suddenly, I felt completely out of my depth, but kept nodding my head at everything he said, rather like one of those awful plastic dogs that sit in the back of cars. He kept staring at my legs while asking a lot of irrelevant questions I really couldn't answer, so I put my glasses back on and went through various notes, basically telling him anything he wanted to hear. By the end of the meeting, I felt we were going round in circles getting nowhere, until he said that he would talk to a couple of his investors and get back to the producer (meaning Andrew) in a week or so. In the film world, those words are certain death and I felt justified in turning him down for dinner that evening.

My second meeting wasn't until Wednesday, and as I knew absolutely no one in Los Angeles, I spent the next day sitting by the hotel pool counting all the actors I recognized and watching the antics that went along with being famous. Still, it was a wonderful glimpse into an exotic world of sun-bronzed men and gorgeous women, all vying for attention and very obviously getting it.

Wednesday morning duly arrived, and I ditched the suit and shoes and went for the more casual approach. Again I was armed with my manila concertina file, having phoned Andrew on the previous evening telling him that I felt this was a wasted journey. I thought, "What the hell, we had a good script, a known actor, and if this person nit picks I'll get up and leave." Well, that's what I thought!

I arrived at a distinctly classier building, and now wished I was more formally dressed. A smart young woman with incredibly large breasts sat at a desk in the foyer, almost hidden behind a huge vase of flowers. I waited while she called her boss, feeling distinctly un-Hollywood and then waited another half an hour until the boss man's first meeting ended. I was then shown into John Pevners' office which was night and day compared to my first meeting on Monday. Now this was what I imagined Hollywood was all about. The office was large, with one side of the room completely glass. The furnishings were grand, and went along with the man sitting behind a huge desk. He was young, energetic and the sort of male you simply dislike on sight. He was arrogant to the point of being rude. He said he had glanced through the script (you hate it when people say that), liked the subject, and if we indeed had half the money, he would be interested in putting up the other half. He then went on to say for that he would want his own producer and production manager. He would also want to distribute the film, which, although it sounded wonderful, meant that he would make all the deals and most certainly take the lion's share. I was learning fast. Again he said he would be in touch with the English production side and the meeting was over. The whole episode took no more than twenty minutes and most certainly could have been conducted by phone. At least Hank invited me out to dinner. This moron didn't even offer me coffee.

Two weeks later Andrew got a call from Hank saying he was willing to put up the other half of the money, provided we got a distribution guarantee. Great excitement! At least now we felt we would have control over the production, and Andrew knew several companies who were interested in giving us a distribution deal for certain countries. Of course they were the countries where they were fairly certain the box office returns would be the best, and Andrew was sure that he could get guarantees on the smaller countries. So, now it seemed that we had the finance and enough distribution deals to go ahead with the pre-production. When one watches films today, it's amazing how many companies are named up-front, all either putting up some of the money or guaranteeing distribution. Now, unless one is lucky enough to get all the money from one source, and indeed, a fair chunk of it up-front, it can be a nail-biting experience.

Andrew duly rang our first investor to tell him the good news, only to be told that he'd made some bad business deals and had pulled out of our film. There was nothing we could do. We were again back to square one, with half of the money now coming from

America, plus some really good distribution guarantees which the Americans didn't want! But no one will go with a project under those terms. It was a salutary lesson about what went into making, or trying to make, an independent film. After many sleepless nights and long weekends waiting for the phone to ring from different sources we never did get that particular film off the ground, and I still admire people who spend years on a project trying to get it made. I know there have been several well-known films that took years to finally hit the silver screen. A couple of years later, while dining with friends at The White Elephant in London, both Hank Sterner and John Pevners' names came up in conversation. Two of the diners who were from California and in the film business said that, as far as they knew, neither had ever invested in any film then or since.

Andrew had worked for Irving Allen for many years, and, through him, had worked his way up to either producing or associate producing. Along with many perks, he had a chauffeur-driven car at his disposal; but the time had come when Andrew felt that he should branch out on his own. I personally didn't think it was a good decision, but Irving was getting on in years, and as Andrew said, one day Irving would retire. I think Irving Allen was sorry to see him leave, but certainly gave him a grand send off and Andrew was then on his own minus the chauffeured car. The first thing we had to do was to buy a car, as I had long since sold my little Morris. Andrew hadn't driven for quite a few years, and after a couple of harrowing experiences, I would always insist on driving. Eventually, we bought our own cars, and even though we still worked together, we very rarely drove together.

By this time, Andrew's drinking was becoming a real problem, and was now being noticed by people he was working with. It was a long way from Shepperton to St John's Wood, and there were so many times I would tell him that it would be such a tragedy if he was killed while driving under the influence, but so much more of a tragedy if he killed someone else. Still nothing worked. And for those who have had this experience, they know they are never going to win. But for me, and so many others, there was always the forlorn hope that through those many hours of talking, pleading, even threatening, something would get through; but it never did.

UNCLE BOB

The last time I saw Uncle Bob he called to say he was going to be in London for a few days, and would like to see me. I remember asking how he had got my number, and his saying that he'd stayed in touch with Ken Brisley. I thought then it was a pity he hadn't stayed in touch with me instead. Still, curiosity got the better of me, and I agreed to see him. I think I wanted him to know that, without any help from him, I was doing fine.

It turned out to be a strange evening. Andrew and I met him at a small bistro in Piccadilly. I was simply amazed that he knew all about me, and throughout the dinner, I could feel the knots of tension bubble up inside me. As the evening drew to a close, I turned to him and said. "I want to ask you one last question. For years I know there's always been talk about who is and who isn't my father. Do you know?"

He nodded saying, "Yes."

At that moment I felt as though I was on the very brink of some important knowledge. "And?" I asked.

It seemed forever he stood looking at me, then said. "I can't tell you. I promised your mother I would keep her secret. The only thing I will say is that he was titled and was French."

I was completely stunned by this revelation, telling him that I needed to know, but he stood firm, and no amount of years of pent-up emotions on my part would budge him. Sadly, it was a stormy parting, and I never saw him again.

Through the night, amid a whirlwind of emotions, I tumbled right back into my childhood, yet again wondering who I was and whether there was still someone out there who would claim me as their child. *She* was everywhere, screaming, laughing and taunting me. I roamed the flat, but she was in every room; there was simply no escape. I fervently wished I'd never seen Uncle Bob on that evening, and can never quite forgive him.

In the early hours of the morning, Andrew found me wild-eyed, rocking in a chair, not quite knowing where I was and why I was there. I vowed never to see any of my family again.

GERRY

It was around 1977 that I started going to California on a fairly regular basis. I had met a man called Gerry Rex who owned a business called Wig Specialities in London. His company made most of the wigs and hairpieces for many films both in Europe and America. Apart from that, his company also made many of the toupees for very famous clients, *both in and out* of the film industry.

Gerry was an incredibly humorous man, who would go to great, and sometimes expensive, lengths to play pranks on his friends.

I first met him with his wife, Helen, and another man called Lawrence at the Elephant on the River, a sister restaurant to the White Elephant restaurant in Curzon Street. Gerry had invited Andrew and me to have dinner with him and his wife. The Elephant on the River was great fun, with a small dance floor, and the sort of music one could dance to. After dinner, Gerry asked me to dance, and reminded me that we had indeed first met at his business, a couple of years before. Later, during the evening, he also told me that, on our first meeting, he had thought I was extremely shy and withdrawn. When questioned, he said that this was certainly not in the way I looked, but in the way I reacted to the conversations going on around me at the time. The barrier went up, and I wasn't certain whether I liked him, and was therefore quite surprised when he asked me to have lunch with him on the following day. My eyes went straight to Helen only to be assured that Lawrence was her boyfriend, and had been for some time. What a very strange setup, and yet I was so easily drawn to it! I was lonely. Gerry was an attractive, successful man, and one of the very few in the industry who knew I wasn't married to Andrew. Still, in any relationship there has to be honesty, so I declined the invitation, and on the way home told Andrew of the lunch invitation. I was somewhat surprised when he readily answered that he hoped I had accepted. He thought it would be good for me to get to know Gerry, and certainly very acceptable that I should have lunch with him. However I did not contact him and in a couple of weeks the incident was almost forgotten – almost, but not quite.

Around a month later, Andrew flew out to Malta to set up the locations for a fantasy film called *The Golden Voyage of Sinbad*, and to have a meeting with a man called Jim Hole, who, back in 1964, had a dream of building the first ever water-filming facility in the world, which was to create a bustle of filming activity on the island and which is, today, taken so much for granted.

The water-film facility was built when the British special effects wizard, Benjamin 'Jim' Hole, experienced difficulties filming out at sea on the Spanish coast when a storm brewed. With another water-based film coming his way, he managed to persuade Malta, then still under British rule, to subsidise a tank built along the island's coast. Jim Hole was to create the world's first special effects water tank. It also became unique for its natural horizon, because it was built against the open skies and sea. This avoided the requirement of painted backgrounds or, CGI (Computer Generated Images.)

What began as a facility with one large 300 x 400-foot tank was later to develop into a second massive tank, built in 1979 for *Raise the Titanic*. Concave-shaped, and thirty-six feet deep, it was ideal for underwater filming. Scores of world-renowned filmmakers have since worked in these tanks along with *The Golden Voyage of Sinbad*. It was written by Brian Clemens, whom I was to meet a few years later, and who, along with his lovely wife, became close personal friends.

Charles Schneer was the producer of our film, along with Ray Harryhausen, an incredible genius, who created the art of Dinamation and would actually make all the creatures for his films. Then after the main shooting was finished, would shut himself away at his London studio, and spend months adding his creatures to the film, one move at a time. With his unique creatures, and through his laborious hard work, they became alive on screen. There was one very special creature Ray made for our film, called Homunculus. He was a scary little fellow, but I fell in love with him, and frequently asked Ray if I could have him. He almost gave in, but not quite, and hopefully my Homunculus is somewhere safe where he, along with all the other wonderful objects Ray Harryhausen made, can be seen as a wonderful part of movie history, now, sadly, gone forever.

On the day Andrew left for Malta, Gerry Rex called, asking me again if I would have lunch with him. This time I agreed, and we met at a little Italian restaurant in St John's Wood. I was charmed by him, and also fascinated to know how he knew that Andrew was on his way to Malta.

His answer: "Andrew called me and told me he would be away for a couple of weeks."

"*And*?" I asked. Gerry shrugged.

It was as if Andrew was pushing us together, which I found very unsettling. Maybe, because he knew Gerry was married, he thought it would be a safe friendship, and then I would stay with him under those circumstances. During the lunch, Gerry made it very plain that he wanted a relationship. I already knew that Helen, his wife, had a boyfriend, and I must confess I was flattered. It was wonderful to be sitting in a nice restaurant being told I was a beautiful woman, for that was something new to me. Andrew always called me his baby doll, and had never truly treated me as a woman. Still, I needed to know a lot more about Gerry Rex, and the very odd marriage he had with Helen.

His answer to my question was. "It's quite simple, we still love each other but we are not in love anymore. We have a wonderful daughter, a lovely home. But we both need more than we can give to each other. Neither of us wants a divorce, so she has Lawrence, and I want you."

I looked around the restaurant, and wondered what the other diners were talking about. Surely no one could be having such a strange conversation as us. I remember thinking *well I guess that's show business for you*, and then I got the giggles. The situation was too ridiculous for words, but I was intrigued. It was rather like having a business discussion as I seriously told Gerry this was something I would have to think about. I didn't tell him that Andrew and I were now nothing more than really good friends, and had been for quite some time. I also didn't tell him that for the first time he had made me feel like a woman and not someone who, to the outside world, belonged to Andrew rather like a prized possession, a paper doll whom he could show around to make him feel good. Even so, getting into another complicated relationship seemed crazy and extremely worldly, which was something I definitely wasn't. Still, I mustered up what little sophistication I possessed, thanked him for the lunch, and was fairly certain I wouldn't see him again.

When Andrew returned from Malta, I told him that I'd had lunch with Gerry, and he seemed very pleased about it. A couple of weeks later, Andrew arrived home from the studio, and said we were having dinner with Gerry and Helen that evening at the White Elephant in Curzon Street. I felt a rush of excitement, apprehension and dread all rolled into one enormous decision which I knew I was about to make.

When we arrived at the restaurant, Helen, Gerry, and of course, Lawrence were already there. It seemed to me that Gerry was labouring the point about Lawrence, but it was quite obvious he was very much part of the family. The White Elephant was a very famous London haunt. One could guarantee that, on any evening, there would always be people from the entertainment world dining there. It was fun, because Gerry seemed to know everyone. They would come to the table, greeting us as if we were all old friends. Everyone adored Gerry, and throughout the time I spent with him, he never seemed to take life seriously. He made me laugh, and I was hooked.

During that time, Gerry asked me if I would accompany him to California for a two week vacation. As Andrew was still in pre-production, I was only working part-time, so I asked him if I should go. What a very bizarre life I was moving into! Thus began an affair lasting for four years.

It was a fabulous holiday, and I met *the Gang*, Gerry's American friends, who were all living the life one only sees on film: Ronnie Lubin, who only ever seemed to play tennis, and had many girlfriends, and Janice Taper, daughter of philanthropist, Mark Taper, who donated a million dollars to build the Music Center in Los Angeles County. The Board of Supervisors voted to reward Taper's philanthropy by putting his name on the seven- hundred-and-fifty-seat theatre in the Music Center complex designated for experimental productions. We all went to many productions at the theatre during my visits.

The person who seemed to reign supreme over this group was a multi-millionaire called Jack Levin. He was to figure greatly in my future life, and eventually became my surrogate father at my wedding to Raymond. Jack's wife was also called Helen, but there the similarity ended. They had married quite young, had two boys and, apparently, were very much in love. Then tragedy happened. Not long after the second son was born, Helen contracted polio, which left her completely paralyzed. During the day, she sat in a wheelchair, but at night she was put on a ventilator. For the first few years, Jack took her all over the world, trying to make her better but it was not to be. It must have been so heartbreaking for this young couple, who had wealth, love and two beautiful children to realize that there was nothing they could do. Helen was destined to spend the rest of her life unable to do anything for herself. Thank God Jack had the money to have every available help for her and the children. Helen was a wonderful person, and I don't ever remember seeing her without a smile on her face. Jack only ever spoke once to me about his despair in those early years, and when he and Helen were together, it was very obvious how deep their feelings for each other were.

On that first holiday, I also met a woman called Anita Ash. She was a true Texan with a wonderful southern drawl, tall, athletic and extremely attractive. She had been Jack's girlfriend for a number of years. The inner circle, as I called them, decided that Anita should be named Sam; that way, when Jack and friends were with Helen, there would be no careless talk in front of her. Over the years, I got to know Helen very well. She was a highly intelligent woman, and I knew she was well aware who Sam was. Also, Helen realized that

Jack needed a companion and I'm quite sure that she accepted it, knowing he would always be with her until the day she died. I don't know how long he and Anita had been together, and I never asked, but I think it was quite a few years. Jack was always so careful that neither life would invade the other. Sadly, a few years later, Helen died, and Jack eventually married Sam.

After that first trip, if I was not working on location, Gerry and I went to California two or three times a year. Each time, during those visits, Jack would always choose a special destination such as Lake Tahoe, Hawaii, Mexico and Vegas. Jack was like the Godfather, and we all enjoyed him immensely. Sam would always join us on these trips, and she and I became very close friends. When they came over to England, Jack and Sam met Andrew, and they already knew Helen and Lawrence. There were times when I would sit in the White Elephant (*which became a favorite haunt of mine*) almost having to pinch myself to make sure this was real, and thinking how crazy was this overlapping life we all shared; but somehow, at the time, it was okay. We were all happy, all having an exciting time, and none of us thought too much of the future.

Around a year into our relationship, Gerry asked me if I would form a company with him, as he had an idea for a script and wanted me to write it. I had never written anything before, but said I would at least get it down on paper, and we could then send it to a professional script writer.

We spent many hours going over the storyline, which was set in California, and was about a man who worked in the industry as a makeup artist. He was also a gambler with huge debts which, if he valued his life, needed to be paid as soon as possible. He was famous for the incredible masks he made for various films and so, in desperation, decided that he would make two or three for himself and become a bank robber. Obviously, it was a comedy, with many exploits and funny situations happening during some of his most daring raids. I wrote the story line, and it was duly turned into quite a good script. The next step was to find an actor with enough star power to hook an investor. I'd been there a few times before, so knew the score! After Gerry read the finished script, he decided that the only actor who could play this part was Peter Sellers. At first, I truly hated the idea, for having met Peter Sellers on several occasions, I had found him very unlikable; but reluctantly, I had to agree that he would be perfect. I knew it would be no good trying to go through his agent, who only accepted scripts from very well-known writers; but I was still in touch with his wife, Lynne Frederick, from our days working together in Spain on *Nicholas and Alexandra*. I called asking if she thought Peter would read a script, if I sent her a synopsis of the story. She read and liked the synopsis, and later asked me to send him the script.

A week later, Gerry and I flew to California. On each visit, Gerry always booked us into one of the most fabulous hotels in the area. This time it was the Bel Air hotel, a beautiful place, steeped in Hollywood history. Jack Levin met us for dinner, and informed us that he was taking us back to Vegas for a holiday.

Jack always stayed at the Desert Inn, and as he was a high-stake gambler, he was treated like a king, along with everyone who accompanied him. The casinos knew how to look after their affluent gamblers, and when we stayed there we were always given the best suites the Desert Inn had. Much to Gerry's delight, our suite always had a grand piano. Gerry, who could play almost any instrument by ear, would sit at the piano each evening while I was getting ready, and played some great music. Those were indeed fun times.

We used to play tennis in the morning, have a light lunch and either sunbathe or shop during the afternoon. Then we would prepare for the evening, see one of the shows and dine at one of the best restaurants in town. The finale of the evening was when we would then go to one of the casinos and gamble. Vegas was incredibly exciting, and, as one walked through the crowded casinos, many people were gambling on slot machines. Colourful people from all walks of life, all hoping their particular machine would win big, and only rarely did that happen but when it did, the whole casino would erupt into loud applause, with ear-splitting whistles. Once, when we were walking through the casino from a tennis game, I put a dollar coin into one of the machines for fun, and, wow! Lights flashed, bells started to ring, and the dollar coins kept coming. In the end, I had five thousand of those coins, and Jack, Sam, Gerry and I all carried them to the cashier to have them changed into hundred-dollar notes. We were all laughing so much, people thought we were crazy.

Jack taught me the correct way to gamble. He liked Blackjack, and rarely played at any other of the tables. He would put a certain amount of money down on the table, in his case thousands, telling me that when the money was gone it was time to leave. He never ever played beyond that amount. Each evening he would give me some cash – in my case hundreds – and then we would have fun. Gerry didn't like gambling, so he and often, Sam, would leave us to wander. We would see him talking to the piano player in one of the lounges that were situated off the main casino area, and while we were playing Blackjack, he would often be playing the piano, to an appreciative audience. I became really good at the game, and in the years that followed, I always remembered Jack's advice, and never bet more than I could afford to lose. Still, it would have been so easy to get hooked on the thrill of a turn of a card.

It was at this time Jack talked to me about a business venture in Vegas. He'd heard that *Frozen Yogurt* was a new food craze and wanted to open a shop there. He bank rolled it but I would have to be the hands on boss, choose the decor, hire staff, and oversee the general running of the business. Not an easy task seeing that I was still living in London and only visited America three or four times a year. It was very hard work and meant I would have to be in Vegas more often but I was lucky and found an exceptional girl who managed the business while I was away.

At the same time, Gerry and I decided to buy a small hotel along with a nightclub in Almeria. We were equal partners with both sharing the cost of buying and running the place. For about eighteen months, I hardly spent any time in England. Luckily Andrew was producing a film in Spain, so I divided my time between working for him, driving to the hotel in Almeria at the weekends and then flying to Vegas whenever I could spare the time. After a couple of years, the hotel and nightclub started to lose money but we were lucky and managed to sell it fairly quickly. I can't say I was sorry this venture came to an end and I think Andrew was more than happy to have me working during the daylight hours and not burning the midnight oil trying to keep up with whatever film we were working on at the time. It truly was a crazy period in my life but I can honestly say I wouldn't have missed it for the world.

FRANK SINATRA

On one of those very memorable evenings in Las Vegas I met Frank Sinatra. We went to see him in concert at the Desert Inn; he certainly was an accomplished performer, and I was absolutely captivated by him. Jack knew him quite well, and after the show, sent an invitation backstage asking him to join us for dinner. Later, as we sat ordering our dinner, I asked Jack why he didn't wait for Frank Sinatra. Jack laughed saying Sinatra got a lot of dinner invitations each evening, and very rarely accepted. I was truly disappointed, until I saw the singer making his way through the room heading in our way.

I know there are many things said about Frank but I always found him to be a perfect gentleman, amusing and very attentive. I saw him on many occasions after our first meeting, and even a few times in London. I will always remember him with great fondness and will always love the framed sketch of him that he gave me, which now hangs in our entrance hall at Fox Haven.

It was during this time in California that I had a message from Andrew, saying that Lynne Frederick had called, and asking me to get in touch with her as soon as possible. I dialled her number, while Gerry and I sat together with our ears glued to the phone. Apparently, Peter Sellers had read the script, and had said he wanted to do the film. Gerry was so shocked that he actually fell off the chair. I told her we would be back in London in a week, and I would call her so we could set up a meeting. We sat looking at each other, completely dumbfounded by this turn of events. We absolutely knew that, with his name, we had a green light. We were so excited, and must have driven everyone nuts during that last week in California.

The day after we arrived back in England, I contacted Lynne and we set a lunch date with Peter, to get the ball rolling. We were to meet him in Soho, at a restaurant called The Braganza. We ordered lunch, then spent at least an hour listening to him telling us how wonderful he was. After we finished lunch, and as the coffee arrived, he told us he had to go, and we should get in touch with his agent to set up the deal. I remember watching him leave the restaurant, fully aware that, if we made the film with him, it would be hell on wheels. Gerry was so excited he ordered a bottle of Champagne, and for a man who didn't drink, he helped me and Lynne finish the bottle.

About five weeks later we were given the news that Peter Sellers had died of a heart attack; and sadly, our film died with him.

ROD STEIGER

On our next visit to California, I met Rod Steiger, who invited us to his beachfront home at Malibu. He was a strange and exciting man who didn't conform to life or person. He did what he wanted when he wanted, and if you didn't like it, well, that was your problem not his. Rod and Gerry had been friends for years, and being with the pair of them was like riding a rollercoaster, never quite knowing when the ride would end. I do remember laughing when he told me that, as a young man, he'd trained as an opera singer; I thought he was joking, but he played Jud Fry in the film version of *Oklahoma* by Rodgers and Hammerstein, in which he performed his own singing. I was duly impressed. I simply adored him; and what fun the three of us had together! From then on, spending time with Rod became a part of our Californian ritual. During one of our visits, Rod was rushed to hospital with heart problems, and it was the start of long periods of depression, lasting for years. At those times, he would take to his bed for weeks, staring at the ceiling, scarcely speaking, not even bothering to wash. I never saw that side of him, for when we were together, he always seemed to be enjoying life to the full.

One hilarious evening, while we were staying with the usual gang in Vegas, Rod decided he would fly out to join us for the weekend. Gerry thought he would play a joke on him and dressed up as a rather greasy Mexican with full wig, moustache, plus tan makeup. I went down to the bar to keep Rod occupied while Gerry put the finishing touches to his creation. I don't know how I kept a straight face as I watched him walk through the bar and sit next to Rod looking like someone out of a third rate Mexican gangster film. He then ordered some obscure drink in a deep Mexican accent, while trying to push Rod away from the bar, muttering to himself about all actors being gay. Now that's something one doesn't do or say to Rod

Steiger and I thought that, at any minute, there would be a punch-up between the two of them, especially when Rod complained loudly that if Gerry was much longer getting ready he'd deck the skinny little Mexican and take me to dinner. As Jack and Sam surreptitiously moved away from us, I frantically signalled to Gerry to stop messing around, for we were beginning to get an excited audience nearby, all hoping that Rod Steiger would do his thing! As Gerry kept pushing him, I could see that Rod was beginning to lose it, and had visions of the three of us being escorted out of the bar, never to return. Suddenly, Rod realized it was Gerry, and literally lifted him off his feet laying him out flat on the floor. Gerry's wig fell off, and the crowd roared their approval. I'm quite sure they all thought it was some sort of cabaret performance. When Gerry asked how Rod recognized him, he pointed to his shoes saying, "I recognized your handmade shoes."

On our return to Los Angeles, Rod again invited us to stay at his home in Malibu for the weekend. He was always a late riser, so on the Saturday morning, we sat waiting patiently for him to appear. His sitting room was small, and dominated by a large painting over the fireplace. It was a portrait of Rod when he had played Police Chief Bill Gillespie in the film *In the Heat of the Night*, with Sidney Poitier. Sitting underneath the painting was his much cherished Oscar for that role.

When twelve p.m. came and went, Gerry got bored with waiting, and walked over to the painting to take a closer look. Before I could stop him he took it off the wall placing it behind a large arm chair in the corner of the room. He then took the Oscar, hiding it in a cupboard. Eventually Rod appeared with a bottle of wine plus three glasses.

Knowing Rod's history of depression, I sincerely hoped Gerry's prank wouldn't send him into one of those downward tail spins. On this particular Saturday he was in high spirits, and looking forward to taking us to one of his favorite restaurants for lunch. We'd almost finished our wine, when Rod suddenly let out a scream like an animal who'd been shot, as he spied the empty space above the mantelpiece, then realized his precious Oscar had also disappeared. I honestly thought he was having another heart attack. Pointing to the empty space, he asked us if we had seen anybody lurking around earlier that morning; to which Gerry replied they would hardly be lurking if they were carrying such a large painting. I thought then that Rod would twig Gerry had hidden the painting but no, by this time, he was in a state of panic, announcing in a strangled voice that he'd been robbed, and was going to call the police. I thought the joke had gone too far, and told Rod to look in the cupboard. As he clutched at the Oscar, raising it above his shoulders I was certain he was going to bash it over Gerry's head; instead he castigated God for giving him such lunatic friends. The painting was eventually replaced back where it belonged, and the only thing Rod said to Gerry was, "You're now picking up the lunch tab, and I'm going to have two bottles of *fucking Champagne*." Each time we went to California, we were always invited over to the Malibu home, but Rod would make a point of checking all his valuables were still where they should be before we left.

The last time Gerry and I were in California, Rod invited us to the Mark Taper theatre for a star-studded award evening. Rod was in no way what one would call a snappy dresser, and as it was a black tie event, I reminded him he would have to dress up and wear a bow tie. When Gerry and I arrived at the theatre, Rod was sitting in his limousine, obviously waiting to make an entrance. As he exited the car, I couldn't believe what I was seeing; yes, he certainly had a bow tie around his neck, but it was minus the shirt and jacket. He bowed low before me, saying he'd dressed just for me, pointing to the tie. Thank God he had the rest of his attire in the car.

It was to be our last visit to California together. A couple of months later, on a sunny Sunday morning, I received a call from Gerry asking if Andrew and I would join him and Helen at Wisley Gardens for lunch, but I declined. A few weeks earlier I had decided to sort out my crazy life and not see Gerry any more, so I thought it best that I didn't go back on my previous decision. We were still great friends, and I wanted it to stay that way. I remember telling him that he would love the gardens, as Andrew and I visited them regularly, and I was glad at last he was going to see them.

Later in the day, Bruce Forsyth, *the famous English game show host,* called to tell me that Gerry had a massive heart attack and had died while walking around Wisley Gardens. I was so thankful Lawrence had been with Helen, and that she wasn't alone on that very sad day.

A couple of months after the funeral, Helen's daughter Robbie told me that Helen knew Gerry had a girlfriend, and she was concerned that this unknown person was suffering Gerry's loss alone. I knew then it was time to talk with Helen. We met for lunch, and over coffee, I told her that Gerry and I had been more than friends. For a second, she didn't say anything, then she said, "Oh, I so wanted it to be you, and I often thought it might be; especially when I used to see you with Andrew. I knew your relationship with him was slightly odd."

It was such a relief to have everything out in the open, and to know Helen was okay with me. I asked her if, later on, she might marry Lawrence. "Good Lord, no! Lawrence is nice, but I would never think of marrying him." Then she leaned in closer and asked, "Did you ever want to marry Gerry?" and my very honest answer was most definitely *No*. We had cried together after Gerry's death, and now we were laughing together. Oh, if life could always be so simple, through very unusual and difficult times.

During the next couple of years, Helen and I didn't see each other very often, but we kept in touch. She sold the house, and a new man came into her life. The last time I saw her, she looked very content, and I think her rollercoaster life had settled into a more normal and happy time.

I saw Rod for the last time in London. He was staying at the Connaught Hotel, and asked me to have dinner with him. It turned out to be a rather sad and nostalgic evening for both of us.

Gerry was no longer with us, and Rod's health was again beginning to be a problem. I feel lucky to have known this very entertaining but extremely complicated man.

·

THE MARTIAN CHRONICLES

The first time I met Rock Hudson was, again, at my favorite restaurant The White Elephant in Curzon Street. Andrew invited him to dinner along with Roddy McDowall, Gayle Hunnicutt, Robert Beatty, Darren McGavin and director Michael Anderson. We were due to fly to Malta within the week, to start shooting *The Martian Chronicles*. Rock was playing the lead in the film, and Andrew thought it would be nice if he met the director and the actress who was to play his wife in the mini-series, along with a few of the other actors who would be working with him in Malta. It was a fun evening, only hampered by me having laryngitis and only being able to croak back at Rock whenever he said anything to me. Over the next few months, he used to tease me, asking where the sexy voice had gone. He also taught me how to play backgammon, and we both became slaves to the game, setting up the board wherever and whenever we could. After I beat him three times in a row, he vowed that he would never play the game with me again, and then unsuccessfully tried to teach me chess instead!

I thought Rock was a very handsome man, with a wicked sense of humor and an easy charm. We became fast friends during our stay. I also simply adored Tom Clark, who was Rock's partner and manager and was with him throughout the filming in Malta and Lanzarote.

Bridget Sellers, who was the wardrobe mistress on the film, fell madly in love with Rock, and followed him around like a shadow. One day I made the mistake of saying that both Tom and Rock were each as handsome as men could be, and what a waste to the female world. It was simply incredible even then that some people didn't know Rock was gay, and Bridget was one of those people. She almost had a nervous breakdown on the spot, hurling abuse at me for telling such lies. I most certainly had burst her balloon, and I don't think she ever accepted the fact. I felt truly bad about it, and told Rock that Bridget was on the warpath, and I was so sorry I'd said anything to her. Thank God, he thought it was quite funny, and was rather surprised, because he reckoned by then that everyone in the world knew, and also said, with a twinkle in his eye, it was sad that she was a wee bit too old for him. Still, he was always so sweet with her, and for the rest of the filming, she maintained he was more heterosexual than any other man she'd ever had the fortune to work with. A few years later, on the day Rock died, Bridget phoned me in California, and cried for at least ten minutes before I got any sensible word out of her. So it proves one thing, *love conquers all!*

Malta was quite a barren island, but the people were so friendly, and after working there on the Sinbad film, it felt like coming home, with many of the residents still there and still remembering us. The restaurants were few and far between, but the small shops would do their best to find us fresh vegetables and fruit, which I would take back to our rented house and cook huge Sunday lunches for the many crew and cast who would arrive, with or without an invitation, expecting a sumptuous meal. Luckily, I always seemed to have and to cook enough food to satisfy all who came. My only request was that they brought a bottle of the local vino, and any fresh fruit for a dessert. We sat at long Mafia-style tables in the garden, ate until we were full, then sang silly songs until it was decided that all should go back to their hotels to get ready for another week's filming. It was such fun, an insulated bubble separating us from the outside world, and a time I wouldn't have missed; sometimes wish I could experience it again, if only for the extraordinary feelings and emotions those memories bring back to me whenever I think about them.

Although, at the time, I was deeply distressed in my private life with Andrew, we managed to patch over the cracks, and would appear happy and content to the outside world. We were both so incredibly busy that personal problems were put aside like unwanted belongings which you knew one day had to be sorted out, but never quite getting around to attacking the task. It was a time where I laughed a lot and cried a lot, but it was all part of this very rich, colourful life I was leading. I guess we all make sacrifices in our lives, and my highlights most certainly outweighed any downside.

It was a very sad day when we finished filming in Malta, and although we were moving on to Lanzarote, most of the cast were not coming with us. As we once again packed up, ready to return to England, I said goodbye to Rock and Tom, and also all the film buddies I'd made over the months of filming, all promising to meet up again either in California, London or wherever. At the time, all the promises were meant, but the sad fact is that one very rarely saw those close friends that were made during the long months together on that or any other film I worked on. Actors and crew move on to other locations and new projects, and although we may not meet again, the memories are there forever.

STANLEY BAKER

Andrew and I were between films when Andrew had a call from Stanley Baker, who was a very well known actor at the time. He wanted Andrew to come and talk about making a film with him called *Zulu Dawn*. Stanley Baker had made *Zulu* in 1964, and now wanted to make the prequel to *Zulu*, called *Zulu Dawn*. We went to meet him at his home, outside of London. To me, he didn't have the appeal that a lot of actors have. I thought him a very curt man, with a heavy Welsh accent. His wife, on the other hand, was charming, and I spent a happy couple of hours with her in their garden, while the men talked business in Stanley's study. Over the next couple of years, there were various meetings between Baker and Andrew about the progress of the project, and making the film in South Africa, where the original film had been made. Stanley Baker was extremely fired up about the project, wanting Andrew as one of the producers. Sadly, Stanley Baker died in 1976 before he could get the project off the ground, and it was eventually made in 1979, starring Burt Lancaster and Michael Caine. Andrew was not included on the production team. I felt truly sorry for him as he had put a tremendous amount of work on the pre-production of the film; with his expertise in maths, he had drawn up a working budget and schedule for the eventual production of the film without getting paid. Andrew took it all in his stride, for as he always said, that was the film industry: good or bad, one had to go with the flow.

A few years before Stanley Baker's death, and while the *Zulu Dawn* project was still very much in the picture, we were working on another Sinbad film in the south of Spain. Stanley was also there, working on another film. With both sets of actors and production teams staying at the same hotel, we would all spend the weekends around the hotel pool soaking up the sun, swapping stories about our respective films. It was always like one large family for, at the time, there were a great many films made in Spain, where cast and crew had almost certainly worked together on many other films.

On this particular Sunday, Stanley Baker was in the pool, flirting with a very beautiful girl who happened to be his leading lady. He kept diving in the pool and surfacing by her side, swimming around her in circles, obviously extremely taken with her. He looked good with a nice tan and well-defined muscles. After yet another dive he again surfaced close to her, but this time, he was minus his toupée. Obviously very embarrassed, the poor girl didn't know quite what to do, so she quickly swam to the edge of the pool, got out and very quickly disappeared into the hotel. I'm afraid there was a lot of merriment that went around the pool, but I watched mesmerized at the black floating mass gently making its way over to my side of the pool. I leaned forward to retrieve the soggy mess and, as Stanley Baker swam over to me, I solemnly handed it to him saying, "Once it's dried, it will be as good as new." He never spoke to me again.

PINETREE LODGE

Having lived all my life in the country, I found the flat in St John's Wood almost unbearable at times, especially in the summer. Though it was large and beautiful, there was no garden. The nearest green belt was Regent's Park, which luckily, was within walking distance from the flat. If I wasn't working at the studio, I would pack a picnic and with Pickles, my Yorkshire terrier, we would go off to the park and walk for miles – shades of Paddy in times gone by. Once again I was leading a fairly solitary life, with Sandra Dorne my only female contact; but then, most of my life had been solitary, so it wasn't something I found too difficult. I think the only sad thing was that I was still far more comfortable in my own company than with other people. Outwardly, I was a woman, but in my head I was that scared child, still trying to come to grips with life, and the sad reality was that I didn't know quite where to start. On one hand, I was living with a man who treated me like his little girl, and on the other, I was being very adult, trying to hold our lives together while watching a truly nice man destroy everything through alcohol. I think one of the saddest times at the flat was when Pickles died. She had been my constant friend, always with me from Devon to London.

One late afternoon, while driving from the studio through the traffic to St John's Wood, I made up my mind that it was time I looked for a house in the country. The surrounding area near Shepperton Studios was really lovely, and somewhat reminded me of Bath. That evening I talked it over with Andrew, who wasn't keen at all, as he was still paying child support for his three children. I told him that, with the money I still had from the sale of my salon and what I had saved on the film *Nicholas and Alexandra* and other films, I had enough to put a sizable deposit on a small country home. He seemed relieved, but said the ball was firmly in my court. It would be my home, along with the mortgage! It was the first time in a very long while that I had felt truly excited.

The following weekend I drove to Shepperton, stopping at various estate agents in the surrounding area, and for the next couple of months, I spent every weekend looking at properties with either excitement, disillusion, or plain disappointment, until I saw a five-hundred-year-old thatched cottage in Horsell, just outside a village called Chertsey. It was situated in a small lane, and completely hidden by a tall thick hedge with a church door gate leading into a very pretty garden, or at least I knew it would be pretty once I got to work on it. There it was, my cottage! The owner, who was leaving the country, wanted a quick sale and had already had it surveyed, so if any repairs were needed, they could be done before it went on the market. The cottage had two bedrooms and a bathroom at one end, with a large main hall in the middle, leading to a huge sitting and dining room with a fireplace you could almost walk into. The small kitchen was at the end of the cottage. Amazingly, all the rooms had fairly high ceilings, but the doors leading into the main part of the house were not! So Andrew and I had to learn to duck through them. It took awhile to remember that little bob, but after a few bumps and bruises, we and our guests got the hang of it!

The sale went through very quickly, and by the Spring, I was the proud owner of Pinetree Lodge. My life changed drastically from then on, and for the better. I also found a kennel nearby that bred Yorkshire Terriers, and my second dog, named Dida, came into my life. She was three months old and so small she could sit in the palm of my hand. She became the love of my life, and eventually travelled all the way to America to live with me there.

Like most newly acquired homes, Pinetree Lodge needed work. I still had a few thousand left so I went ahead with some much needed renovations. The kitchen was very small and old-fashioned. Still, there was another unused room leading off from the kitchen, which was opened up, turning the area into a good-sized kitchen and breakfast nook. By the time all the modern units, that were in keeping with the cottage, were finished, it looked simply beautiful. It was my very private haven.

After work at the studio, I would drive back to Horsell, turn my key in the gate lock, and once again, hide myself away from the world, except this time, it was a wonderful world. I spent almost every weekend working in the garden, and as Autumn came around I'd already planted a huge vegetable area, and with Andrew's help erected a new greenhouse at one end, hidden by a Leylandii hedge, turning the rest of the garden into a beautiful fragrant setting with rose beds and lawns surrounded by flowering bushes and shrubs. Even Andrew was impressed with all my hard work. This was a very happy time in my life. As the lease of Wellington Court was now up, we moved the remaining furniture into Pinetree Lodge. I now had my own home, with, at last, a garden. For me, being without a garden was like being half-alive. When I was not working at the studio, my little Yorkshire terrier, Dida, and I would go for long country walks; then I would sit in my garden, knowing all was well with my world.

Because the cottage was so near to Shepperton Studio, Andrew spent more time there and less at the cottage. Although he always said he liked it, Pinetree Lodge wasn't really important to him. It was somewhere to come to at the end the day. I don't think a home life was as essential to him as the studio. Still, we had many happy times there, and I know we both loved living in the country and away from the city.

YOCKLEY

Pinetree Lodge was lovely, but quite small, and after a couple of years, I had a yearning to have a bigger home. Again, I talked this over with Andrew, telling him that I was thinking of selling the cottage for a more traditional home. His answer was the same as before. It would be up to me, and if there was a mortgage, it would be mine not his. So again I started looking for a new home. I loved the area, and didn't want to move too far away from Shepperton Studio. Again I felt the rush of excitement. I knew the cottage would make a profit, and I also knew the kind of home I was looking for. My weekends were once again taken up with estate agents and viewing houses. Sad to say, Andrew didn't accompany me at all. In fact it was Jan Dorman, a friend of mine, with whom I worked with on location in Malta. Jan was also the hairdresser on one of the Sinbad films, and it was she who came with me to view most of the houses.

Eventually the day came when I saw Yockley for the first time. I drove down a long drive turning a corner to reveal a lovely formal house with a beautiful mansard roof. The house was surrounded by three acres of garden. There was a galleried staircase from the main hall, with another staircase at the other end of the house, leading to the guest wing. The house consisted of five bedrooms with three bathrooms upstairs. On the main floor a sitting room, dining room, study, powder room, a huge kitchen with a day room leading off the kitchen, plus a laundry room – and, yes, the whole house needed a lot of work! But I wanted it. That evening, I excitedly told Andrew about it, and asked him if he wanted to see it. His interest was not impressive, and again he said it was completely my decision and my financial burden. Unlike me, Andrew was not a man who was governed by his surroundings. As long as he had somewhere to sleep and dinner on the table, life was okay. I sat back and thought about the decision I was about to make. It was a big step, especially as I would be doing it alone, but I felt it was the right decision. I put Pinetree Lodge on the market, and made an offer on Yockley. Within six weeks the cottage was sold, and my offer was accepted on Yockley. I was both excited and extremely nervous.

The move to Yockley took place on a very icy February morning. So to move from a small, cosy warm home to a large, empty and very cold place was a shock, both physically and mentally. There were many days when I wondered if I'd made the right choice, as I divided my time between the studio and the house, trying to organize the renovations that would make Yockley into my home. It took almost a year of living on bare boards with minimal furniture and workmen hammering, stripping out and redesigning almost every room, but, in the end, it was worth all the hard work and sleepless nights. Yockley became a beautiful home, with gardens to match. While the work went on in the house, every spare minute away from the studio was spent in the garden working on flowerbeds to the rear of the house, then painstakingly weeding an overgrown Japanese rock garden and bringing it back to its former glory and into a beautiful setting for the entrance of the main house. It was a very challenging year, with Andrew in pre-production for a new film called *The Zany Adventures of Robin Hood*, while I tried to make our lives as normal as possible.

Every so often, on a Friday evening, we would drive into Shepperton and have dinner at the Warren Lodge, a well known small hotel in the square in the heart of the village. It had a quaint, old-world atmosphere, and one could imagine people of yesteryear dining in the restaurant. We would sit at our usual table, order our favorite meal, then somehow, the conversation would inevitably drift yet again to the decision which we both knew would have to be made soon. We were friends, and always would be, and although Andrew was quite happy with the way things were, I certainly was not. We had got ourselves into a ridiculous situation, a couple to the outside world, but not in our world. Andrew's drinking had now become full blown. Each morning he would get up early. He seemed very alert and raring to go. He would have a good morning, working in his office but then, at lunch he would start to drink. By the time he came home, after a few more drinks at the studio bar, he would be well under the influence. It was both heartbreaking and frustrating to watch this man slowly disintegrate with no amount of talking or pleading for him to stop making the slightest difference. Joanne Stewart's words about Andrew being an alcoholic always came back to haunt me.

On this particular evening, I think we both knew our relationship was at an end, and this time, it was me who said that I would wait until after the film was over for us to go our separate ways; and at last Andrew agreed. There were no tears, just a firm resolution we would stay friends. It was as if the weight of the world had been lifted, and now I could move on; my only hope was that in the next few weeks Andrew would not renege on our decision. We were living at Yockley, and the work on the house was almost finished. It was a really beautiful house, but it needed life and laughter; and above all, it needed to be lived in.

After dinner, we arrived back at Yockley, and armed with very strong black coffee, we sat talking until the early hours – which in itself was a miracle, as Andrew hardly ever made it beyond eight p.m. We discussed the house, and I told him that I would probably sell it and move back to London. At the time I remember thinking that I should have kept Pinetree Lodge and not bought such a large house, but it was too late to think about what one should have done. On looking back, it's sad to say that Yockley brought me no happiness; as beautiful as it was, one cannot put into a building what isn't there. It wasn't a home, it was a home in waiting. I can only hope whoever owns it now has the happiness I never quite achieved.

We started pre-production on the new film, and for a few months Andrew curbed his drinking, managed to stay awake during the evenings, and I could see that he yet again thought I would forget about our decision and carry on as if nothing had happened. Every so often I would remind him that although we were working long hours, he still had to start looking for another place to live, but it never quite got through to him.

One weekend, Andrew's mother came to stay. I liked her tremendously and I knew she liked me. She often told me I was good for her son, but this weekend she could tell there was something drastically wrong. After preparing dinner, we all sat in the garden, enjoying a perfect English summer day. Andrew went inside to make some phone calls, though I suspected he really wanted to have a drink.

Andrew's mother touched my knee. "What's wrong?"

I certainly had no intentions of telling her about Andrew so I shook my head. "I'm not an idiot and I have known for some time things are not right."

"Andrew and I have decided to separate."

"I wondered how long it would take you to come to that decision."

I sat and stared at her. This was her son, and I'd just told her I was leaving him.

"I've watched you for the last three years, and although I love my son, I know you can't go on like this."

"I've tried so hard to make it work, but I can't do it anymore. I can't cope with his drinking, and whatever I say or do he won't or can't stop."

"I can assure you it's a bit of both, and you will never stop him. I've tried." She took my hand in hers. "Although I hate to say this, I'm begging you to make a fresh start before it's too late."

RAY AUSTIN

On a lovely sunny Sunday in June, Andrew and I were enjoying a relaxing afternoon in the garden. The pre-production at Shepperton was almost finished, and in three weeks we were due to start shooting *The Zany Adventures of Robin Hood* on location in England. We had a really great cast, with George Segal playing Robin Hood, and Morgan Fairchild, Maid Marion. Roddy McDowell, who was a friend of the director Ray Austin, had agreed to come over to England to have fun with his long time buddy, as he put it! And my old friend Tom Baker was playing the villain. We also had some other great English actors who would be making up the rest of the cast. The director Ray Austin was due to arrive that afternoon from Los Angeles. I knew nothing about him except that he was English and had moved to America a few years ago.

It was around mid-afternoon that I got a call from Ray Austin, saying that he'd arrived at his hotel, which was near the studio, and wondered if I knew anywhere in the area where he could have dinner. I gave him the names of a couple of restaurants, then Andrew asked why we didn't ask him over for dinner at Yockley. It would be a nice, relaxing way to get to know him before meeting him at the studio. I must confess that I really didn't want to play the hostess. I wanted to relax, have a quiet dinner and go to bed; still, I duly asked, hoping he would refuse, but no such luck. I reluctantly laid another place setting at the dinner table, prepared more vegetables and waited for him to arrive.

I stood at the hall window of Yockley as a dark blue Mercedes came to a stop outside the front door, and an extremely tanned man with curly blonde hair, dressed completely in white stepped out of the car. I noticed he had a couple of gold chains around his neck plus a gold bracelet. My very first reaction was *oh my God, he must be gay!* I opened the front door and said, "Hello, you must be Raymond

Austin." His answer was, "Please tell me you're the au pair and that you're not married."

"It's no to both those questions," I answered. And so Raymond Austin had come into my life with a bang.

Over dinner he told me that apart from his mother, I was the only person to call him Raymond. In the industry, he was Ray Austin. I said I never abbreviated names and to me he would be and to this day is Raymond. The dinner was interesting, to say the least, and our director was mesmerizing, he kept asking me if I would be his secretary, I think more in fun; but Andrew took it very seriously saying that, by now, he couldn't manage without me. What he really meant was that he'd been through all my teething problems, and he wasn't about to break in another production assistant at this late stage.

As I watched Raymond leave, I knew I was treading on dangerous ground. I had made up my mind I was going to get through this film with Andrew, then at long last, sort my life out. In the meantime, I didn't need any distractions, no matter how charming our director was. Besides, he lived in California, and I lived in England.

Throughout the next week, Andrew brought work home to me, and I happily finished the contracts in my new study, telling him that this was good, as there were no distractions, and I could finish my work much faster. It was in the middle of the following week that Andrew asked me why I wasn't coming to the studio and said that, obviously, I couldn't work from home much longer. Up until then, I hadn't voiced the reason even to myself, but I knew deep down I didn't want to see Raymond Austin. Still, Andrew was right; once shooting started, I would have to be on location with the rest of the cast and crew.

The first morning back at work was fine. There were no distractions, and Andrew was happy to have me working alongside him again. At one p.m. Chuck Fries, the American producer, stuck his head around the door, and invited us to have lunch with him at the studio restaurant.

I sat in a booth, while Andrew and Chuck got drinks at the small bar adjoining the restaurant, and then saw Raymond Austin making his way toward me. He sat next to me, and then said, "What am I going to do about you, young lady?"

I feebly answered, "I don't know." I think it was then I knew I'd fallen in love with him; in fact, I really knew the minute I opened my front door on that Sunday afternoon. How can one look at a complete stranger and know? I've absolutely no idea, but at the time I knew nothing would come of it. I didn't need any more complications; besides, I had too much to sort out in my life, and I had no idea what his life was like, apart from the fact that he was married, and lived in California.

With pre-production finished, we were ready to move to the country for the location of the film. Our location manager found us a really nice house, where we would stay during filming. Raymond joined us, and shared the other half of this large house.

It was obvious that Raymond and I were attracted to each other, but we were much too busy to take it further, and besides, I truly didn't want to get into another relationship with someone who wasn't free. Raymond was funny, dynamic and an innovative director. All the cast and crew simply loved working with him. Though he kept everyone on their toes, it was a happy set. He had to watch schedule and budget, while getting top performances from his actors. I had worked with a few directors, but none of them brought out the best in an actor like Raymond Austin. It was definitely one of the happiest experiences I'd had in the industry.

Raymond rarely talked about his marriage, but late one evening, after we'd finished shooting on location, and Andrew had gone to bed, we stayed up talking about our respective lives. I told him that Andrew and I were going our separate ways after the post production on the film. He told me his marriage was virtually over. We talked about the what-ifs, but were so wrapped up with the problems of our own relationships that neither of us could think any further. I remember Raymond saying he would not marry again, he then said that four times was enough, especially as none had worked out.

When he told me that, I almost fell off the chair in shock. For me, marriage had always been a scary word of commitment, and, as I have said, having been someone's property for all of my childhood, to me marrying meant just that: I would be someone's property once again. And although I had lived with Andrew for a number of years, even with the problems we had, I never felt he owned me. I always thought that making a vow to live with a man for the rest of my life would never bring lasting happiness. Once again, it was a shadowy figure who every so often would come stealthily into my life and rob me of *me*. Though I craved for a life where there would be a complete partnership, from what I saw in my world, and I can only talk about my world, relationships were very haphazard or exceedingly lopsided. My total fear of complete commitment had indeed thrust me into those very scenarios, so here I was, deciding to clear the debris that had built up around me and move on. My love for Andrew will never die; even after his death it is still there. There are many people who have come into my life, men and women whom I love dearly; some, like Judith Halsall, now so far away, with many years between us, yet love has not diminished, and never will.

While we were talking about our respective lives, Raymond told me about Cary Grant, and how they met. I told him that on my eighteenth birthday my grandmother took me to The Hole in the Wall, a famous Bath restaurant, for dinner. As I walked past the window of the restaurant, I saw Cary Grant sitting at one of the tables. He looked as handsome off screen as he did on. I don't even remember what I ate that evening, I sat staring at Mr Grant. Raymond asked me if Cary was with anyone and I remembered that he was with a young man. "That was me." He said, "I always drove Cary to Bristol to visit his mother, then we would stop in Bath for dinner on the way back to London." He then said, "Did you notice me?"

My answer was, "Of course not I was too busy looking at Cary Grant to notice anyone else." How very strange to think that I actually saw my future husband on my eighteenth birthday!

It was during this film that Andrew and I actually finalized our separation. It had taken him a very long time to come to this realization. Parting from someone you no longer care for must be so much easier. Parting from someone you still care for is very difficult, for there was no conflict between us. Our feelings were those of very deep friendship, and I did worry about him, and wondered how he would manage on his own, *and* how I would manage. There was an apartment in Paris which I'd bought after we'd finished filming *Nicholas and Alexandra*, and I also had Yockley. All this was going on while we were on location, and, as usual, toward the end of the work day Andrew would be asleep by the time he reached our accommodation. At weekends we would talk for many hours, trying to sort out what our next move should be. Andrew wanted to stay in the house, and came up with ridiculous ideas of how we could still work together and share Yockley, with him living in one part of it and me in another. It was a sad revelation, and I knew that for Andrew this would mean nothing would change; I would still be in his life. In the end, I told him I would probably sell the house and the apartment, but he couldn't come to terms with the fact that he would then have to find somewhere else to live. We spent hours going over his finances, and I knew he could afford either a small town house or flat near Shepperton, which was his stamping ground. It was at that time I realized I *would* have to sell Yockley, and probably the apartment, for my total investments were in both properties.

The film and post-production came to an end, and Raymond left for his home. A couple of days later, Andrew took the negative of the film over to California. During this time, I talked to a couple of estate agents, and started thinking seriously of what I was going to do moving forward. I wanted to stay in the film industry, and was offered a job as a personal assistant to a director who was about to make a film in Australia, of all places. I had little time to make my decision, and I wanted to wait until Andrew had returned from America. Talking for so long about life's decisions was one thing; actually making those decisions was something else. While Andrew was away I was so unsettled that I felt like doing something drastic to myself, so I let a friend perm my hair. Oh, what a disaster! I rushed off to the nearest salon, and had the frizzy mess cut short. It was a very different- looking me who left, but at least the frizz was gone.

Three or four days after Raymond left, I suddenly got a phone call from him, and, as always, he was quick to the point. He told me that his wife had a boyfriend, who had actually been living in his home while he was working in England, and was still there when he returned a day too early! His manager, David Licht, had already set the wheels in motion for a divorce, and his wife had immediately moved into an apartment with the boyfriend. Raymond then asked me how quickly I could fly out to California. I remember my brain spinning in all directions as I tried to listen to what he was saying, but I knew instantly what I would do, I *would* fly to California. This was the one person in my whole life who did not cast a black cloud over my future. This was a man who, again, I hardly knew; yet his past didn't worry me, nor my past him. I'm sure that all people who enter into a relationship such as ours are convinced it will be forever and sadly it does not always turn out that way. Looking back on those early days, how crazy were we to think we could build a life together on such little knowledge? Was it just the incredible attraction we had for each other? Would it burn brightly for a while, then dwindle like a flickering candle, before it finally fizzled out? But you see, we both knew it was an everlasting candle. I told Raymond I had to wait until Andrew got home to tell him I would not be staying in England.

Andrew duly returned, very buoyant from his travels. He chatted about this and that, and the promised meetings for *our* next project. It was so sad, for even after all our talking, he was back again, thinking he could pat me on the head, not even noticing my extremely short hair. He would tell me I was his baby doll, and we would carry on living separate lives together. I sat watching as he poured his second drink, knowing I must tell him soon. It was very difficult watching the light go out in someone's eyes and knowing I was the cause. I gently reminded him that we had made our decision to part even before Raymond came into my life, and try as he might, he could not and must not ever blame Raymond. We sat in silence for what seemed like hours; then Andrew said. "I want you to be happy, and I've known for a very long time I could never do that for you. It was enough to have you here beside me, and I always hopelessly believed it would be enough for you. I put you on a leash, telling anyone and everyone you were mine. That way they would stay away from you." He then said that he wanted desperately to blame Raymond. It was so much easier than blaming himself; and I told him that, really, no one was to blame. It was life, and life happens. I reminded him that our decision had been made long before Raymond came to England. Over the next few years, Andrew came to California a couple of times, and always visited us. I was glad to see he was getting on with his life.

I put the sale of Yockley on hold, to give Andrew more time to find somewhere to live, and left Dida dog in his care until I could work out how to get her to California. I packed my suitcase, and within a week, I was on my way. Andrew insisted on coming to the airport, and even sat with me until the plane was announced. Tears were again shed as we said our goodbyes: so many years together, starting in Devon and ending at Heathrow airport.

Raymond was at Los Angeles airport to meet me. My first thought was that he looked very thin, and probably hadn't eaten properly since he left England. I think his first thought of me was probably shock, because I suddenly had short hair, and I know it took some time for him to get used to it. He drove me to his home in the Hollywood Hills; there was no garden, just a jacuzzi outside the master bedroom leading to a very steep rocky hill going way up, and looking very unstable. I'd left my home to come to a home that wasn't mine. I could see Raymond in the house, and I could also see his soon-to-be ex-wife there but I couldn't see me.

That evening, Raymond took me to his favorite Italian restaurant, named Giuseppe's, after the owner. We ordered cocktails, then Giuseppe brought over the menu. Hidden underneath it was a Cartier box with a Santos watch inside, and on the back was the date of our first meeting at Yockley. I was simply speechless, as I had often admired Raymond's watch and always wanted one. What a lovely present! After dinner, Raymond asked me to marry him; I said yes before he even had time to finish the question, for there was absolutely no doubt in my mind this was the man I wanted to spend the rest of my life with. Giuseppe arrived with champagne announcing to the restaurant that one of his best friends was getting married again!

We had a couple of weeks together before Raymond was off to the studio for a new show. I felt like an alien on another planet. Although, over the years, I'd spent many months in California, I was not yet ready to get in touch with any of my American friends. Later on, I called Jack Levin, to tell him that I was now living in California, and wanted him to meet Raymond. They became firm friends from the very first meeting. Raymond also met Anita, Sam and the lovely Helen.

It was at this time that I first met David Licht's wife, Inge. Right from the beginning, she took me under her wing. She knew I had no transport, and would arrive at the house to whisk me off to lunch at one of the restaurants on Rodeo Drive, then take me shopping. She was a truly special person, and from the first time I met her, I knew we would become firm friends.

I had never driven in the States, and even if I had, I didn't possess a car, so for five days of each week, I was a prisoner in Raymond's home, wondering what the hell was I doing; but each evening, when he arrived back, everything always fell into place. And I knew somehow that we would survive. We would go out to dinner and I wondered if we'd ever settle into a normal life together. One of Raymond's favorite foods was sushi. Now I'd never even heard of sushi, and the thought of eating raw fish every evening did not appeal to me in any way. But for the first few weeks I picked away at the different types of fish the Sushi chef named, Nobi, offered, never having the nerve to tell Raymond that if I had to eat any more raw fish I'd throw up. Another week came to an end, and we were again off on our way for sushi and I knew this was the night I would have tell him that I simply hated sushi, and couldn't take any more of it. I decided to wait until the end of the meal, for it was rather like giving Raymond one last taste of his favorite diet, because once I told him, I knew he would never take me there again. I sat watching Nobi prepare the sashimi, knowing this would be my last visit. Then, a strange thing happened. I tentatively chewed on various fish, while Nobi made me an Eel hand roll. Heaven! I truly thought I'd died and gone to heaven. I suddenly knew that if I chose carefully, I could enjoy the food, and Raymond would not be deprived of his then staple diet. I never did tell Raymond I was about to drop the hammer on his beloved sushi, and from then on, Nobi always cooked me some tasty delicacies, which I enjoyed immensely.

It was around this time that I told Raymond I had to get mobile, if only to get to the shops and buy us some proper food so I could cook dinner, and also not feel such a prisoner. Later, Raymond confessed to me that, each evening, when he arrived home, he always dreaded that I might have packed up and gone back to England.

One Sunday morning, while we were on our way to the Beverly Hills hotel for lunch, Raymond told me that he was going to buy me a car. I was so excited, and couldn't quite believe that, at last, I would be mobile. On our way to the hotel, Raymond suddenly stopped the car, got out, and walked around to the passenger side. Now at the time, he had a Mercedes 350 SEL, a big car which was absolutely immaculate. It took me a few minutes to realize that he wanted me to drive the rest of the way. I firmly stuck like glue to the passenger seat, telling him I would never dare to drive his car, especially in Beverly Hills. I had never driven on the other side of the road and the thought of doing so absolutely terrified me. His answer was.

"Well darling, if you don't drive, we won't be going to lunch, in fact we won't be going anywhere. We'll sit here for the rest of the day."

I knew Raymond well enough by then to know he meant what he said, and we would be sitting there until I moved over and drove his wretched car.

Raymond has many incredible qualities, and one of them is patience. He must also have had great faith in me not to wrap his beloved car around the nearest lamp post! But after a quick lesson, I started tentatively down the road, with encouraging words from him and drove all the way to the hotel as if we were in a funeral procession; but we arrived there all in one piece, and I was in need of a very stiff drink, only to be told that alcohol was out, as I would be driving home. Two days later, a small BMW was delivered to the house, and I felt like a bird who had found out that it could fly.

I was now mobile, and each day I would plan an outing. I had become good friends with Kiva Lawrence, who was the girlfriend and later wife of stuntman, Robert Hoy, a lifelong friend of Raymond's; in fact, their friendship went back to the early fifties, when they were both starting out in the industry as stuntmen. Kiva, an actress and a sculptress, was an incredibly attractive woman and though, sadly, she died in 2016, after a long fight with cancer, and I lost a most beautiful friend, I will never forget her voice; it was soft and melodic, and whenever I think of Kiva, I can still hear that wonderful voice on her answer machine, saying, *this is Kiva, please leave a message.*

I would get into my little BMW, drive over the mountain and arrive at Kiva's home, incredibly pleased with myself for having made the journey in one piece and, above all, not getting lost. We would then venture forth on to Rodeo Drive, and join all the glamorous people who never let themselves get or look a day over thirty, and troll the streets feeling like a million dollars. Like young children, we would breathe all over the shop windows looking at the designer clothes we could neither afford, nor indeed wanted, to buy! We would then have lunch in one of the small bistros that dotted the area. Kiva and I had the same sense of humour, and we would sit for hours, mulling over our lives and what we both wanted for our future. Hers was to marry Robert and carry on with her acting and sculpting. Mine was to become a whole person, and, if I ever could, to let the past go. I loved Raymond to distraction, but now I had no stability in my life. Raymond was a very dynamic and driven man, and at the time, I felt I could very easily be swamped by him. I did not want to become the little housewife who stayed at home waiting for her man to come home each evening. On the other hand, I knew I could no longer work in the film industry. Raymond was in television, and if I went back to work, it meant we would do what so many others have done, meet up every so often while going off to our various locations around the world. Besides, for me, leaving England meant I had virtually given up my film career.

It was an unsettling time. We both wanted to move into a home of our own, and after Raymond talked with his manager David Licht, it was decided it would be best if Raymond gave his now ex-wife the house and a hefty settlement, for California was a no fault state, and although her boyfriend had moved into their home, while Raymond was away on location, it didn't matter. He railed against it, but the law was the law. I would hate to think of another woman moving into my home, and I'm sure Raymond's ex felt the same way; also, I was very happy with the decision. I wanted a home of my own.

During this time, I realized that Andrew could not cope with work while trying to find somewhere to live and looking after a small dog, so I decide Dida should come to us in California. Raymond was not too sure that he wanted such a small dog in his life for he had always had what he called manly dogs! But Dida duly arrived, and I picked her up at the airport, none the worse for her long journey. I was so happy to see my little Yorkshire Terrier, and pleased she settled in so well. Animals always amaze me, they can be transported from one side of the world to the other, and as long as they are fed and loved, they are fine. At first, she didn't take to Raymond, she would snap at him if he tried to make contact with her. He found this very upsetting, as all animals usually gravitated to his side, then would stick to him like glue. I kept telling him that, in time, she would get used to him, as she was really my dog, with Andrew only a passing human in the scheme of things. It took exactly three weeks for this tiny little dog to become besotted with her new owner, and me coming a most definite second. He would take her to the studio, and on location, where she would sit quite happily in his trailer, waiting for him to come back. I know she still loved me, but she was now Raymond's Yorkie!

Christmas came, and we spent it together, not really celebrating but enjoying being together. We decided to go back to England in the New Year so that I could meet his two daughters and put Yockley on the market. I also knew that Raymond had three sons by two other marriages, but, sadly, he hadn't seen them for many years.

Raymond had often talked about his friend Brian Clemens, whom he'd known for years, and who was more like a brother to him. Brian was a writer and showrunner for a number of television shows. He was also one of the early producers and writers for *The Avengers*, and will always be remembered for that particular show.

We stayed at Brian's flat in London, with both daughters coming up from Somerset to visit for a holiday. I remember first meeting them in San Marino, a restaurant just off Piccadilly. Araminta was the eldest, and I think far more concerned with what she was going to eat than anything else.

Johanna was younger by a couple of years, and a little more inquisitive. I felt sorry for them, for I know they must have been wondering if I was going to be yet another stepmother! It was a fun time, with Raymond buying them presents and obviously spoiling them. At the time I must confess I didn't think too much about them, for they lived with their mother, only staying with their father on school holidays. I felt I could cope with the girls for short stays, but was secretly relieved that there was an ocean between us. I knew that Johanna often travelled with her father on various locations during her school holidays, and when I was first with Raymond, she would usually come alone, for Araminta mostly wanted to stay in England, with her friends. I enjoyed her visits, and we had a lot of fun together. Sadly, I didn't meet his sons until quite a few years later.

I knew from a very early age that I would never have children of my own. Most certainly, my adolescence had coloured my feelings about bringing a child into the world, and for a very long time, I never truly felt an adult. I guess that, never having had a normal childhood, there was and still is always a small part of me that didn't grow up, still clinging to some dream I would capture those lost years and be nurtured as one would a small child; besides, I was still battling my demons even after all these years. I realized that I would live with them for the rest of my life, for they were always there, just below the surface. It only took a certain look from someone, a whiff of a remembered perfume, or a voice somewhat like hers, to set me off with all those terrible nightmares. I would once again wake in the night, shivering under the bedclothes, wet with sweat, seeing her standing over me, hearing her say I would never get away from her. And she was right. She was never far away. A few days, a few weeks or months would pass, and then there she was, with those black empty eyes and those thin lips, almost laughing at the sheer audacity of my thinking I was free.

While in London, and after the girls had gone home, we drove down to Ampthill in Bedfordshire, for me to meet and stay with Brian Clemens and his wife, Jan. I fell in love with them on sight, though again, I think they were a bit more wary of me. Maybe a fifth wife in the wings was a little too much for them at that moment in time. Through the years we have spent many happy holidays with them, antique-hunting in the various towns and villages around Bedfordshire, and listening to Brian and Raymond regaling many stories of their past while sipping champagne and doing the rounds of the local restaurants. It was always a fun time with many precious memories I will forever hold close to me.

PALM SPRINGS

Raymond always liked Palm Springs. He'd lived there in the early fifties, and also bought his first house there opposite Cary Grant and Betsy Drake.

Patrick Macnee, the star of *The Avengers,* was a very close friend of Raymond, and had his home in Palm Springs. We both decided it might be fun to move there, so Raymond called Patrick, who immediately asked us to come and stay. I remembered the last time I visited Palm Springs and had stayed at the famous Racquet Club, where I often met Frank Sinatra. Little did I know that one day I would be living there. What a very strange world it is!

Patrick's home was small but charming, with orange and lemon trees surrounding a pool at the back of the house. Each morning I would find Patrick *stark naked,* sitting by the pool reading a pile of newspapers, and hidden under a sun hat. I very quickly got used to his wonderful parties, where many actors of all ages would arrive, strip off and spend hilarious weekends telling funny stories and drinking copious bottles of champagne. I managed to go topless, but drew the line at that!

Patrick was a very funny and eccentric man, who Raymond called Bits, because he would read his papers almost from cover to cover and then spend the rest of the day quoting useless bits and pieces from the news that no one cared to listen to.

It was during a lunch outing with Patrick that we saw Joseph Cotten sitting with his wife, Patricia Medina, in the corner of the restaurant. Raymond had directed him in a show called *Love Boat.* At first we all thought he was somewhat inebriated, as we could hear him slurring his words; and though Raymond was hesitant, he decided to go over and say hello. Later we found out that Joseph was getting over a stroke, hence the speech problem. How quickly people can be labelled, before knowing what problems they may be enduring!

What a joyous meeting it turned out to be! Joseph and Patricia became two of our closest friends during our time in Palm Springs. In fact, when we told them that we were looking for a house to rent, their answer was "Look no further. We have a house in Regal Drive that's for rent." No sooner said than done! We saw it the next day and moved in a week later. Regal Drive became our home for the next year. Life in Palm Springs was fun and extremely hot.

Raymond still owned the house in the Hollywood Hills while the settlement with his ex-wife was being sorted out, so he would often stay there during the week while shooting whichever episode he was working on, and would spend the weekends with me in Palm Springs.

We decided on a date for our wedding, so for me the next couple of months were taken up with wedding preparations. For most girls this is a happy time; for me it was an *unbelievable* time. This was something I said I would never ever do, and at the time, I had truly meant it. But here it was. I was getting married and giving my very soul to another human being, something I also said would never happen; and yet I knew that these years to come would be the happiest years of my life. This colourful, talented, knowledge-hungry man was going to be my husband. Yes, he would be a handful. He was not the usual male one met in the supermarket. He had an agenda of his own. His whole life had seen an extraordinary sequence of events which he made happen by his talent, his necessity to get somewhere in life, and the need to succeed in everything he did. I'm sure that some people, especially the women in his life who had gone before me, thought I was crazy, but I was the stabilizer Raymond had never had, and he was the one person who would bring love and meaning to my life; together we made a good team, and I thank God we both wanted the same things at the same time.

We were married in Palm Springs on 3rd November, with Joseph Cotten as Raymond's best man. How classy was that? To think that, as a young girl, I had seen him in the movie *The Third Man*, and now here he was, standing in a beautiful setting, handing the groom my wedding ring, which had once belonged to Raymond's grandmother. A glorious day, no bride could wish for better! I was marrying my Prince Charming. Jack Levin was my surrogate father, and Lynne Burk my Maid of Honor.

Yes, our wedding day was perfect. Do all brides think this? Of course they do. The ceremony was held in the gardens of the Ingleside hotel, a most beautiful setting under an archway full of flowers, with many of our close friends there to join our celebration. For Raymond, it was his fifth marriage, for me my first, and for both of us, *our last!* The wedding breakfast was held at the hotel, and in the evening we had a buffet dinner at our home in Regal Drive. I spent the whole day singing "Sadie, Sadie, Married Lady." I had at last married the love of my life, and I was happier than I could ever imagine possible.

While we were living at Regal Drive, Johanna, and sometimes Araminta, would fly from England to stay with us during their school holidays. It was fun having them around, and I got to know them better. Araminta was a problem child with, sadly, many hidden agendas. She would shut herself away in her room and not communicate for hours, but if she wanted something, like money or attention, she could be charming and stick to me like glue. Even at a very young age, I could see she was travelling along the wrong road, which was heartbreaking, because she was an intelligent girl, and I always felt that she could really have done something with her life. Sadly, over the next few years, Raymond spent many harrowing hours either on the phone or flying to England trying to sort her out. She was with the wrong crowd, and heavily into drugs, and no amount of talking or pleading would ever change her. It took a very long time for Raymond to come to terms with the complete mess that Araminta was making and has made of her life.

Thank God Johanna was different. I don't think they were ever very close, so it wasn't a question of the younger sister wanting to copy her older sibling. After a couple of holidays with us, Araminta stopped coming to America, choosing to stay in England near her friends, where her lifestyle would not be under constant scrutiny by her father.

We spent a lot of time with the Cottons, either dining at their home, or taking them out to various restaurants. Joseph was still struggling to regain his speech, spending many hours with therapists, and at times he found it so very frustrating; but oh, how he loved Raymond! He would laugh until he couldn't laugh any more at the silly jokes Raymond would tell him. Patricia would often say that whenever we were together, Joseph said he felt like a young man again.

On Joseph's eightieth birthday we were invited to a party. It was a surprise event, with many famous actors attending. Colorful people like Don Ameche, Farley Granger, Cesar Romero, Anthony Perkins and Janet Leigh, and the list went on. We all silently waited in a darkened room for the birthday boy to arrive. As he walked through the doors leading into the ballroom, the lights went on, and he looked across at the crowd and said. "Oh fuck, I thought I was going to see Cats." It was a wonderful evening.

VISITING BATH AGAIN

At this time, England was still very much in our lives. We often went back at least a couple of times a year to catch up with family and friends, or Raymond would be directing one of the English shows there. It was on one of these vacations that Raymond decided that he wanted us to revisit Bath and also to find my mother's grave. Since leaving *the woman*, I'd been back only once, with Andrew. It wasn't a pleasant experience for me and certainly not for him. He simply couldn't understand while staying there, and really didn't want to know, why I suddenly morphed into a completely different person. I was the awkward child again, and as far as I was concerned, *she* was still around every street corner, every shop and every restaurant. I would see her walking toward me, and could hear her voice mocking me, telling me I was back, and this time would never leave her. I couldn't sleep at night, and after a week, felt like a zombie. I wanted to get as far away from her stamping ground as possible, and never return. After that, Andrew and I didn't talk about the visit or the circumstances surrounding the city.

Apart from Judith, Raymond was the only other person who knew what my childhood had been like, but still I never went into glorious technicolor. It has taken me all these years to truly face the past and write this book.

I told Raymond it wasn't a good idea visiting Bath, but Raymond, being Raymond, said it would be therapeutic for me and we would go through it together. So the visit was planned, and as we drove nearer and nearer to the city, I could feel my blood pressure rise.

We arrived at the Crescent hotel with Raymond booking us into the best suite. I felt strung-out and very tense, remembering my last terrifying visit. As we set off to explore the city, those old memories quickly came to the surface, and no matter how hard I tried they wouldn't leave me; then Raymond started talking. He asked me to tell him about my feelings at that particular time, and he especially wanted me to talk about *her*. Then, together, we would take it one step at a time. With much trepidation I agreed. As we entered each shop he would say, "Look around, see? She's not here." As we walked through the city of Bath he would say, "She's not here either. She can't hurt you any more, because you're with me, and I won't let anything happen to you. Tell me exactly how you are feeling." Gradually, I started to relax, and I would talk about my abject fear of seeing her again. Gradually, through the next few days, I began to realize that she couldn't hurt me because I was with Raymond. I have to say he is the only person who ever *truly* understands me. He never once said that I must stop thinking about her, because he knew I couldn't. He would listen, and then give me constructive advice. Gradually, we both began to enjoy being there, visiting the Pump Room, eating Bath buns, hunting for antiques; I went to Russell and Bromley to buy shoes. For me, it was rather like visiting a new town, with memories fading away and new, fun memories taking their place.

During our visit, we went to Haycombe cemetery, to look for my mother's grave. When we eventually found it, it was just a mass of broken stone. To see it in such a very sad state was absolutely heartbreaking. I sat in the car while Raymond went to the office at the cemetery entrance. To my surprise, he ordered a beautiful granite head stone, and we had the original words, plus our names and love added at the bottom. We have visited her grave many times since, and it always gives me such a warm feeling to see Raymond's name along with my own, sending special love to the mother I sadly never knew. Over the years we have often returned to Bath, and I now have only happy memories of our holidays there.

Bath now holds no bad memories for me, and I have my darling to thank for that; and although many readers may not understand, my going back to my childhood home with Raymond has filled in a huge black void in my life.

LEAVING PALM SPRINGS

After a year in Palm Springs, the Cottons told us that they were selling their home and would like to move back into Regal Drive. As our year's lease was almost up, we decided not to stay in the desert; the two hour drive to and from the studio was becoming a little too tiring for Raymond. With the sale of Yockley, we eventually found a house in Tarzana that we called Petit De Veauce, and again, even though it needed much work, we bought it. It was a one-storey home, and although I simply hated it on sight, we eventually made it into a beautiful home. During the three years we lived there, we had a lot of parties and a great deal of fun.

It was a whirlwind life, with Raymond working flat out with hardly any breaks; and it was then that I decided I would start writing, mainly to still be my own person. At the beginning I finished writing a book of poetry which I had started a few years before. I found it very satisfying, for I was still chasing my demons, especially when Raymond was away on location and I was still struggling to become a whole person, though the missing pieces were never visible to the outside world. Like lost parts of a jigsaw puzzle, my life would probably never quite fit together to portray a finished picture. Uncertainty and a feeling of complete worthlessness would often sweep over me, and I would be held captive, unable to break free while it lasted. There were times when desperation would grip me so tightly that, as each year went by, I wondered if the day would ever come when I would be a completely free soul; but as I get older, I've learned to accept that it will never be. The footprints of my childhood will stay with me for the rest of my life; they just become more infrequent, and the things I can't change, I can now try to understand. I am always at my happiest when either with Raymond or alone working in my garden. Except for a few very close friends, I still do not need the outside world. Indeed, for me, it is often a treacherous place, where I am still very much the lonely child in an adult body.

OUR MOUNTAIN HOME

Although we were enjoying *Petit De Veauce*, being English, we were both missing the four seasons. It's always fun thinking of living in a climate that hardly ever changes, but there comes a time when rain, grey days and chilly mornings start to become an obsession. Some friends told us about Frazier Park, which is in the mountains, and was only two hours drive from our home in Tarzana. It certainly had the four seasons, with temperatures at least twenty degrees lower in the summer, and wonderful snow in the winter. After a couple of visits, we decided it was perfect for a weekend home. We found a very pretty house with breathtaking views, which we named *Pinetree Lodge* after my first home in Surrey.

After Raymond finished work on a Friday, we would load the car, plus Dida, and drive to our mountain home. The weekends there were fun, with long country walks and renewed energy.

When Raymond was away on location, Dida and I would drive up to Pinetree Lodge and often spend weeks at a time just being away from the world. Yes, I was still fighting my demons. There would be months when *the woman* wouldn't be in my life, and I could almost forget that she had ever existed. Then, quite suddenly, something would happen, and there she was, once again, standing over me, immobilizing me, telling me what a worthless creature I was. So I would shut myself away where no one really knew me. I would walk the mountain trails with Dida, and tell myself soon she would leave, and I could be myself again.

When Raymond was not away on location, we would plan weekend parties at Pinetree Lodge, with many friends coming for either summer breaks or winter skiing. Poor Raymond did once try to teach me cross country skiing, but after I got completely stuck, head first, under a tree I think he realized that winter sports were definitely not my strong point.

We had a wonderful last Christmas at Pinetree Lodge, with Johanna and family coming over from England; and on Christmas Eve, it started to snow. We all awoke to a white wonderland, with Father Christmas arriving on skis, and Raymond's granddaughter, Rebecca, in awe that he should actually visit her, and wondering why her grandfather was not there to witness such a momentous occasion!

It was a happy, busy period in our lives, where we were always ready to party at either house.

VIRGINIA

California was fun, but not a place where we wanted to spend the rest of our lives. There were times when we wondered whether we would go back to live in England, especially as Raymond was a well known director, and through his agent, could work anywhere in the world (and actually did, throughout his career). As it turned out, it was a decision we never really had to think about.

RJ (Robert Wagner) and Raymond had been friends for many years, and had worked together on several shows, including the pilot and various episodes of *Hart to Hart*. In the late eighties, RJ called Raymond, saying he had a project called *Lime Street* that was to be made in various parts of the world, and that he wanted Raymond to direct them. The story was about a large insurance company investigating scams. RJ's home was to be set in Virginia, where a lot of the main filming was to take place. While looking for locations in the area, Raymond found a house in Middleburg that was right for the story line, and was used as RJ's home in the series. Middleburg looked very much like a typical English village. I think at the time the seeds were sown, and the eventual move to Virginia set.

While filming some of the locations at Brocket Hall in England, I first met Samantha Smith, the girl who had become famous for going to Russia as a goodwill ambassador and participating in peacemaking activities in Japan. She had never acted before, but RJ, along with Raymond and the network, thought it would be wonderful to have her play his daughter in the series. On our last day of shooting at Brocket Hall, I was sitting with RJ, and watched Samantha walk across the lawn with her father; she was thirteen years old. I remember thinking that she was one of the most beautiful girls I'd ever seen. There was an aura about her captured in that moment in time.

She was not needed for the next show, so Raymond agreed that she and her father could fly home for a couple of weeks, then meet us in Switzerland for the next episode. That evening, she left with her father, while Raymond and I flew to Switzerland. I had never been to Switzerland, and as it was dark when we arrived at the hotel, I was looking forward to seeing it the next morning. I remember waking, and Raymond opening the curtains, then saying, "I give you Switzerland." The scene was quite breathtaking, for our suite looked out onto the mountains, and in the distance I could hear the cow bells ringing. It was a magical moment for both of us.

Later that morning, Raymond received the terrible news that Samantha's plane, Bar Harbor Airlines 1808 had crashed. Samantha, along with her father, were killed; he had held her in his arms, shielding her face as the plane went down. When they found her, that beautiful face shone through the wreckage, completely undamaged. The reporters and photographers who were on the scene zoomed in on a script of Lime Street that was lying fluttering in the wreckage. My heart ached for the lost possibilities of this beautiful child. She was much too young to die, with all the potential of becoming an incredible adult. Our hearts also went out to her mother, who had literally just moved into a new home, and now had lost both her husband and daughter. What a terrible tragedy. Raymond spent most of the day trying to get in touch with RJ, who was due to fly out to Switzerland the following day. He didn't want RJ to hear the news on television before he had had a chance to gently tell him what had happened. Although the network tried to carry on with the series, from then on it was really a doomed series, and (I think much to everyone's relief) it was shut down after only a few episodes.

On Raymond's first visit to Virginia, and while looking for locations for the series, he absolutely fell in love with the country, saying that it was more like England than England. I flew out there some weeks later, and yes, it certainly was a most beautiful area. Raymond often said when he retired it would be wonderful to make our home in that part of the world, and I readily agreed. With our very hectic lifestyle, the thought of moving was put to the back of our minds, only coming to the surface every so often, like a warm bed into which we eventually knew we would snuggle into.

The day soon came when I realized it would be years, if ever, before Raymond would retire. We talked it over and decided, to the shock of most of our Californian friends, that we would take the plunge, and look for our home somewhere in Virginia. So over the next eighteen months, we spent every spare moment flying to various parts of Virginia, to find a place we could call home.

Eventually, we arrived in Albemarle County, and fell in love! We found Jane Fogleman who was a realtor with an office near a hotel called The Boar's Head. We told her we were coming to live in Virginia, but when we said that we came from California and that Raymond was in the entertainment industry, we could see her eyes gradually glaze over. Obviously she had experienced *the Hollywood crowd*, as she called them, before, and was not too sure of us. When I then told her we had two houses there and wanted to sell them before we moved, I could see that she wrote us off immediately and was sure she would never see us again. Both our houses sold in record time, and when, a few months later, we again walked into her office, I think she was stunned to see us. At the time, I'm not too sure whether she was happy about this or not. She and her husband, James, have become very close friends over the years.

Virginia is very eclectic, but one soon finds out that no one is particularly interested in who you are or what you do. Albemarle County is home to a great many people who come from all walks in life, and as Jane got ready to show us some homes in the area, she made a very interesting statement. "One can be very social here, or if you prefer not to socialize, you will be left alone; it's entirely up to you." We were both excited by the prospect of a new life in a part of America, so like England and having four seasons, something we sorely missed in California.

Raymond had now become an instant Virginian, and wanted a home with acreage, but I was not quite so sure that that would be a good thing. He was still working non-stop, and I had visions of being somewhere deep in the country for months on end with only a tiny Yorkshire Terrier for company. Between us, Jane and I managed to talk him out of his dream of being Lord of the Manor, and in a fairly short time we found a house in Earlysville with just under four acres. I truly don't know why we both instantly fell in love with the home we now call Fox Haven, for there was simply no garden, just a field at the front and back of the house, plus it was in need of quite a lot of work to make it into the sort of home we both wanted; but the good vibes and the feeling that we both belonged there was instant. The owners wanted a couple of months to sort their lives out, so after we had packed up the two homes in California, putting the furniture in store until it could be transferred to our new home, Jane found me a small cottage to rent near The Boar's Head, while Raymond went back to California to carry on working. It was a strange and very lonely time for me, suddenly being deposited in a part of America where I knew no one, and had absolutely no idea what the hell I was doing there. Still, the cottage was very cosy, and I had Dida dog with me. Each day, we would venture out to investigate a new area of Virginia, and I was always very thankful when I managed to find my way back to the cottage. Although there was one morning, after taking Raymond's car to have the phone number changed, when I got completely lost. I simply had no idea where I was. In desperation, I called Raymond, who was finishing shooting a series called *Our House* in Los Angeles; God knows what I thought he could do, especially as he was already on the set at studio ready to shoot a scene. Of course he couldn't help, but happily assured me if I drove around I would soon see something familiar. As I said goodbye I lamented that if he didn't hear from me again, I would still be trying to find my way back to the cottage.

In September of 1989, we moved into Fox Haven, and on that day, we sat on the grass in front of the house, while the removal vans drove in, ready to unload two homes into one. As I had earlier marked each box, I felt it would be easy for the boxes to be carried into the correct rooms, etcetera. We both started off the day being very efficient, but by early afternoon it was obvious each room was becoming over filled with all our belongings. Thank God for Jane Fogleman, who brought us lunch as the three of us sat and watched the men unloading box after box, not to mention all the furniture. By the middle of the afternoon a bright young man asked me where I wanted a particular box to go and I politely told him anywhere he (expletive) wanted to put it.

To say that the next few months were chaotic would be an understatement. One week after we moved into our new home, Raymond was off to Spain to shoot the television series *Zorro* and would not be back until Christmas, while I was left with a house still full of boxes plus stacked up furniture in every room, and around twenty workmen, who would descend upon me at some ridiculously early hour every weekday, only leaving me free at the weekend trying to regain my sanity. Monday would come around all too soon, and we would be back on the merry-go-round, with something happening in every room, as well as a master bathroom being installed. Decisions had to be made while keeping an eagle eye on the cost of this rather expensive remodelling. Cars and trucks would come and go at regular intervals, with me continually telling myself it would all be worthwhile, and some day in the not too distant future, Fox Haven would be rid of workmen, and would start to look and feel like a home.

While all the work was going on inside the house, I started work on the outside. It was literally a blank canvas, with both Raymond and me wanting very much to turn it into an English garden. At first it all seemed a wee bit daunting, but Jane introduced me to WA Wells, who was an excavator and landscaper. He took yards of earth away from the house, opening up the surrounding area. Jane also told me about Peter Hallack, who owned the Garden Spot in Charlottesville, and, between us, we started to shape the front field into a garden. I knew nothing about American trees, but did fall in love with the Bradford Pears I saw around the area. I told Peter I wanted six trees, but I wanted them established, meaning fully grown. A week later, each tree arrived on a huge truck, and they were duly planted. Suddenly, the field didn't look like a field any more and the first signs of our English garden had begun to materialize. Upon Raymond's return to his new home he drove past the house twice, telling the driver he knew the house was somewhere along Buck Mountain Road, but it certainly didn't have any mature trees at the front. While he was away, I'd told him about the trees, but little did he know the trees that were planted were around twenty feet high! As we have grown older, our gardens have changed. We've remodelled and put in various little areas where we can sit, to enjoy and marvel at the now fully mature gardens we have made.

Having sold the two houses in California, we decided that it was now time to sell the small apartment I still had in Paris. We had fun staying there for holidays, or when Raymond was working in the area, but it was somewhere we knew we would now rarely visit, and was expensive to keep.

It went on the market, and was sold within a month.

During Raymond's second season of filming in Spain, we both decided to have a swimming pool. Needless to say, Raymond wasn't at Fox Haven while the pool was being installed, and while it was being built, the back garden looked like hell, with mountains of red clay at one end and an army of men at the other. During this time, Benny Byler brought our lovely Gazebo all the way from Stuarts Draft, and placed it with loving care slightly off centre, in front of the humongous clay mountain, with me praying that it would be in the exact position Raymond wanted. It was a very exciting time, especially when, one week later, Raymond surprised me by arriving home from Spain for a long weekend, to assure me that the gazebo was indeed in the most perfect position. How can one not love a man who would fly halfway across the world to spend a weekend making his wife happy? In fact over the years Raymond has flown home from various parts of the world for short stays, and then spent hours flying back to those locations to continue his work.

Around this time, we received the dreadful news that Inge Licht had suddenly died on her way to play tennis. I often wonder why lovely people go too quickly. She will always be a special person in my life. She was there for me when I needed a friend, and she is still sadly missed.

Over the years in Virginia, we have made many friends, from all different walks of life. Although I enjoyed my time in California, it's so refreshing not to be continually closeted with would-be actors or people looking for work in the industry. Life is very different here, and people are not interested in what work you do. They either like you or not, and the nice thing is that if they become friends, it's certainly not because they want to work on the next television project.

I guess one of the very few drawbacks was that Raymond's work always took him away from home. He was very much in demand, so I seemed to spend a lot of time packing suitcases and waving him goodbye for months on end. I looked forward to the work's being finished at Fox Haven, leaving me free to join him at various times on some of his locations.

During his third season shooting *Zorro*, I decided to close up the house for a few months, and join Raymond in Spain. Jane offered to have Dida while I was away. Raymond had a really nice apartment in Madrid, and, as I'd spent a year there on *Nicholas and Alexandra*, I was excited to be back. Pepe, his driver, met me at the airport, and was ecstatic to see me, remembering that he often drove me to and from the studio in Madrid when I worked for Andrew. After an effusive greeting, he took me to the apartment to freshen up, and then on to the location. It was always exciting watching Raymond work, and I was looking forward to being with him and meeting crew and cast. Some I already knew from my work in the past.

Now Raymond was always very mischievous, and loved to play tricks on people, and I was certainly not excluded. The actor Adam West, from the classic television show Batman, was making a guest appearance on the episode being shot at the time. I'm embarrassed to say that the name meant nothing to me as I had *never* watched *Batman*, and knew nothing about the series. After being introduced to various members of the crew and cast, Raymond called Adam over, telling him that I was his greatest fan, and had actually watched *every single one* of his shows. I was completely dumbfounded and dear Adam, utterly bowled over by this revelation, clutched me to his chest, telling me what a joy it was to meet someone who had followed *Batman* so ardently. He then proceeded to ask me which of the shows I liked best, and I really had to tap dance through that, vowing I would kill my husband at the very first opportunity. After that, whenever I saw Adam a flurry of excitement would run through the cast and crew who, by now, knew my secret and watched as he would rush to my side telling everyone I was his greatest fan ever. I so enjoyed my time again in Madrid, especially going to the market each day to buy dinner for the evening. It was also nostalgic being taken to the restaurants where I had so many fond memories of times gone by.

It was at this time I decided to start writing in earnest, and not just dabble in it. Although Raymond would have loved me going to the location every day, I was definitely not one of the location wives who would sit around all day watching their beloved partners do their thing! So it was at this time that I wrote my first book, *Leave the Killing to Me.*

Through the next few years, our life in Virginia was becoming established, and now we can't think of anywhere else in the world we would rather be. Although all of Raymond's family still live in England, with at one time, a slim hope of Johanna's moving here permanently, we know we would never be happy living anywhere else.

AUSTIN AND ANTHONY

Although I knew Raymond had sons, I didn't meet them for a number of years. Austin first came into my life one day while Raymond was away on location. His mother called asking to speak to Raymond, and I explained he would be home in a couple of weeks. She never did call back, but later, we found out that Austin had not been well, and I feel she wanted some contact between father and son.

Eventually, we met Austin in England, with his partner Sharron. It took time getting to know Austin, for I truly believe he was wary of yet another wife coming into his father's life, and I completely understood. I think that, if I'd been in his shoes, I would have felt exactly the same. Still, over the years, I now feel and hope there is a strong bond between us; and the more I see him, the more I understand him. I also think he knows that, by now, I am the last wife in his father's life, and will always be there for him.

It took a little longer for Anthony to get in touch, and, as neither boy had seen his father for a number of years, I'm sure they felt that they were doing fine without him. As in all relationships, one has to build trust; also they had to start from scratch, with both Raymond and me getting to know each of them as grown men. I hope they enjoy coming to see us, and I hope they know how much their father and I love them.

TROUBLING NEWS FROM MY DOCTOR

On a late Autumn day, with the garden still looking beautiful, rather like English Summer at its best, Raymond and I were planning our winter holiday in Barbados, where we usually celebrated our anniversary. One morning while showering I found a lump in my breast. I made an appointment to see my family doctor, who assured me that it was nothing. After worrying about it for a month, Raymond and I went to see him again. I remember the doctor looking at me as if I was a hypochondriac, but I quickly reminded him that the only time he ever saw me was once a year, for my annual visit. Again he assured me there was nothing to worry about. As we left the surgery, Raymond asked me if I felt more reassured, and as I nodded, I remember thinking, "No, this is something serious."

We had our holiday in Barbados, and did all the usual things, like walk the beach, and swim each day, read copious books, and dine at our favorite restaurants, while I tried to put the nagging fear of something's not being quite right with my body out of my mind.

When we returned home, I told Raymond that I truly thought I should have a second opinion, and thus started the roller coaster of hospitals and doctors, with all that it entails. I was told very early on that I had breast cancer. While I was going through the initial stages of meeting with the doctors who were going to look after me, Johanna suddenly arrived on our doorstep. I remember looking at her and thinking I was hallucinating, but there she was, she had dropped everything, got on a plane and come to help me and her father through a very unsettling time. I will be forever grateful for all the help and support she gave us, especially with her nursing experience. Also going with us to each hospital appointment and explaining exactly what was happening, for at the time, both Raymond and I were a little dazed, and not truly understanding any of the discussions taking place at the various appointments.

I thank God I was lucky, and listened to my body. I can only hope other women do the same. It was caught in time, removed, with no chemotherapy and limited radiation. I can't speak more highly of Linda Sommers, my wonderful surgeon, and all the other caring people who looked after me. How thankful we are to be living in America! Everything was done in record time, and we were very soon ready again to get on with our lives in Virginia. Through all this I had Raymond by my side. During each hospital stay or visit, he was there with such love and gentle care, although I know he was a complete basket case, he was my rock, and without him by my side it would have been an exceedingly difficult time in my life. I feel secure in the knowledge that he will always be there for me. How incredibly lucky I am.

FAMILY VIEWS MANY
YEARS LATER

Recently I had a couple of emails from my half brother, Peter's daughter, Linda. The one thing that stood out in the last email, which was vitriolic and so very unkind, was a paragraph where she said she couldn't understand why I had stayed so long in the abusive situation with a woman who was so cruel. If it had been so terrible, why hadn't I left years earlier? Well, it is obvious that this female plainly has no idea what my situation was like, or indeed she simply has no idea what any person goes through under those circumstances. Whether it be a child, or adult in an abusive marriage, why do we stay with the abuser? I can only speak for myself. If a child, and in my situation from the age of four years old, is constantly abused mentally and physically, she becomes completely indoctrinated. She also becomes worthless, a frightened child watching, waiting and hoping each day will pass without doing something, however innocent, to set off that terrible wrath. Her whole life is controlled by the controller, and her whole life is spent trying to find out *why*. What had she ever done to deserve this treatment, and above all, when will it end? The child dreams of being free, but knows nothing of freedom; it's simply beyond their comprehension. It's there, but you can't grasp it, no matter how much you desperately want it. I spent many years plotting my escape, throughout my childhood and then into my teens. To someone who has never experienced what it is like to be absolutely controlled, how dare they be so flippant, with their throwaway accusations? Let them walk a mile in my shoes. And then let them ask *why*?

LOSING JUDITH

Some time ago, I received an email from Judith's son, telling me the terrible news that his mother had died from a sudden heart attack. To say I was stunned by this is an understatement. Just a few short years ago, she'd come back into my life and now she was gone. I thought of her husband Joe, and how devastated he must be by her loss. She was truly a special person, a girl who helped change my life giving me the courage to move on. I will never forget her and will always thank God we have had some time together, through Skype, where we could laugh, remembering the past, and holding those memories so very close to our hearts.

HOME IS WHERE
THE HEART IS

It's almost unbelievable to realize that we have lived in Virginia for nearly thirty years. Where does time go? But they have been the happiest years of my life. I am still madly in love with Raymond, and treasure each and every day we spend together. He cares so much for me, he makes me laugh, he makes me glad to be alive. Can a once skinny introverted child ask for more? No. I have so much more than I could have ever hoped to have. Life is serene and happy, and I thank God for each and every day I share with a most incredible man who completely understands me, has listened to my insecurities with a gentle patience, and is the only person in the world who has helped me become who I am today. I so enjoy the close relationship we have with some wonderful friends we call our family. They bring joy, much laughter and happiness into my world, and I love them deeply.

As I sit in my lovely English garden and think back over my life, I know that I am one of the luckiest women alive to have led such an interesting life, and, I think, living proof that a childhood such as mine need not taint nor ruin the rest of one's life. Oh yes, there are still nights where dark rooms will always be there; but those long grey corridors of loneliness and misery have got so much shorter, with bright lights leading me through them, and sunny mornings where I wake to find my darling lying next to me. I don't know how long this journey will take me, but I am content living each day with the man I love.

Other Books by
Wendy DeVere-Austin

Leave the Killing to Me by Harlon Publishing Company

Dead on Cue by Publish America Baltimore

Walking the Ladies by Publish American Baltimore

94114254R00192

Made in the USA
Middletown, DE
17 October 2018